CRITICAL ACCLAIM FOR

THE COLDEST WAR

"Brady has an uncanny ability to evoke a time and mood, a talent he puts to exceptional use in *THE COLDEST WAR*. . . . What he brings to the mix are a keen eye for the detail of a soldier's life, the ability to present it skillfully and, above all, honesty."
—*Philadelphia Inquirer*

"A MARVELOUS MEMOIR. A sensitive and superbly written narrative that eventually explodes off the page like a grenade in the gut. Taut, tight, and telling. History up close and personal. History from and for the heart . . ."
—Dan Rather, Managing Editor, CBS News

"Brady's Marines were real people, and that's part of why this story rings so true. Brady's account of his own actions and attitudes during this time is remarkably candid and objective. . . . Brady jogs our memory in A FIRST-RATE BOOK."
—*San Diego Tribune*

"TERRIFIC . . . Page after page of close-up, vivid recollection. This is an account about growing up. Most war memoirs are. But, this is also a celebration of a man's appreciation of the hard catechism of combat and . . . the hard beauty of the wintry landscape of the strange, perilous place he found himself. . . . MARVELOUS."
—*New York Daily News*

A Military Book Club Dual Selection

(more . . .)

THE
COLDEST
WAR

A MEMOIR OF KOREA

JAMES BRADY

POCKET BOOKS

New York   London   Toronto   Sydney   Tokyo   Singapore

POCKET BOOKS, a division of Simon & Schuster Inc.
1230 Avenue of the Americas, New York, NY 10020

ISBN: 0-671-72525-4

First Pocket Books printing July 1991

10 9 8 7 6 5 4 3 2

POCKET and colophon are registered trademarks of
Simon & Schuster Inc.

Map by Alan McKnight

Cover art by Dominick Finelle

Printed in the U.S.A.

This book is for my daughters, Fiona and Susan.

But it is dedicated to those who fought in Korea, especially the men of the First Marine Division and of Dog Company and the Second Battalion.

Memoirs are about remembering. I wish I could recall all the names. If the book has a hero, it is Capt. John H. Chafee.

These are some of the men who fought, and whom I remember: Lts. Maurice J. (Mack) Allen, Robert Simonis, Red Philips, Tex Lissman, Ed Flynn, Jack Rowe, Stewart Boone McCarty, Pierce Power, Jack Vohs, Dick Brennan, Nathaniel (Taffy) Sceva, Al Myers, Lou Faust, Carl Ullrich, Joe Buscemi, Ernie (Mouse) Brydon, Tim O'Reilly, Robert Bjornsen, David Gally; Capts. Ramon Gibson, Charles Logan, Bob Baker, Alvin Mackin; Col. Noel C. Gregory; Maj. Dennis Nicholson; Sgts. Ronald Stoneking, Wooten, John Fitzgerald, Porterfield, Green, Blasco, Wright, Gagnon, Jay Scott; scout Rudy Wrabel; machine gunner Herb MacDonald; marine Joe Saluzzi.

And it is for the 54,000 of us who died, two of whom were my friends, Lt. Jim Callan and Lt. Douglas H. T. Bradlee.

Shortly after he got to Korea in the spring of 1951, Bradlee, a Bostonian and a Harvard graduate, wrote home: "Try not to be overly upset by my present mission. I have felt during the last seven years or more that I might have been cut out for things away from the beach and the country club . . . this might be a good foundation. I look to the principles of a Christian life, not stopping at a 'gentlemanly' Christian life but working toward a saintly one. I hope one day to find and work toward God."

Later, while fighting the Chinese, Bradlee wrote: "I've lost five men in the last three days through heat prostration and exhaustion." Yet he spoke of horseplay and laughter on the march and was still able to see country and enjoy it. "Amazing thing here is that there are mocking birds exactly the same as in Colorado."

The Chinese killed him June 3, 1951. He was not yet twenty-four.

*Some names have been changed
The rest is as I remember it.*

J.B.

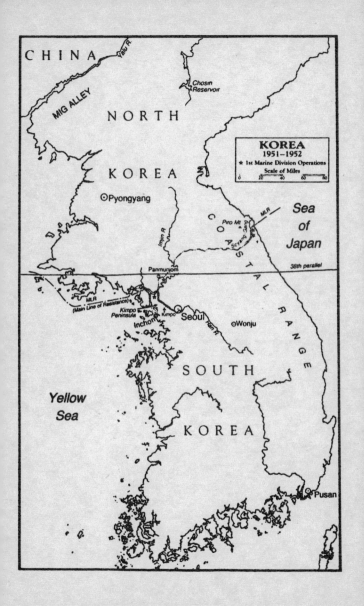

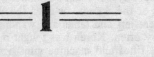

1

The Korean War, which President Truman called a police action and Averell Harriman "a sour little war," and which today is largely forgotten, began forty years ago, on the morning of Sunday, June 25, 1950, when 90,000 North Korean troops pushed across the 38th Parallel and came south.

Before it ended thirty-seven months later it killed more than 54,000 Americans. In the three years of Korea nearly as many of us died as in the decade of Vietnam. No one will ever know how many Koreans and Chinese we killed.

Korea gave us a brief shelf of history books, no great war novel or film, not a single memorable song, a wonderful combat journal by Martin Russ called "The Last Parallel."

And it gave us "M*A*S*H."

Because it began along an artificial frontier dividing a single nation effectively into Soviet and American zones, a deal cut in part to lure the Russians into attacking the Japanese in 1945, Korea might be thought of as the last campaign of World War II; because of the vague way it ended in 1953, as the opening battle for Vietnam.

Korea was a strange war in a strange land, a war the generals warned we should never fight, a ground war on the Asian mainland against the Chinese. It anointed few heroes, ended MacArthur's career, helped elect Ike. Korea didn't arouse America as the Second World War did, nor did it, as Vietnam would, scar a generation. There are men today lying in VA hospitals who were broken by Korea, but those of us who came home intact pretty much picked up our lives and went back to school or out to look for a job.

They didn't stage any parades, but then neither did people spit at us in the streets.

In some ways, it wasn't a modern war at all, more like Flanders or the Somme or even the Wilderness campaign. There were jets and tanks and warships but you didn't see them very often. Korea was fought mostly by infantrymen with M-1 rifles and machine guns and hand grenades and mortars. There was artillery, of course, quite good on both sides. And barbed wire, lots of that, and mines, always the mines. We lived under the ground, in sandbagged bunkers, and stood watch in trenches. Men who fought in France in 1917 would have understood Korea; Lee's and Grant's men would have recognized it.

The war in that first year was a dashing affair, at least until the snow came, a war of movement, tanks and planes, up and down the peninsula, with Seoul fought over and changing hands four times. The armies marched up the land and marched back down again. There was much fervor and martial oratory. MacArthur thought the "boys" might be home for Christmas. When the marines were surrounded up near Manchuria at the "frozen Chosin," General Smith said, "Retreat, hell"; they were advancing in another direction. Col. "Chesty" Puller remarked of the encircling Chinese, "Good, now they can't get away."

By November of 1951 there was no more oratory. The line had stabilized, partly from exhaustion and cold, partly because the truce talks occasionally flickered into promise. The Chinese, a million of them, and what was left of the North Koreans dug in. And we dug in, six American divisions and our UN allies. Two armies stood and faced each other in the hills with another damned winter coming out of Siberia.

That was when I got there, Thanksgiving weekend, 1951.

Most of us hated the war or feared it; a few loved it. No one was neutral on the war. Sergeant Wooten, who had fought in the Pacific, said people shouldn't knock Korea:

"It ain't much but it's the only war we got."

2

=====2=====

In the second year of the war, with November near wasted, the plane turned east from the sea and crossed over the coast. Before it left Japan someone said there were enemy jets, Migs, out over the water, and I was afraid of the Migs and glad to see land. From the starboard windows you could see real mountains in the north, hunched and white-robed like Dominicans at prayer. I didn't like the look of them. Here near the coast the hills were only hills, no Gothic menace about them, but even on the low hills there was snow. Only in the flat of the valley where the plane would come down was there bare earth, brown and frozen hard. We banked and came in low over the hills. A sort of landing field was marked out, flanked by agricultural terraces reaching gently for the hills, the terraces lined with dull ice in the furrows and the wind chasing little whorls of brown dust. Up and down the valley you could see huts and tents and a few unsuccessful fires giving no apparent heat and little light in the gray morning. Small snowflakes blew past the windows.

Heavy with men and goods, the plane touched down, slowed by a shoving wind, wheels chewing into the earth, powdering and splintering the ground into frozen bits that skidded away in a brown wake. No paved landing strip here. There were some Korean troops in the plane coming back from hospitals, and they started being sick when the plane was still taxiing and had not stopped. Mack Allen

3

thought this was jolly, but I was still whisky-sick from the geisha house and nervous about the Migs and did not think it was at all amusing. When the plane stopped, there was a meditative moment during which nothing moved, a world all gray and brown and cold, no pastel hint of joy or movement, as if we in the plane and those in the huts and tents wanted to consider further before committing ourselves to anything rash or irrevocable.

No flags, no wheeled gangway, no great thing of a welcome. From a dun tent came one small man in a too large overcoat, his hands jammed into pockets, shoulders rounded against the wind, wandering toward the plane. The hatches opened, and men and baggage dropped lumpily to the ground. The small man looked at us, his hands staying in his pockets. I felt the wind for the first time and understood. Still silent he motioned us with a cocked head and a shrugged shoulder toward the straggle of tents and corrugated huts, and without waiting to see if we followed, moved off faster than he had come, away from the plane and out of the wind. I looked around, and we picked up our goods and snaked off the field toward shelter. Behind us the plane was already moving down the strip for takeoff. No one stayed here who had opportunity to get out.

The huts were nothing, but they cut the wind. We went into one and the sergeants into some others. The Koreans drifted away in another direction. There were no signs, only instinct and the military caste system to direct us. I dropped my rucksack on a cot and rolled the seabag underneath. Someone asked what this place was, where we were. No one answered. I was just glad to be there, on the ground, the flight behind me, my stomach settling. Mack Allen looked across the potbellied stove, his flat face opening and happy with its broken nose. Mack was the only cheerful thing I'd seen that morning. He was happy; I was only relieved.

"Well, we got here. We didn't miss it after all." His Virginia voice was alive and I knew he meant it. I was not so sure, but I gave him a nod.

"I'll be back."

Outside the hut there was again the cold and behind it the wind. Korea looked like what I expected and then it didn't.

Maybe I didn't know what to expect. The smell was new, for one. I liked to catalogue things, and the smell didn't fit anywhere. Neither did the quiet. There should have been activity but there wasn't. I moved down the line of huts still a little shaky in the wind but with the ground solid under me. There was talk coming from one of the tents, and I leaned inside, got directions, and went on.

The chaplain had a tin hut near the end of the row. I found him poking up a plugged chimney and told him what I wanted. He said sure and put down the bayonet and we walked together into the dim at the end of the hut. I knelt and the chaplain sat on a cot. He was smoking a cigar, but he took it out and set it very carefully on the wood frame of the cot so it would continue to burn but not start a fire. A little smoke rose like incense in the dark of the hut.

"Bless me, Father, for I have sinned." I went through the routine. Then I got to where I was going.

"I fornicated once."

"Are you married?"

"No." I would have said adultery if I were married.

"Was the woman?"

"I have no way of knowing. I don't think so."

The priest hitched himself forward on the cot, sneaking a look sideways at his cigar. It was still burning.

"You know, in committing sin with a woman of this type, you are responsible for her act as well as your own."

"Yes, Father." I don't know how he knew what type she was, but this was no time for a theological debate.

"Had you instead given good example, well, one never knows. It might have touched a chord, made her realize her sin, altered her life for the better."

"Yes, Father." I was thinking that if I were into good example I would not have been in a whorehouse, would never have met the girl, my good example the famous philosophical tree falling silent in the forest with no ear to hear.

"Say ten Our Fathers and ten Hail Marys and say a prayer for me."

"Yes, Father," and I bowed my head to mumble the Act of Contrition. At least the priest was not sanctimonious, just slightly out of touch. Then I caught myself thinking that

5

and knew it wasn't right, not in the spirit of contrition, and I stopped thinking it. I was contrite, I meant it truly, and was glad to have confessed. The sin was a sin, but the act itself fine, and now the slate was wiped and the fear of a guilty death gone. I could go north without worrying about it. We stood up, both of us relieved the cigar was still going. He asked where I was headed and offered a cup of coffee, but I thanked him and went out. He'd picked up the sooty bayonet and was again working at the chimney.

In the cold and the wind walking back down the strip I remembered how that morning began, the day I went to war, an enlisted man coming through at six and shaking me awake. "Plane's ready, Lieutenant. You go out at eight." I woke to a morning long awaited and went into the bathroom. There was an open line of toilets without partitions, but even so I considered trying to be sick, trying to get the booze up. I was not much of a drinker. But then fat Hutchins came in, naked as when I'd last seen him in his obscenity at the house, shouting filth at his girl. Hutchins scratched his big pimpled rump with pleasure, maybe remembering what he'd had the girl do. It decided me to fight down the nausea. I didn't want to vomit with Hutchins watching. As I was leaving the toilets an old Japanese woman came in with a mop and pail to do her chores. I was glad again about not being sick.

There was a spit of snow in the air as we walked across the endless concrete of the air base, past the neatly aligned fighters to our plane. The luggage was heavy and I walked under it with an exaggerated straightness. Mack Allen walked with me, and I wished I'd stayed with Mack and not gone to the house. Mack's opinions were important to me. He could have gotten laid and hadn't. Someone brushed by with a valpack. It was he who said there were Migs out.

"That's great." Now I felt worse than ever and thought how right Mack had been. But the flight was fine except for the sick Koreans. Because of the snow we were routed south instead of going directly to the division in the north. It was at this sideshow field that I found the chaplain.

The hangover was gone and I'd confessed and hadn't been shot down over the Sea of Japan, and with the real business about to start, I tried to get hold of myself. It was

Thanksgiving 1951 and I'd just turned twenty-three, and for nearly a year I'd been getting ready to go to war, preparing for this day. For the next hour I walked up and down the empty, windswept little airstrip alone, feeling the wind, shivering in the cold, testing myself against Korea. I was here now and no way out and I'd better begin learning to live with it.

Can you be scared by pictures in a magazine? Ever since November a year ago I'd been afraid, literally, of the Korean winter. It was those David Douglas Duncan photos in *Life* magazine of marines up in the mountains of North Korea fighting the Chinese and dying in the snow and the cold. It was strange. Since childhood I'd loved winter, the snow, skiing, ice-skating. But the pictures of that first winter up here terrified me. I knew I was coming to Korea to fight, and the way the calendar fell it would be winter. And in some surreal way I associated with those photos in *Life,* seeing myself dead in the snow, arms and legs frozen straight out, my body tossed up with others like cordwood on the trucks grinding slowly down the narrow roads from the Chosin Reservoir to the Sea. It was like looking into my own coffin.

At Quantico in Virginia, where we trained, men talked endlessly about that first winter, imagining what the cold must have been like. Hard enough fighting a war; in Korea the cold could kill you. At Camp Pendleton, dry, hot and dusty, near desert, the Korean winter remained with us in imagination. It was with us at Pickle Meadows, the cold-weather training camp up near Tahoe where we had two feet of snow in October and the thin air burned our lungs. The training films, at Quantico and Pendleton, were meant to help, to teach us how to survive the cold. They sickened me. There was an especially gruesome film clip in color of a marine's toes being removed on an operating table. The foot looked normal, but the toes, all five, were swollen and black. Frostbite. The surgeon didn't have to cut them off; he simply bent them back and they broke off in his surgical glove, all five toes, bloody at the stump but otherwise black and dead.

Avoid this, the training film advised: keep your feet dry, change your socks, don't get frostbite.

How did you keep your feet dry or change your socks when you were on the march in temperatures below zero, when to fall out at the side of the road was to risk being ambushed or, worse, to fall asleep and be left behind to freeze to death in an Asian ditch? There were other things we heard about that first winter, that march south from the Chosin, how the mortar tubes shrank in the cold so the shells wouldn't fit, how men's skin stuck to metal when bare flesh was exposed and the whole palm of a hand tore away like a bloody glove, how you couldn't pull the pin on a frozen grenade, how men pissed on rifles to thaw them for firing.

Now I was a character in this chill nightmare.

Finally the wind forced me back to the hut. Mack and Hutchins and the rest of them were flaked out on cots, Hutch reading a dirty book but the rest asleep. I actually felt pretty good. I'd confessed, the hangover was forgotten, I'd been in Korea a couple of hours and had forced myself to stay outside in the cold and the wind and hadn't frozen to death.

Or even been shot, I thought, trying to laugh off fear.

It might have taken three or four minutes before I, too, was asleep. It helps to be young.

3

Men joined the Marine Corps for many reasons: because of John Wayne movies or to keep from being sent to prison or because they were bored or because of the uniform or because they were the kind of men who enjoyed discipline and really wanted to serve. A few sought adventure. I joined to avoid the draft.

I was in college in 1947 in New York when they reinstituted the draft after a brief, postwar interlude and we were all going to have to go in for two years. A classmate came back in September of our sophomore year suntanned and raving about something the marines had set up called the Platoon Leaders Class, the PLC. A college boy who spent two summers in the PLC at the Marine Corps Schools in Quantico, Virginia, would be commissioned a second lieutenant in the reserve the day he graduated from college. He would have to attend weekly meetings and go for summer training afterward, but he couldn't be drafted.

I had no desire to spend two years in the army, I thought being an officer sounded better than being an enlisted man, and the Marine Corps had a certain glamour. Others thought the same way, and Pierce Power and several more and I went down to 90 Church Street to sign up. We were sent for physicals, and out of six of us, four failed. We had heart murmurs. I was eighteen and terrified. When you are eighteen and a doctor says there is something wrong with your heart, you have visions of invalidism and sudden death. I was afraid to tell my family and for several days went around in a funk, envying total strangers their good health, until Pierce had the good sense to check with a family doctor and was told heart murmurs in teenagers came with growth and would go away. I'd grown eleven inches in five years, and when I got myself an electrocardiogram, I was fine. There were two sorts of heart murmurs and mine was the benign sort, so I took the EKG back to 90 Church Street and passed. Then the navy dentist flunked me. I had an overbite. My own dentist was apoplectic: "Do they want you to shoot people or bite them?" He filed my front teeth a little and I passed.

The next summer I was at Quantico, a member of the PLC.

In June 1950 I graduated and was handed, along with my B.A., a commission in the United States Marine Corps Reserve as a second lieutenant. That was clever, I remember thinking, how nimbly I'd avoided two years of military drudgery. A week or so later the North Koreans crossed the 38th Parallel and the war was on. Within a few months my class was mobilized.

I'd joined up to dodge the draft and ended up being sent to war.

People said the worst job you could have was marine rifle platoon leader. Life expectancy was supposed to be very short. Most marines did not think this was so and believed it would be much worse being a platoon leader in the army. Marines were better trained; their NCOs were superb; and there was discipline. Men just assumed the platoon leader knew his stuff, and they did what they were told. In the army it was different. If a platoon leader gave an order, they would all have to sit down and discuss it and then perhaps vote to decide if they would carry it out. This was more democratic, but good officers got killed that way in the army. Maybe that's why the West Point class of 1950, the same class in which I graduated from a civilian college, would lose so many of its young platoon leaders in Korea.

At Quantico there were many theories to explain why we were better than army troops.

There was always talk of esprit de corps, of being gung ho, and that must have been part of it. Better, tougher training, more marksmanship on the firing range, the instant obedience to orders seared into men in boot camp, more automatic weapons in each platoon, and so on. The NCOs must have been another part of it, hard, tough, experienced men, most of them regulars. So many of the officers were reservists, civilians called up, kids like me, that we leaned on the regular sergeants, the career marines. Army officers, young ones, had to do nearly everything themselves. That's what got so many fresh West Pointers killed.

But beyond such things, there was arrogance and pride. No matter how insecure an individual marine might have felt, how scared and confused, there was strength in the mass, in the unit. Men really believed we were better than the enemy, or anyone else, smarter and quicker and harder, more professional. Just better. That was contagious, it could carry a weaker man along. It didn't mean each man was braver or stronger or cared more, just that he was part of something larger that was all those things.

Those were questions we grappled with at Quantico, at the Marine Corps Schools. A hard catechism. Now we were going to get the answers.

4

Korea is a slender country which on a map resembles a somewhat smaller Florida, about the same shape but with the panhandle up in the northeast instead of reaching west toward Alabama and the Redneck Riviera. It is washed on one coast by the Yellow Sea and on the other by the Sea of Japan. To the north is vast China and beyond that, Siberia, from where the cold wind came. The whole country is maybe five hundred miles north to south along the long axis of the peninsula and not more than a hundred miles wide at its waist, about where you would find Orlando on a map of Florida. That was where they divided the country after World War II, at the 38th Parallel, with the Russians putting in a communist government north of the line and the Americans installing old Syngman Rhee in the south. And now, as the war's second November waned, with winter coming, that was where the two armies stood, on a diagonal roughly approximating the 38th Parallel, dipping below it in the west and extending some miles above it in the east. All that fighting and the country laid waste and all those people dead, and both armies were still just about where they stood when it began seventeen months before.

There were said to be a million Chinese, some forty divisions, north of us with the nine or so divisions that survived of the North Koreans. Facing them were five American army divisions, a British Commonwealth division and a mixed bag of brigades and regiments of Greeks and

Turks and French and others, in addition to what was left of the ROKs, which was what we called the Republic of Korea's army. And there was the First Marine Division which now in the second year of the war meandered over a terrible length of line, its right flank anchored on the Sea of Japan, its rifle regiments strung out across the high ridges of the coastal range, its left flank tied in with the ROKs. With its own regiment of artillery, its Marine Air Wing, its naval gunfire and an additional rifle regiment of Korean Marines, it was, even bloodied by the hard fighting that took those ridges in September, as powerful an infantry division as there had ever been in combat anywhere.

Divisional headquarters lay in a pleasant wood of evergreen in low, rolling hills ten miles south of the front. The woods were deep in snow, the pines glittering crystal. It was like every Christmas card you ever saw. We flew from the south on a clear morning, about thirty of us, lieutenants such as Allen and Hutchins and myself, staff sergeants and gunnery sergeants and master sergeants. These were the ranks and grades of which the division had run short. Now we were separated, the sergeants chivvied in one direction, the officers in another. I was relieved to see the master sergeants go. It made me uneasy to be saluted by men of such distinction.

We expected some sort of address by the general commanding the division but were spared. No one told us anything, no one asked anything, and in the whole, bustling, impressive winter camp there was nothing for us to do or say or hear. We ate and slept and in a light snow the next morning were fallen out, issued rifles and three clips, and packed into open trucks to continue north. Mack had it there would be an armistice before we caught up with the war. I had similar fears until a helpful soul had the kindness to inform us there were guerrillas out in the hills between Division and Regiment. During the truck ride I worried alternately we wouldn't get to the war and that we would.

The guerrillas, like the Migs over the sea, never appeared. The road north was dirt but well laid and ballasted, and the convoy of trucks moved smoothly and at a fair pace. From time to time on the right were glimpses of the sea, gray and looking cold with no great surf and what seemed like fishing villages at the head of every cove. There were no fishermen. Except for a few native hangers-on at the airfield no one had seen any civilians. We didn't know it yet but we wouldn't be seeing any for a long while. They'd been rooted from their homes and packed south out of the zone of battle. This was humane, I supposed. Around midday the snow petered out as the convoy halted at a fork in the road. There were shouted orders from the lead jeep, and our truck and one other swung left away from the sea and began to grind up the slope of a rougher road through timber. It was very cold now as we climbed, and I held the rifle between my knees with my hands in the pockets of the parka. Even through the pockets and the mittens the cold worked at my fingers. Mack and I were being sent to the same regiment. We were not that close, but I knew him from Quantico and respected him, and we got along. It would be nice to have Mack in the same regiment. I did not really know the others in the replacement draft, but already in a small way I missed them. Not Hutchins, though. The thought of being in combat with Hutch, his pale face and watery eyes and the quick fat hands on playing cards or on that girl, none of it went with how I felt about combat, about the war. I was glad he was gone. Probably we wouldn't see Hutchins again, or any of them. Maybe I wouldn't see Mack for long. Even ships that pass had schedules and routes and sailing orders and would pass again. Not so with us. I did not waste emotion worrying about it. Everyone goes to war alone.

Now we heard artillery for the first time. It was dull and sparse and far off, but it was a tremendous thing to me, a sound I'd waited nearly a year to hear, and dreaded, but now that it was there ahead of us I was curiously pleased. Deep inside maybe I never really believed in the war until now. I wanted to ask Mack about it, what guns they were, ours or theirs, but there were enlisted men in the truck and I did not like display in front of them. They teach young officers restraint.

Regimental headquarters was more warlike than Division, more satisfying. There were fewer people about and they wore helmets and carried weapons and were less neat and tailored. The road pinched out at the head of a very narrow valley, really just a two-bit ravine with tents, and the first bunkers chopped into its flanks. Strung through the air from one side of the ravine to the other were wires at a height of perhaps a hundred feet. At first I thought they were snares for low-flying aircraft and considered it a clever idea. But they were only part of the communications setup.

An enlisted man asked for our orders. We were officers, but no one seemed terribly respectful. We handed over the bundles of paper without which we didn't move, papers ordering us, in a marvelously romantic phrase, to "duty beyond the seas," and he pointed out the adjutant's tent halfway up the north slope. Steps were cut into the steep hillside, frozen earth braced with metal stakes, and a light line running along knee-high as a kind of casual bannister. The adjutant's tent was a cave of gloom. A clerk told us to sit down. He was not at all impressed by second lieutenant replacements, having seen too many of us come and too few go. The papers were sent deeper into the gloom. There was a bark and Mack Allen jumped up and went back. He was gone five minutes and then it was my turn, like waiting for the dentist. I understood the tent now, the gloom. The back of it opened into a narrow bunker, very deep and gouged into the hill, the tent itself just a sort of canopy. Giddily, I thought of those white canvas marquees erected before generals' quarters in the Revolutionary War, pictures in children's history books. It was not General Cornwallis but an ordinary major in an overcoat and a helmet pulled tightly down. He informed me I should sit down, that this was a fine regiment, finest in the division. I told him I was sure this was so.

"What job are you looking for?"

I knew the expected answer and snapped it back.

"Rifle platoon leader, sir."

The major said this was excellent, that I was a hard charger, that they needed hard chargers.

In the Basic School in Virginia where they train marine lieutenants they ask you every few hours that same question. Then they push a form at you to write down your first three choices of duty. There were several schools of thought about this. One held you should tell the truth. Those who subscribed to this odd notion put down communications or tanks or mountain training, anything that might delay assignment to a replacement draft and the war. Another advised diplomacy, a first choice of rifle platoon leader to show your spirit, then what you really hoped for, logistics or motor transport. A third school felt you should lie brazenly, indicating ferocious belligerence by demanding a rifle platoon, on grounds this might impress people and get you made a general's aide. Mack Allen achieved something of a name at Basic School by stipulating, quite honestly each time, "rifle platoon leader, rifle platoon leader, rifle platoon leader." I didn't worry about it much, not out of fatalism but simply because I believed the Marine Corps discarded all such forms without reading and it didn't matter much what you wrote. This close to the line I was too embarrassed to give any answer but the one the major obviously wanted to hear.

"Splendid," said the major, "we have an opening for a hard charger. Second battalion, Colonel Gregory's battalion. They want hard chargers up there, they need them. That's where you're going. Second battalion. Short of company grade officers." Then, sensing curiosity, "That's where I'm sending both of you, you and Allen. Hard chargers."

Mack was outside on the slope, hunched down on his heels like a cowboy. It was only three o'clock and the ravine was already in dusk.

"Man, we're going up there. A rifle battalion. We'll get platoons, just you see."

He sounded really happy. I asked if he thought the major wore his helmet to bed. Mack whooped joyously and then, remembering where he was, punched me on the arm and took off down the chopped-out steps three at a go. I went after him. Well, it was what we came for. I tried to be as pleased about it as Mack, but somehow I don't think I succeeded.

5

Colonel Gregory was a disappointment; his executive officer, Colonel Youngdahl, an immediate success. Later, we would know better. But now, joining the battalion for the first time, a battalion in combat, we knew only what we saw. The battalion commander had an old man's freckled face, a shapeless, rather silly grin, and a turkey neck. He cackled when he laughed, and he laughed often during a wandering talk of welcome. There was nothing laughable in what he told us, but he laughed nonetheless. Youngdahl did not laugh. He was a fine-looking man, blond, blocky, an older edition of the Naval Academy halfback he might have been. People who did not know Youngdahl predicted he would one day be commandant. People who knew him thought there was little danger of that. But the way he looked, the things he said and the way he said them, moved and impressed me and even Allen. If inspiration had not been currently in bad odor, both of us might have admitted to being inspired.

The battalion CP was again in a valley, a snug, snow-covered glen with pine trees and in the bottom of it a frozen creek. It was all very much like New England, northern Vermont, where I'd skied. Here artillery fire was less a novelty but still not heavy. Of course, it was louder. I tried to see where they were firing from but there were no batteries in sight. The two colonels shared a large tent fifty yards up the east slope of the valley. Neither wore a helmet. In contrast to the formal indifference of Division and Regiment, here was genuine welcome. They were short of officers. When we had presented ourselves and the rituals had been observed, we were told to come back after dinner and talk.

Gregory did some more cackling and Youngdahl talked.

He said it was a fine battalion, understrength following the September offensive, but a strong unit holding good positions.

"You'll see tomorrow. You'll go up in the morning with the gook train and some marines rejoining their companies. We're sending you both to Dog Company. They're down to five officers with two of them due to be rotated home."

Mack said we were pretty pleased at that. We wanted a rifle company and it was extra nice to be sent to the same outfit.

"There's a fine company commander," Youngdahl said, "a reserve, like you. Doesn't matter, though, we're all of us professionals. In fact in the whole battalion I think there are only five or six regulars, Colonel Gregory and myself and a few others. None in Dog Company. I'm really pleased, very much so, that you want rifle platoons. That's just the kind of young officer we want out here, that we need. Let me tell you about a young lieutenant in Dog Company and what he did just last night."

Youngdahl got off his camp chair and went to a map stand with a large-scale map under a plastic sheet. I knew how to read maps; at Quantico they made a fetish of it. There were grease pencil overlays, and with a stubby finger Youngdahl traced out for us the lay of the ground, the enemy lines, the positions of the battalion and its flanking units.

"We're down here right now, about two, two and a half miles back of the MLR." The MLR was the main line of resistance. "Now look at this ridgeline, where Dog Company ties in with Fox. You see this nose reaching out north. It drops away pretty fast, drops 600 meters right down to the flat and then on the other side the ground climbs again and steep. The gooks are there, of course. Well, last night this lieutenant, Simonis, only here a month, took a combat patrol down that nose, across the flat, and right up to here."

The finger stopped. There was no mark on the map but I leaned forward without saying anything, waiting for Youngdahl. Six hundred meters was 2,000 feet down, two thousand back up. That was a lot of climbing, in snow and at night. Mack and I knew Simonis. He'd been with us at Basic School at Quantico, a quiet, controlled sort who'd been an enlisted man in the war.

"There was a gook trench at this point with bunkers dug into it every seventy-five, hundred yards. Simonis got up there around midnight with no one the wiser, picked out two of the bunkers, and dropped grenades right down the chimney. He had a light machine-gun section set up, and when the gooks began to boil out, they cut them down. Got back here without a casualty, without a tear shed. Fine operation."

He let it sink in for a while.

"You see in this kind of stable warfare we've got right now, with the peace talks on and winter down on us, you don't really think in terms of a major offensive. That's for spring. But even in winter you can't just go to ground. That's no good for morale, no good for marines. You keep on the prod, jabbing away at them, keeping them off balance and nervous, bringing in prisoners, maintaining the aggressive spirit of the men. This is the sort of patrol you two will be sending out, leading yourself in some cases. Sometimes a combat patrol like this one, sometimes a reconnaissance, just getting out there and snooping around without a shot. Whichever, it's a game for young officers, tough young men who stay cool and think fast, like Simonis. Like you two, I'm sure. Wouldn't you say, Colonel?"

Colonel Gregory cackled pleasantly and Youngdahl smiled at him and went on. I'd listened to hundreds of tactical lectures at School and more at Pendleton, just the sort of talk Youngdahl was making now, but here the grease pencil was a line of men, the problem real and not academic, and the "School solution" not simply smart-alecking. Here you had to be right. My eyes traveled back up the plastic sheet along Simonis's route. He'd gone a long way out, Simonis. A long way out and back safe, a mission accomplished. I'd never considered Simonis anything special at School. Apparently the criteria here were different.

There was more chat, intimate and casual. The Corps was small, it was family, and regulars like Gregory and Youngdahl, men who might not even like each other, shared memories and curling snapshots of the past.

"I was so glad," Gregory said, "when Guadalcanal came along. Because then the old-timers would have to stop talking about 'how it was in Nicaragua.' Then we got so sick of hearing about the 'Canal.' Then it was Iwo and Okinawa. I was glad last year when the Yalu came along and now I'm fed up with the Yalu and how cold it was and the chinks on their Mongol ponies blowing bugles in the damned night. I wish we'd have another decent scrap so we could put the Yalu back where it belongs. With Iwo and the 'Canal' and Nicaragua. In the history books."

Mack and I just listened, mouths open. Later we learned Colonel Gregory had been on Guadalcanal as a platoon leader and had led the hard fighting in September when the battalion took losses taking these ridges. He was pushing forty and he hoped if the Division were going to do anything dramatic they would do it soon, while he could still sit up and enjoy it and not leave it up to these young kids they kept sending up.

He didn't say this to us now, of course, but issued a good-night cackle, and Mack and I were sent off to unroll sleeping bags and turn in on the dirt floor of a supply tent.

The morning was crisp. Outside, there was sun and people moving. Mack had lost his razor; he borrowed mine and promptly sliced a piece out of his earlobe. Blood streamed down his neck.

"My God, Mack, what happened?"

"Dammit, why didn't you warn me it was double edged?"

He wouldn't go to the battalion surgeon. With much dabbing and handkerchiefing he got it to clot.

"In the First War they used to shoot off their toes," I said.

"Well, I'd advise that. This hurts like hell."

Handkerchief to ear, with the cold helping stop the bleeding, Mack led the way to the supply tent, where we drew carbines, thermal boots, compasses, and canteens. We packed our seabags with stuff we couldn't carry and wouldn't need on the line and padlocked them against the next time the battalion would be in reserve. Mack had a .45 automatic from the war, and I'd bought a .38 Smith & Wesson revolver in California. An officer at that time could carry whatever side arms he chose. Carbines, pretty useless things, were issued regardless. We were happy to have thermal boots. We'd worn them in winter training in the mountains above Tahoe and knew the worth of them in snow. The first winter of the war men lost their feet to frostbite. These new boots were so good you could wade an icy stream with the water coming in over the top and within a few minutes be sloshing in water heated to body temperature. We packed our field shoes, boondockers, as a change-off or to wear in a thaw.

At the colonels' tent a half dozen marines had fallen in and Colonel Gregory was talking to them. We stood off to the side. The colonel's cackle was less evident in the morning. On each man's chest he pinned a medal, Purple Hearts, given for wounds received in the September jump. These men had been in hospitals in the south or in Japan, and now they were rejoining the battalion and being sent back into the line. It didn't seem fair, sort of like double jeopardy, but that was the system. They would march with the gook train to which we'd been attached. Youngdahl walked over to us when the little ceremony was finished.

"You won't have commands until you join the company and the captain assigns you platoons. So don't give any orders this trip. Just tag along and go where they take you. The sergeant will deliver you to Dog Company. Good-bye and good luck."

He shook hands, and we saluted, and the gook train moved off up the valley.

Mack carried a packboard slung with a rubberized waterproof bag holding his goods. I'd brought over a rucksack used by mountain troops, bought secondhand at an Army-Navy store. I'd used it skiing. Each of us carried maybe fifty pounds plus weapons and ammunition. The gook train moved steadily up the valley and then began more slowly to climb a well-traveled trail in the snow under big pines.

The gook train, and no one ever called it anything else,

James Brady

was made up of Koreans, service corps personnel, men for
one reason or another unsuited to active soldiering. I was
surprised how old some of them were, literally old men.
They carried tremendous loads on A-frames: rations, ammo,
oil, rolls of barbed wire, shovels, tents, empty sandbags,
the stuff of the army. I was sure their burdens weighed
more than mine, and when we'd been on the march for an
hour, climbing all the time, I wondered how the old ones
cut it. I was also watching the wounded marines. For the
first few minutes I was in awe of them, their combat experience and their wounds, much as I felt toward the NCOs in
our replacement draft. But the longer we marched the less
vivid was the difference between us. None of the six was
very big, several were pimpled boys, and in their faces there
was nothing distinctive. They were just marines, marines
here before me who had been in the fighting, but nothing
more. I started to feel better about it, less defensive.

Still, they were different. Their wounds set them apart.
They were veterans as I was not. The fact they were younger, eighteen or nineteen, that they had no college degrees,
no commissions, mattered less than the chance which put
them into the September fighting while I was still training in
Virginia. They had pimples. My adolescence was less obvious, but just as real.

The trail was easy going. Gook trains passed over it, a
hundred laden men or more, every morning going up, every
afternoon coming down. The snow lay a foot deep off to the
side, but the trail itself was a sidewalk. I walked along, not
thinking about the march, one foot in front of the other with
the legs of the man ahead going steadily up through the
pines, my eyes slitted against the bright sun coming off the
snow. I thought I'd better remember to grease my face
against sunburn when we got to the ridges about the tree
line. I had to smile at that, thinking like my mother:

"Don't forget your rubbers. It looks like rain."

I mouthed the words heard so often. It was strange being
here instead of home, among people who loved me. Here
were only strangers in a strange land, and up ahead, worse
than strangers. Mack Allen was a friend, in a professional
way. But he'd been in a war before, on Okinawa and then
in North China, and he had his own concerns, maybe his

22

own doubts. The wounded marines had no interest in me, why should they? The company commander to whom I would report, what could he possibly care about a young lieutenant with nerves? The company needed a body; they had sent him a body. That was all.

I had enough sense to be realistic about myself. I was still unformed as a man and knew it.

I turned twenty-three the day we flew north from Camp Pendleton to San Francisco to catch the navy plane to carry us west. There was nothing behind me more meaningful than puberty, a quietly broken home, and a pleasant college with summer interludes of marine training. In the plane, which I dramatized as perhaps the start of a last journey, I wasted an hour writing a sentimental letter to a girl I liked who was marrying someone else. I didn't love the girl, hadn't yet really loved anyone, but it seemed a shame on my birthday not to have had the opportunity of talking myself into love. I was embarrassed by that letter now, wishing I hadn't sent it. Now also behind me was the little Japanese girl in a geisha house. I was sensible enough to know that didn't make you a man, one note in a chord of maturity. Up ahead on the ridges would be plenty of opportunity to complete the process. Youngdahl said we were all professionals; I knew better.

Now, without any sudden change of direction, the long train was actually on the ridges for the first time. The valley had slipped away and we marched along a spine of ridge that climbed gradually north. Full of tactical strictures, I was wary of this exposure on the skyline. But I had my instructions on not interfering with the conduct of the march, and anyway, we were still screened by other, higher ridges farther north. The trail was neat, none of the flotsam of war you expected, the smashed guns, the torn sandbags, rusted barbed wire, none of that, only clean, smooth snow. Of course there might be things under the snow, but from what you could see you might be climbing Mount Mansfield, up in Vermont.

After a while someone up ahead gave the word and the column halted. Dutifully every gook dropped his A-frame and moved to the edge of the trail to urinate. Steaming yellow holes appeared in the snow. There was some talk, a

23

few laughs. No one wandered off the trail. I wondered about that and then concluded they were careful about mines, even in the mountains. This ground had been fought over before. The gooks stayed with the path and didn't roam. I moved up to where Mack was standing.

"Want to sit?"

"Nope. It's better to stay up with a load like this. You sit down and it's hell getting back up."

Mack looked fine, even with his bloody ear. He was short and barrel-chested with a cropped bullet head. I wondered if he felt the climb. I felt it myself, in the back of the legs, in the shoulders where the straps cut, but it was a good feeling, not fatigue, just the recognition of genuine exertion. None of the marines looked tired. I made my way back down the line, not waiting for the column to catch up. They taught officers to do that. As I passed one old man he was leaned over nearly double under his load and coughing heavily. There was one final cough and he hawked up phlegm and spit in the snow. The phlegm was bloody. I started to say something but lacked the language. The old man saw my interest and tried to straighten up, smiling, under the A-frame.

"Cigarette?" he asked in English.

I shook my head, patted the old man on the arm and moved down past him to my place.

6

Captain Chafee, the Dog Company commander, came a few hundred yards down the trail to meet the gook train, shaking hands with Allen and me.

"I'm very pleased to have you both here. I simply wanted to say welcome and to get you off to a proper start."

Chafee was a Rhode Islander of French descent, with a high color, a large nose and a splendid mustache. He was very lean, very dark, a handsome man. He didn't seem to have a weapon of any sort, only a kind of alpine stave that he used as he loped, his long legs covering the uneven ground in great strides. Going uphill he was fast and coming down he nearly ran. Later I would learn he was Skull and Bones at Yale and had a law practice and political ambitions. He now took us on a guided tour of the company front.

It was clear that Basic School notions of defensive warfare were to be put aside. They had drilled us in the need for defense in depth, a main line of resistance protected to the front by an outpost line and supported in the rear by various strongpoints wired-in, and by counterattack units. There was none of that here, only the MLR, and that stretched thin. The reserve battalion held a blocking position on another ridgeline entirely, miles back, too far to be of any immediate use in case of a breakthrough. There was no other reserve. In front of us was a no man's land and, beyond that, the enemy.

25

"We're a trifle understrength at the moment," Chafee told us. He didn't sound apologetic or dismayed by this. Just stating a fact. He took off as he talked, swinging along the top lip of a shallow trenchline that followed the ridge, linking large and small bunkers twenty to fifty yards apart. The bunkers were all on the ridgeline proper or slightly down the forward slope, joined to the trenchline by brief stretches of crawling ditch.

"There are sergeants commanding the mortar section and the machine-gun platoon. Lissman has the second platoon and he'll be going home soon and one of you will take that over and the other the machine guns. Don't worry about it. Whoever doesn't get the second platoon will pick up the third when Ed Flynn is rotated. He has the third and Bob Simonis the first. I understand you know him."

Mack said we did and had heard about his patrol.

"Colonel Youngdahl told us about it."

"Ah, yes, Colonel Youngdahl," Chafee said. "Well, now here's one of the machine-gun sections. They're all attached out to the rifle platoons. No point bunching them up with the line so long. The mortars are behind the third platoon on the reverse slope. From there they can hit anywhere along our front."

As we moved along the length of the company line, Chafee stopped to talk with marines at each bunker. He called each man by name, not Christian names or nicknames as they do in war movies, but the man's proper name. He didn't make introductions but was businesslike in a cheerful way. At the bunkers marines were shifting sandbags, cleaning rifles, cooking rations over small primus stoves, one marine cutting another's hair. No one seemed fussed by the captain's presence, none of the obsequiousness or make-work you saw at Quantico, intended to impress. Chafee's questions dealt with enemy activity to the front, the conduct of an ambush sent out the night before, the possibility of getting some mortar fire laid in on a suspicious-looking piece of ground off to the right, and so on. No chat about rations or leave or letters from their girls. They were all eating the same rations, there was no leave, a man's mail was private.

Here and there, I noticed, there were blackened places in

the snow, where incoming shells had hit. No one mentioned them.

The company frontage was astounding. Once again, the School solution was in discard. Dog Company, understrength, was covering about a thousand yards of front, more than half a mile of rough ground. In front of the line down the forward slope, two or three strands of barbed wire were stark against the snow. Here and there a tin can or a cardboard carton had been tossed out in front of the line. Otherwise it was surprisingly neat. I wanted to see what the enemy positions looked like, and during Chafee's stops I stared north to the line of hill and ridge running opposite our own. I could see nothing, even though the two ridgelines could not have been a mile apart, closer at some points. Before I could ask where it was Simonis had gotten to, the captain was off on another lope and I hurried to stay with him. I was starting to tire now, feeling in my legs the long climb and the pack, the early wakening, the tension, the novelty of it all. I looked over at Mack but there was nothing to see. His stubby legs were carrying him along as easily as Chafee with his long strides. Now the company commander jumped into the trench, a dirt corridor waist deep with dirty snow piled on either lip.

"Got to stay in the trench from here on," Chafee said. "Show you why in a minute."

The trench deepened to shoulder height as we moved toward the left flank of the company. We were in the third platoon's sector now, Flynn's platoon, which either Mack or I would have in a matter of weeks. Chafee stopped in front of a bunker to talk with a big, balding young man. He gestured to the left front, nodding vigorously.

"This is Lieutenant Flynn," Chafee said, "you're in his area now." He introduced us and we shook hands. Flynn, too, had a mustache but it was scruffy, lacking Chafee's elegance. He wore no insignia of rank, not even a collar bar, and looked like any other marine. He had a good smile.

"This sector Flynn holds is a tough one," Chafee said. "This is what we call Hill 749. Isn't really a hill. just a more prominent part of the same ridgeline. It was 749 that this battalion and another battalion took in September. It was a

27

hard piece of fighting. Those marines who came up with you in the gook train today, they were hit taking this hill.

"Well, they took it," Chafee said, "but not quite all of it. You tell them, Flynn."

Flynn grinned through chapped, cracked lips as if embarrassed. He waved a big red hand vaguely to his front.

"Really, we and the gooks share the ridge along here, or rather just to your left front. You can't see it from here. We'll crawl up and take a look later, but our lines and the gook lines are both on the same ridge for a few hundred yards. We're as close as eighty or ninety yards for a bit. We tried to dig them out in September and we've tried a couple of times since then with night work. They've tried to dig us out but we're both in too deep, too solid. It would take a real effort to clear this ridge. They can't get us out without bringing up more people, and neither can we. So we share the ridge, so to speak."

"Live and let live," I said.

"Not quite," Chafee said. "I guess Flynn's perfectly willing, but they're busy people and nearly every night we get activity here. Come on, let's take a look."

We got back in the trench. Chafee let Flynn lead the way; it was his neighborhood. Now the trench was head high and even deeper, with ammunition boxes set in here and there as firing steps. We passed two bunkers, each with a heavy machine gun emplaced. Here there was no haircutting and the men were all underground. In each bunker one marine had his back to us, his face toward the firing port. Open boxes of grenades stood inside the bunkers. At the third bunker, Flynn tapped the shoulder of the man on watch. He backed away and Chafee squeezed in to peer through the port. He knelt there for what seemed a very long time, then he squirmed back out and waved me into place.

For the first time I was looking at ground that matched my notion of what it would be like. There were three untidy fences of barbed wire a few yards to the front and some rusty concertina wire looped farther out. Beyond that were a field of snow pocked by shell holes, a few scrub pines badly chewed, and, about a football field away, a long, dirty mound of snow. I turned back and found Flynn's face very close to mine.

"Those are the neighbors," the platoon leader said.

I nodded, not knowing what to say. Since September, for two months, the two armies had been this close? I backed out and Mack replaced me at the firing port. A poncho covered the floor of the bunker, and I sat cross-legged on it and leaned back against the wall of sandbags and earth. The bunker may have been four feet high. Over my head a rough board shelf held stacks of ration cans and more grenades. Chafee squatted in the doorway, talking to the marines who lived in the bunker, professional talk, about wire and mines. Mack had seen enough, and one of the marines crawled in to return to his post at the port.

"Flynn, I'm going to send you some more wire. Tomorrow night before the moon comes up, try to get another couple of strands out there. It's a bit fragile as it is now."

"Aye, aye, sir," Flynn said. In the Marine Corps you said yes to a question, "aye, aye" to an order. It was clear this was an order. Flynn went with us as we worked our way back down the trench to the limit of his sector.

"The wire will be here by noon," Chafee said.

"Thanks, Skipper."

We shook hands again and Flynn wished us well. As we moved through the second platoon area Chafee said, "Flynn lost a man out there the other night trying to put in more wire. The gooks come up pretty close as soon as it gets dark. They crawl across the snow. But you need the wire. When the lines are this close, you need wire."

Now it was late afternoon, with the sun falling at our left, and we were back at Chafee's command post, the CP. It was a larger bunker of logs and sandbags on the reverse slope. You could walk around here; you didn't have to stay in the trench. A pudgy redhead, again with the inevitable mustache, came out.

"I'm Red Philips, the exec. Glad to have you aboard." He had the cheerful manner of a good salesman. Chafee had gone inside and we could hear him talking on the telephone. His soft voice carried, the words indistinct. I wondered if I could sit down, but anxious not to make the wrong impression, I stood while Mack and Philips exchanged small talk. Chafee came out.

"We'll skip the right flank tonight. You know Simonis

already. Besides, we have only a little daylight and I want
you settled in by dark. You know the division order, replacements don't go forward of the MLR their first five
days. It's a good order, lets you get the lay of the land. Last
summer we lost some new people just because they got
mixed up and made a wrong turning. They just plain got
lost. Not their fault, of course, but they're gone nonetheless." Mack looked downcast at being shackled. "Don't
worry," Chafee said, "five days go pretty fast and we'll
count this one day so you have only four to go."

He left us to Philips. For the moment Mack would bunk
in with the machine-gun sergeant and I'd stay with the
section leader of the mortars.

"Don't give any orders," Philips said, "just hang around
and keep your eyes open."

I wondered if I were ever going to give an order in this
war, not that I'd know what order to give. We slung our
packs and Philips assigned a company runner to guide us.

The mortar sergeant was a staff sergeant named Porterfield,
a good-looking, apparently educated man, very polite. His
assistant was named Dodge, a tiny fellow with sandy hair
and wild eyes. Both men had mustaches of extraordinary
length. I could hardly wait to begin cultivating one.

Dodge was also polite. "We're going to make you comfortable here, Lieutenant. So cozy you won't ever want to
leave us for one of those rifle platoons. We ain't crude
fellows like them, no, sir, mortarmen are more like technicians, you know, like scientists. Not just running around
shooting and yelling. When we fire, it's for a reason. And
usually it's for keeps."

The bunker was a big one ten yards down the reverse
slope of the ridgeline. It had no firing ports. Below the
bunker on the slope three 60mm mortars were dug in about
twenty yards apart, each ringed with sandbags. I looked
around but it was getting dark. And colder. The bunker was
warm and cheery, with candles, but I was uneasy with the
mortarmen. Aside from their politeness, which I didn't trust,
they were dealing with a weapon I did not fully understand.
At Basic School mortar instruction was cursory and I had
particular difficulty lining up the sighting bubbles that deter-
mined accuracy. I was a good shot with the rifle and the

BAR and had all the marksmanship medals, but the technique of the mortar eluded me. We ate dinner together, Dodge rattling on about what he claimed had been a promising career as a pitcher in the Southern Association. Baseball had ended for him when he punched out his manager for some ignorant but unspecified slight. Porterfield spoke sense, but I had the feeling I was being patronized. Both men were older than I was.

I was glad when dinner was over. I unrolled my sleeping bag and blew up the rubber air mattress. Porterfield gave me a clear space against the wall.

"Now don't fret, Lieutenant, if we're up during the night. It'll probably just be we're firing a mission in support, nothing to concern yourself with. Just get a good sleep and we'll show you around in the morning."

I said that was fine and lay down, my mind churning with events of the day. Hopes and fears, both. But I was very tired.

Then the air was full of sound. I sat up. Porterfield and Dodge were gone. I pulled on boots and snatched my helmet. You slept fully dressed with your web belt on, so I had the Smith & Wesson. Outside it was black and then just below me a blinding glare as one of the mortars fired. It was followed by another off to the side and then by a third. Somewhere over the ridge there was a rip of machine-gun fire and unfamiliar-sounding fire from another weapon. I started down the hill to the mortar emplacements, half sliding on the hard-packed snow. Porterfield grabbed my arm.

"Lieutenant, you didn't have to stir yourself. You need your sleep. Didn't I tell you we'd probably be firing a mission?"

"What is it?"

"Gooks are pestering Mr. Flynn again is all. Listen, you hear it? That brrrrpppp? That's a burp gun. Once you hear it you'll never mistake it for anything else."

Marine officers below captain's rank are properly called either "Mister" or "Lieutenant."

The firing went on for another ten minutes. Except for the distant artillery, it was the first hostile fire I'd ever heard. It was only eleven o'clock. When I woke I was sure it was around three. Gradually the firing faded and Sergeant Dodge climbed out of the sandbagged emplacement. It was a clear night with stars but very cold. Dodge was sweating. He looked happy. When they went inside, I could hear Porterfield on the phone.

"Yessir, Captain, we've secured the mortars. Fired around forty rounds. How many? Dodge, how many'd we fire?" Dodge told him thirty-eight. "Thirty-eight, sir, yessir. Good night."

I stood there outside the bunker a few minutes, looking down at the mortar pits where the crews were cleaning the weapons and talking low and then up at the immense sky full of stars. I did not feel tired anymore, or feel the cold, but then I turned back to the bunker and went inside, pushing the poncho curtain aside. Dodge and Porterfield were already asleep.

7

The morning offered no evidence of the night. Porterfield made coffee and said there were no casualties anyone knew of, though the mortars might have gotten people on the other side where they could not be seen. "The other side." They called them that, or "gooks," or "people." They also called our Koreans "gooks." The Chinese were "chinks." But we weren't facing them right now. It was all very matter-of-fact, how we spoke of the enemy.

Dodge was down in the mortar pits already, canteen cup of coffee in hand, cursing and waving his free arm at the mortar crews. Porterfield took no interest in Dodge's tantrum or the crew's subsequent sulky drill. You could see Dodge was the real mortarman, passionate about his trade, and Porterfield section leader only by virtue of his higher grade. I puttered around the bunker for a time and then strolled off toward the company CP. It was awkward being in the company without a defined responsibility. The next four days would pass slowly. I felt self-conscious about the simplest things: should I walk in the trench or atop it? If I stayed in it people might think I was afraid; if I stayed out someone might accuse me of drawing fire and being a damned fool. They didn't teach you the finer things at Quantico. I compromised by walking atop the trenchline but walking slumped.

The day before it had been terrain I noticed, the trenches and the bunkers and the hills where the enemy waited. Now I saw the men.

I supposed there had been motlier armies. The Chinese of the Long March; Lee's people at the end; the militia at Valley Forge; the Italians after El Alamein. But you had to go some, really work at it, to beat Dog Company's marines. Fresh from Quantico, I knew I should be righteous about it, but it was Chafee's company, not mine. Some men wore knee-length parkas, others pile vests or field jackets, one a forest green overcoat to his ankles. There were stolen army jackets, turtleneck sweaters, a plaid mackinaw made respectable by an issue green scarf tossed jauntily over one shoulder. There were fur hats and hats with earmuffs, ordinary fatigue caps and a baseball cap, wool stocking caps, overseas caps, and helmets, some with the green, some with the tan, some without any camouflage cover. There were thermal boots and ordinary boondockers and jump boots "liberated" from the army. Men wore no insignia, or black stripes painted on the sleeve, or metal badges of rank I didn't recognize that they'd gotten from the South Koreans. From every breast pocket gleamed a brass spoon, hammered from an old shell casing, a "gook" spoon. I did not know what they were and finally asked. One marine wore his Purple Heart, another a 1948 "Dewey for President" button. Barely credible was a navy corpsman in blues and flat hat. It would be some time before I would meet Jay Scott, who wore a Brooks Brothers button-down shirt and repp tie under his winter uniform.

Mack Allen shook his head over it. He'd been out early scouting along the line and had seen the disregard for uniform.

The sailor bothered him most. "I'd run that swabbie up the mast."

Mack was remembering spit and polish as an enlisted man in North China.

As we talked, a marine with a BAR (Browning Automatic Rifle) came along wearing blue jeans and cowboy boots.

"Goddamn," Mack said softly. He didn't curse much and I knew he was upset. I sympathized with Mack, not only a marine officer but a Harvard graduate school alumnus and a product of VMI.

Philips took us out to the right flank to see Simonis. He seemed glad we were there, but to me he looked wary, tired, though physically in good shape. He was the only Dog Company officer not sporting a mustache.

"I had one for a week but food kept getting hung up in it," Simonis said.

Mack said something about his patrol, the one Youngdahl was bragging about.

"We were quiet and we were lucky," Simonis said. It was obvious he didn't want to talk about it. He excused himself, saying he was inspecting weapons this morning. Philips took us out on the point, the nose off the ridge down which Simonis had taken his patrol.

"This is an abbreviated version of the nose Flynn's got up there, but the difference is, here we've got the whole ridge. No gooks to share. See how it falls away steep and that's the valley way down there, about a hundred yards of open ground to cross, and looky here, follow my arm and you see where a new ridge begins to grow out of the flat right there and go up. That's where Simonis went up. Quite a job at night and slippery as the snow is. You can't see their bunkers from here without glasses. Those gooks, gotta give it to them, they camouflage better and they observe skyline discipline. We don't."

Philips turned to look around and I realized we were all three on the skyline. Off along the ridge were other marines. No one used the trench at this end of the line. When it had to be crossed, men jumped it and kept on going. We turned back from the nose, and as we did there was a loud whiz and Philips, moving faster than a plump man should, dropped into the trench.

"Down!" he shouted. Mack and I jumped in after him. There was an explosion and black smoke rising somewhere behind us and then another whiz with a bang on the end of it.

"Seventy-sixes," Philips said, squatting in the bottom of the trench. "Flat trajectory weapon, not as fast as it sounds. If you hear the whiz you can usually beat the bang."

I looked past him at Allen. Mack was beaming. "Were they shooting at us?" I asked Philips.

"Likely. They only wasted two, so they couldn't have been serious about it, just trying to instill a little discipline into three damnfool marines."

He didn't seem angry at being shot at. But we stayed

in the trench for a hundred yards, until it dropped away below the skyline. It was all very casual. Mack's pleasure at being shelled puzzled me. One thing to be gung ho about going to war, another to be delighted someone was shooting at you.

We had lunch with Lissman, the second platoon leader. He was a huge, happy man, all Texas accent but without the boasting. "Hutchins," Mack whispered. But Lissman was no Hutch. He blended charm and humor and good sense during the meal. He understood the job and gave an impression of competence, his explanation of the platoon's disposition and its problems clear and instructive. My opinion of Captain Chafee rose another rung. Mack and I were getting the best possible feel of the line simply by wandering about like this, guided but not lectured at, from one platoon leader to the next. Chafee could have sat us down in front of maps as Colonel Youngdahl had done, and it would have been Quantico all over again. This way it was real, and I did not think I would forget. I wasn't tired anymore, but my heart ran a little rough still. Being fired at the first time was not as terrifying as I expected, nor as effective, but it was something you had only once and I kept thinking about it. I didn't talk to Chafee again but saw him when I passed the CP on the way back to the mortars. Chafee was stretched full length on top of his bunker, slowly scanning north with big glasses, and calling down remarks to one of his runners, who noted it in a pocket book as he sunned himself in the lee of the bunker.

The night was quiet. I sat up awhile with Dodge and Porterfield, chatting more normally. I wanted to think it was because I'd been under fire, but they could not possibly have known this. It was probably that I'd been around for two days and the novelty had worn off.

Dodge even tried to educate me a little.

"Most of the enemy weapons," which he pronounced "weepons," "are Russian. And the Russians are pretty smart about weapons. Their mortars are one millimeter larger in diameter than ours. We got 60s and 81s. They got 61mm mortars and 82s. So they can use captured American mortar shells. They slide in easy and just a fraction loose, but we can't use *their* shells. They're just a tad too big for our tubes.

"Maybe," said Dodge, reaching back, laboring, into history, "they come up with that idea during the Big War, when they was fighting the Germans, so they could use German ammo when they got some. Of course the North Koreans and the chinks got plenty of American ammo. They got it from old Chiang Kai-shek when they kicked his ass out back in '49, and the Russians got lots of American shells from the war, from Lend Lease.

"And don't worry about how old ammo is," said Sergeant Dodge, "ammo, you keep it nice and dry, keep it clean, it lasts a long time. A twenty-year-old mortar shell? Why, that'll kill you as nice as one just out of the factory."

Flynn's platoon tried during the night to erect an additional barbed wire barrier on the nose, but the Koreans heard them and a flare went up and they had to cut and run. A few shots were exchanged but no casualties. The mortars hadn't even been called in. Philips told us about it in the morning at the CP.

"More to the point, there's talk of another patrol the same route Simonis took."

If Battalion decided the patrol was on, Philips said, Lissman would go. Chafee and Lissman were out now, going over the ground with glasses. In another few days Lissman would be bouncing around in a truck headed south and either Mack or I would have his platoon. Give or take a couple days, this patrol would be our problem, not Lissman's, and one of us would be out with Chafee and the sergeants, straining to pick out landmarks we would need in the dark. It gave you a rooting interest.

Just how Chafee would decide between us for the platoon was unclear. Based on experience, Mack deserved first crack. As the day wore on Mack worried he would not inherit the second platoon and I worried, but only to myself, that I would.

The afternoon was unseasonably pleasant, strong sun, no wind, and warm enough to begin melting some of the mountain snow that by rights was there for the winter. We were in North Korea, the chunk of it hung on to when the Chinese came south a year before, and I guess all of us remembered the horror stories of that first winter, the ambush at the Chosin Reservoir and the cold and the pictures of frozen marines in *Life* magazine. I'd started thinking about the North Korean winter at Quantico and never stopped. Now I was strolling around a North Korean ridgeline in a wool shirt and one sweater.

Around three o'clock, off to the left there was a sudden smash of incoming mortar fire, then a distant shouting. Chafee, just back from scouting with Lissman, took off along the ridge toward Flynn's position. I started to go but Red Philips barked at me. "Stay put till we know what happened!" Then Philips's phone rang. It was Flynn. Four of his men, sunning themselves on top of a bunker, had taken a direct hit from an 82mm mortar the gooks had thrown up without notice. Just one shell but two of the marines were dead, another had lost both legs, and the fourth was badly holed. They brought them down past the CP, the dead shrouded in ponchos, the wounded conscious and in pain. I stood watching, feeling a stranger. One of the dead was cousin to the man whose legs were gone. They came from a town in Massachusetts. The marine without legs didn't seem to realize about his legs but was talking about his cousin.

"Poor Eddie," he said, "what's Eddie's mother gonna say?"

Chafee was with them, at one corner of the four men carrying Eddie in the poncho. He turned it over to someone else and went into the CP, Philips and I following.

"Get Simonis," Chafee said, "tell him to send three men up to Flynn for tonight to fill in the line. Tell him thin out his own people where he can. I'll try getting him some more men in the morning. He can have my runners if I can't get anyone else. They'll have that bunker okay before dark. It wasn't banged up too badly. The men took most of it."

While Philips made the call Chafee turned to me.

"Well, that happens. No one to blame. Blame the sunshine if you have to lay blame. Truman himself couldn't keep marines from getting some sun. Good men, too. You hate to lose them anyway but losing them like this is stupid. It hurts even more. We learn, though. You won't see anyone doping off on top of a bunker for a while."

He picked up the battalion phone to call in the casualties.

Except at family wakes and once in a car crash, I'd never seen anyone dead before.

8

It was Lissman's day. Battalion confirmed that another combat patrol should retrace Bob Simonis's steps and attack with concussion grenades to try bringing back a prisoner. Armies love prisoners, the best intelligence there is. The patrol would jump off directly last light faded. Lissman would have three or four hours to descend the nose, cross the open space, and climb to the enemy lines. He should be there by nine, back at midnight. Coming back they could move faster with less need for quiet. Remembering what we'd seen, Mack and I agreed three hours wasn't much for the outward leg. Big, fat Lissman would have to move. Chafee told us to take our bedrolls to Lissman's bunker for the night. He wanted us to get the feel of what it was like running a patrol. It was late afternoon when we got there and squeezed in. Lissman and Red Philips went over the map again while Lissman's platoon sergeant listened and the runner cooked dinner, passing around the tin cans.

"Nothing for me," Lissman said. His face under the tan and the fine mustache was pasty and he talked more than seemed necessary, the Texas accent more pronounced. Philips kept telling him it would be a cushy thing.

"Hell, Tex, if Simonis could pull it off you won't strain yourself at all. We'll have some bourbon on the ice for you. I'll be here my own self, midnight. That's a date."

"Sure, Red, sure. I know. Only thing worries me is taking the same route. I don't like that. Pushing our luck.

39

Those gooks are probably still pissed off at Simonis and we're going to walk right up the same street. That's what I don't like."

Philips kept at it, soothing.

"Why, Tex, that's the beauty of it. Just what they won't expect. It's just lovely. You'll fool 'em dead."

There was more of this, Lissman worrying and Philips scouting the worry. I didn't say anything but it scared me. Here was this big, extroverted Lissman, after nearly a year of war, courage and confidence oozing out of him by the minute, with Philips, his superior officer, trying to wean him off his fear, down to the promise of a drink when he got back. How bad could it be out there to frighten Lissman? I looked at Mack, who had his own memories of war, but could read nothing in his face. I thought he might be embarrassed to be hearing all this. Now Lissman started again.

"Maybe you could phone Simonis again, Red, for me. Just ask him what he thinks. You know, what does he think our chances are."

"Now, Tex, if a kid like Simonis can do it, you'll breeze through. Give Bob a chance to ride you tomorrow? I wouldn't do that to you."

The talk went on and I crawled out of the bunker. In the west there was a last streak across the sky, the east black with the first stars showing. It looked like a sky at home, a sky anywhere. There would be a moon, but much later. After they got back. If they got back.

It was a reinforced squad Lissman was taking out, and now the squad leader was there and the corporal of the machine-gun squad. They were taking two .30-calibre light guns for covering fire when they hit and then to support them getting away. The same drill, exactly, as the Simonis patrol. I knew too little to say anything but enough to be uneasy. The battalion might have varied the exercise a jot, giving them a new set of bunkers to hit, a new approach, something different. It was this seemed to bother Lissman most, that he'd be a carbon copy of Simonis. He was crooning this still to Philips.

"You never would have tried the same stunt twice with the Japs, Red. You know that. John knows it, too. He should have stood up to Battalion on this."

"Now, Tex, I'm not going to listen to any talk about the skipper. You know if Gregory didn't order him to stay off patrol, it'd be John Chafee and not you going out tonight. He gets an order from Battalion, he carries it out. They ask his opinion, well, that's another matter. He tells them. This patrol's an order. Else you wouldn't be going. Flynn can't do it. He's got his plate full just hanging on to his share of 749. Simonis pulled the last raid. Now stop worrying, it's going to be fine."

"Fine." Lissman snorted a half laugh. It was the first echo of the Lissman of the day before.

"Now you bring us back a real talkative gook so we won't have to go out again till spring."

"Sure, Red, sure we will."

Lissman was making a big effort at control. I sneaked a look at my watch. It was just five, full night.

"Well," Philips said.

"Yessir," Lissman said, not to Philips but as if to himself. He turned to the two squad leaders. His voice was reedy, funny coming out of that big gut. "Saddle up, it's time."

We all got up and I backed against the wall to be out of the way. I didn't know if you were supposed to wish a patrol luck.

Outside we watched them move off. The rest of the patrol had been out there waiting. I didn't have my night vision yet, but I could sense the bulks there around me, could hear them. There was little talk, then Lissman's voice, steadier now, deeper.

"Come on, let's move out. No talking. Don't bunch. Let's go."

The column moved down the line, walking in the trench to stay in touch, twenty men moving quietly in the dark, no sound but the creak of web gear and the shuffle of thermal boots on frozen mud and crusted snow. I sat down atop the trench, looking north. I had vision now and could see the loom of high ground out there, the enemy ridge up which Lissman would soon be creeping. There was no wind, which was not so good. A little wind covered sound. But it was colder, the day's thaw having seeped away as if drawn into space, and after a few minutes the patrol was gone and I went inside. Mack was there over coffee, but Philips had gone back to the CP. Lissman's platoon sergeant was in command now. He was at the phone, listening to nothing. The runner gave me some coffee. I drank it, feeling sleepy but not wanting to sleep. I would have felt guilty sleeping with Lissman out there.

"A couple of days and we'll be doing it," Mack said. I didn't say anything. At least he wasn't being enthusiastic about it. Neither of us would say much, anyway, not in front of the sergeant and the runner. Though Lissman had said plenty, said what he thought. Of course he'd been around for a while, this was his sergeant. Lissman hadn't come in on the last plane. And it was Lissman out there, not Mack or me.

The telephone rang and we all four straightened, expectantly, though it was too early to know anything. The sergeant took it. I relaxed, slumping back against someone's helmet. It couldn't be anything; we would have heard firing, and so far the night was quiet, even in Flynn's sector. The sergeant just kept saying, yessir, yessir. He sounded excited.

"They called it off," he said. He hadn't even hung up the phone. "The patrol's off."

"Why so?" Mack asked.

"Battalion canceled it. Something about the truce talks. They got Mr. Lissman by radio before he was off the nose. He's on his way back."

Mack shook his head. "Hot damn, they cut them close."

I got up and yawned, stretching nervousness out.

"I'll bet Lissman can use that bourbon." Then I remembered the enlisted men were there and I shut up.

"He's not the only one, Lieutenant," the platoon sergeant said.

I grinned, deciding maybe I worried too much about rank, and stayed long enough to see Tex when he came in. He wasn't grinning, didn't seem interested in the drink, a big man thoughtful and subdued, still thinking how close they'd gone to the edge. His platoon sergeant said something to him, something routine, and handed him a canteen cup of coffee, knowing what to do and what to say. And what not.

42

"Good coffee," Lissman said, brightening a bit.

It was terrible coffee. I'd been drinking it and I knew. But I knew Tex was just trying to say thanks.

I wondered if this would be my platoon, my platoon sergeant, before the week was out.

I began to wish that it would.

We forgot a lot of what they taught us at Quantico. But I remembered Joe Will's lecture. Will was a captain who'd been in the hard fighting around Pusan the first summer of the war. There were pictures of Will and his men in *Life* magazine. Will had really been to Korea and had fought and so we listened and took notes. Will didn't talk about war aims or strategy or even small unit tactics. He told you what to take to Korea in your pockets.

Nail clippers. If your nails grew too long they caught on things and became jagged or maybe even were ripped off. One-a-day vitamins. You were going to miss meals and there was no fresh fruit or milk and you needed vitamins to keep you going. A knife. Not to kill people with but just a boy scout knife with a couple of blades and a screwdriver and an awl. Toilet paper. There was a package in every ration box, but there was never enough. A flashlight, sheathed in black rubber for insulation and against hard knocks. A pen and a small spiral notebook. You wanted to keep track of your men and to be able to write lists, to leave notes for people. A good watch with a luminous dial you could read at night. A couple of good-sized bandanas you could use as handkerchiefs. You were always wet and going to catch cold and your nose would run. A toothbrush and paste. A small bar of soap. A razor, of course. The soap also worked as shaving cream. Some rawhide leather thongs, in case your shoelaces broke or you had to make jerry-rigged repairs to something. A plastic bag to keep your wallet in when you got wet. An extra pair of wool socks. A Zippo lighter, for smoking and lighting fires.

Marine uniforms have plenty of pockets. All this you could carry without having a pack. Sometimes you'd lose your pack or have to drop it behind for a time, but what was in your pockets you always had. I carried a compass and because it was winter some handwarmers that worked with lighter fluid. A dozen extra .38 cartridges on a strip of belting material. I also had a hunting knife that hung with the canteen and the holster on a web belt. Everything else went into the rucksack: the sleeping bag, the change of clothes, the extra sweater, the rations for that day, the rubber air mattress, the poncho that kept off some of the rain. A book. Some flimsy airmail writing paper. You didn't need stamps. Or money. There was nothing to buy, no place to spend it.

The dog tags went around your neck. You hung them from a leather thong at different lengths so they didn't clink together and make noise. You wore two dog tags so that if you were killed they would cut one off and turn it in to graves registration or some other authority and leave one on the body to ensure accurate identification. The Marine Corps had a system for just about everything.

People at Quantico said Joe Will did some drinking nights at the officers' club. But he gave a good lecture and most of us remembered what he told us. As I was pretty sure I was going to remember what I was learning now from Chafee and Philips and Tex Lissman and Sergeant Dodge.

9

The next day started off as Sergeant Dodge's day and ended as something quite different.

It was mid-morning. Porterfield was reading and Dodge was down in the pits, alone and puttering. He would fiddle with the mortar, making infinitesimal alterations in its aim, then scramble back up the slope to the ridgeline, throw himself flat on the ground to stare north through eight-power glasses, then go back to the mortar for more computation and aligning of the bubbles, then back to the ridge and the field glasses. Under the baseball cap Dodge's eyes were darting and he was crooning to himself, unaware of me or anything beyond his project. Several more shuttles between pit and ridge and then Dodge was ready. Without looking up he waved me away and picked up a shell, licked his lips, and dropped it down the tube. There was the usual thud and then the dull cough of a mortar's firing, and Dodge leaped from the pit to scramble up the ridge with his glasses. Seconds passed and then, way off to the right, in the flat of the valley, there was a red flash and a splash of white, a white phosphorus shell exploding. Dodge jumped up.

"Got the son of a bitch! Got them, four of them! Right down the hatch."

He did a little dance there on the ridge. Porterfield came up.

"Were you close?"

"Close? Close? I was right on. Right on, man. Four of

45

them palavering down there and in she came. Oh, it was sweet. Extreme range. Two thousand yards, not an inch less. And it was sweet. Looky, looky here. Take the glasses. There they are, all four of them spread out, still a-smoking. One was rolling around on fire for a minute, but he's stopped now. Four with one shot. Oh, but it was sweet."

When Porterfield finished with the glasses, I took them. Sure enough, there were four bodies lying out there blackened against the snow, lying still. Smoke was still wisping up from one of them. Dodge had hit them dead on.

"Pretty fair shooting, Dodge," Porterfield said.

"Pretty fair? Fair? Why, that's great shooting," Dodge shouted.

I said the proper thing. It had been an astounding shot. I didn't know mortars but I could tell that. Dodge was either very good or very lucky.

I thought back to the four marines hit by a similar shot from the other side. Dodge had evened the score this morning. And of course the enemy shot, good as it had been, might have been zeroed in earlier. Dodge's shot was dead reckoning, as he said. Porterfield got on the phone and reported the shot, and the four gook casualties, to Philips at the CP. They kept lists of the dead, on both sides. I was starting to learn that was how the dead added up in this war, people sunning on a roof, or sitting around palavering in a valley, while mortarmen guessed at ranges and played games with bubbles in a glass. Dodge probably would have gotten along quite well with his counterpart over there, had more in common with a gook mortarman than he did with me.

Porterfield was asleep. Dodge was out, probably caressing one of his tubes. I was writing a letter home. It was ten o'clock. The firing began somewhere close. You could hear the spit of the burp guns, the heavier crash of rifles, then the short controlled bursts of a good machine gunner. I pulled out of the sleeping bag and slipped into the boots. Porterfield was up, too. Outside there was the initial black, and then, as our eyes adjusted, I could see men jumping into the mortar pits.

"They're after Flynn again," Porterfield said.

Dodge was on the phone, getting a call for mortar support

from the third platoon. The first rounds were pumping out even before I got to the pits.

"Probing Flynn," Dodge told Porterfield. He didn't bother explaining anything to me, to the amateur, wheeling from us to curse out the squad in the next pit. To his ear something hadn't sounded right about that last round.

"Two charges, you meats! I said two charges." You could adjust the amount of powder to alter the range.

The rounds went chunking out, one tube then the next then the third, and then the first again. You could hear them crunching on the other side of the ridge. Dodge's men were firing so fast they had four or six rounds in the air all the time. There was plenty of flat trajectory fire off to the left, both sides firing. I was beginning to know the sounds. I left the pits and climbed to the ridge. I knew what night firing looked like from Quantico and Pendleton. The sustained firing was the machine guns, maybe the burp guns, some of it very close. It sounded the way it did on the rifle range when you were pulling targets in the pits and the bullets whipped overhead through the paper bull's-eyes and you could hear them sing.

"Hey, Lieutenant, get off of there."

It was Porterfield. I slid down the reverse slope to where he crouched.

"What are you doing on the skyline? Don't you know those people are firing at you?"

"Well." I didn't know what to say. I supposed maybe they were firing at me. It was dumb standing up there, but I'd gotten excited trying to see. "Well," I said, "I guess they were."

Porterfield looked disgusted. Then the firefight was over.

"Secure," Dodge said, "seeee-cure."

In the sleeping bag it kept going through my head, being shot at, being chewed out by Porterfield, the shooting up close and not at a distance and mechanical as happened with the whiz-bang 76s. I could have been hit. That was how it happened, when you didn't expect it, when you weren't thinking, like the marines on the roof in the sun. I was dreaming, a confused dream, when the bunker phone rang. Porterfield picked up and was saying, "Okay, okay." Dodge was already up and out.

"Second platoon is getting gook sound," Porterfield said. "Exec thinks they'll get a probe. We're alerted."

It was two thirty. Very cold but again no wind, the sky clear, spattered with big stars. No moon yet. I took the phone in the pit. "Red, this is Brady. What is it?"

"Second platoon hears gooks. Maybe they're wrong but they're pretty cool boys. Lissman thinks they're coming in."

"Red, could I come down there? I'll stay out of the way. I'd just like to be there."

"Sure, what the hell. Come on down. But come quiet and stay in the trench or someone's liable to take a piece out of you. Don't forget the password."

I handed the phone back to Porterfield. He looked at me as if I were demented. Inside the bunker I took the carbine off the wall and stuck two extra magazines in my pocket. I crouched and moved fast along the trench. No one challenged me, there was no firing anywhere except miles over to the west, where you could see artillery flashes, so far away you couldn't hear them. Lissman's place was quiet. I stuck my head in and Lissman told me welcome. But it was too crowded and I didn't want to break their concentration. Two men hunched at the firing port, trying to see something against the snow, in among the dwarf pines. I backed out and sat down in the trench. It was cold against my ass. Another marine was there, a few feet away, one of Chafee's runners. I listened hard but there was nothing to hear, only myself breathing.

Then came the whir-whir-whir of an incoming mortar shell and another and another, all before the first hit. It wasn't far off. I could see the flash. Then came another and another, and in among the whir-whir you could pick out the whiz bang of flat trajectory fire and 76s began to slam into the ridgeline. I crouched lower in the shallow trench, trying to count the rounds, but there were too many. Now they were hitting nearer. The ground shook, and then some dirt slapped down on my helmet, and Chafee's runner was moving off. I moved, too, low. Any lower and I would have been crawling. Now the mortars were coming in so fast you couldn't separate the hits. The whiz bangs, too. More dirt landed on me, big chunks. I found myself up against a bunker. There were voices inside.

"Room for one more?" I said, feeling silly but trying to be cool and not urgent about it. Someone shouted something and I took it for welcome and scrambled in. I would have gone in anyhow. There were four or five men in the bunker, practically sitting on one another. I huddled just inside the entrance.

Someone said, "You know that's just a poncho hanging there behind you."

More shells hit. I felt naked, sheltering behind canvas. Then there was a commotion and another marine scuttled inside, knocking me farther into the bunker and taking my place in the doorway. "Good morning," he said. I was sitting on someone's leg, but I was relieved to have a body between me and the canvas doorway. The mortars and the 76s came in for another few minutes and then abruptly cut off.

"Now they'll come," someone said, very quietly.

"Yeah," said the marine behind me. It was Chafee's runner. I wondered how I'd gotten here before him.

There was silence and then, seemingly right above us, came machine-gun fire, then burp guns, rifles, and now the crack of grenades exploding.

"Let's get out of here," someone yelled, and the runner and I were pushed through the entry. We were just barely on the reverse slope, a few feet below the ridge. Over the ridgeline everyone was firing. I slipped the safety catch off the carbine and threw myself down and started crawling on my belly to the ridge, the firing all around and confusing me. I lost direction momentarily, then realized up was front and resumed crawling. It was something you did a lot of in training. But then they weren't firing live ammunition. There was burp-gun fire everywhere now, some of it behind me, on the reverse slope. There was a man standing on the roof of the bunker I'd just left. What a damn fool thing to do. Then the man was gone. The machine guns were no longer cool and controlled, firing short, disciplined bursts. They were chattering off long *rrippps*. Grenades crashed, and in front of us mortars were coming in. Ours, I thought, probably that crazy Dodge. A flare went up and I pressed my face into the snow not to be blinded. While it hung there swinging on its parachute the fire became more intense. Then, without any signal, it piddled out. I was still flat on my belly but over the ridgeline, a few yards down the forward slope, no damned place to be. I scurried back and dropped again into the trench. I could not remember crossing the trench on the way out. I must have, but I could not remember it.

10

Captain Chafee and Red Philips were there now. Lissman was checking his platoon front and his sergeant was making the report:

"We figure between four and five hundred rounds of incoming, Captain. All in fifteen minutes. Most of it mortar, some 76 in there, too. Far as I know to date, no casualties. Mr. Lissman's checking the squads now. We figure we got four, five gooks. Maybe more. But we can see four hanging on the wire and what looks like a piece of another one."

Chafee listened carefully, nodding as the sergeant catalogued the action. His mouth was pursed under the mustache, and he was swinging a stick against his leg. He was neat and pressed, and I wondered if he stayed up all night so that he was never rumpled and creased like the rest of us. He was asking questions, feeling out the platoon sergeant. He and the sergeant were smoking, sitting there nice and quiet.

"You want me to go out there with a fire team and bring in the bodies, Captain?"

"No, I think we'll wait for first light. It's now, let's see, just on four o'clock. We'll have light, enough light anyway, by five, five thirty. Then I want to go after the people who probed us. We might still catch up to them before they reach the valley. They'll be carrying wounded and that's going to slow them. How many do you estimate there were, Sergeant?"

"Well, the boys along here, they think maybe a platoon. But you know people get excited. Me, I figure a squad, maybe reinforced. And a machine gun. Say a dozen, fifteen men. So there might be nine or ten left movin'."

There was a shout from someone to the right and Chafee was on his feet instantly. I never saw a man move that fast. Philips moved along behind him.

"It's another gook, Skipper. Dead on top of this here bunker."

It was the bunker I'd sheltered in during the firefight. A man lay facedown across the roof, arms dangling. There was no sign of blood. He didn't look dead at all, just very limp. He was the first North Korean I'd seen up close.

"He's got a sack full of grenades, sir. Probably going to stuff them down the chimney."

"Just like Santy Claus," someone said. Behind me there was a snort of laughter.

"Well," said Philips, "that makes five, maybe six."

I wasn't counting. I was thinking of what a grenade down the chimney would have done to us crowded inside the bunker. The gook, the dead one, must have been the man I later saw standing on the bunker, the man I thought was a marine being stupid. If I'd been alert, I might have gotten him myself. Then, the gook might have gotten me if he weren't preoccupied with his grenades and the chimney. There was some conclusion to draw, but I didn't.

Chafee had given a few precise orders and no one was standing around now. They were all back in the line. Lissman came up and saluted. We didn't salute up here as a matter of course but once in the morning and once at good night. Lissman must have been thinking about something else.

"No casualties, Skipper, not a one."

"That's fine," Chafee said.

"They throw in four, five hundred rounds and don't hit anyone, and the other day they toss up one shot and get four men," Red Philips said.

"Well, Red, if wars were logical we wouldn't fight them," the captain said. "Now suppose you make up a patrol, three or four fire teams and a gook interpreter, and shove off at five. Use your own judgment in the pursuit, but no matter what, turn for home when you get to the valley. I'd like to sort of discourage those people from coming back."

"Yessir."

"Of course, if it looks fishy, turn back before that. Try to get a prisoner. Take a stretcher. They may abandon their wounded if you press them."

"Aye, aye, Skipper." Philips went off to round up the men for the patrol.

"Skipper?" It was the first time I'd used the familiar address to the company commander.

"Yes, Brady, you want to go along. Go ahead. Just stick. close to the exec and don't tell Battalion."

"Aye, aye, sir. Thank you, sir."

I guess I was pretty obvious about it, but I was glad Chafee was letting me go. The night's action, the mortars, then the firefight, made me feel terribly sure and relaxed, as if burdens had been shed. Not nervous the way I'd been since the plane touched down. Mack came up now at a trot.

"Hey, Jim, I hear you got a dozen of them."

"Well," I said, grinning. I felt pretty good, having seen it all while Mack didn't.

He seemed to understand. "It's something, isn't it?"

"Yes," I said, "it sure is."

Philips was back now, the patrol rounded up. Nearly everyone wanted to go. This wasn't like crossing the valley and going up the other ridgeline in the dark. This was ground they knew and it would soon be dawn. To men who'd shuddered under the incoming and then beat back the probe, it was a satisfying notion to go after a retreating enemy, nice to think of trying to hit them even harder than they'd been already hit, to hunt them down and kill them. An hour ago they'd been up here cutting through the wire, tossing grenades, trying to blow up our bunkers, trying to kill marines. No one was talking about prisoners now but Chafee. The marines wanted kills. At least that was how I read them. Remembering the gook on top of the bunker with his grenades made me feel that way.

"Saddle up," Philips ordered, "saddle up. Moving out in five minutes."

I unslung the carbine and made sure there was a cartridge in the chamber and the safety engaged. It was brightening in the east, the night sky breaking up. Chafee came over and told Philips something. Then he nodded to me.

"Bring one of them back alive if you can," he said, and I said I would. I would have gone up the hill on the other side of the valley if Chafee asked me right now. Almost instantly, I dropped that notion of killing the gooks if we caught up. A man like Chafee tells you something, you do it.

"Okay, moving out," Red Philips said, and we moved, bunched, through the first barbed wire fences. The dead were hung on the second stretch of wire. Philips told a sergeant to go through their pockets. He came up with cheap wallets and some papers and some paper money. Chafee had come out with us this far, and he took the lot to send back to intelligence. Some of the money was soaked with blood, dried and the color of rusted iron. I made myself stand close to one of the dead and look into his face. I thought it would be hard but it was nothing. It was just a wax face. The top of the man's head seemed to have been shot away, but a marine had stuck the cap back on him at a cocky angle and you couldn't see the wound. Seeing the dead up close wasn't as bad as I feared. Philips told us to move along now, we were wasting time. Chafee waved a hand. The snow was hard packed and not deep, but I walked carefully, not wanting to slip or make noise. When I looked back, a hundred yards down the hill, Chafee had some marines dragging the bodies off the wire by their feet and up the slope. It was machine guns had done the work, catching the four gooks with fixed fire in near total darkness, firing prearranged bursts over luminous aiming stakes, down the outside of the wire. That way you didn't have to see gooks to kill them; you worked by sound. It was below the wire the enemy patrol had died as they tried to cut their way through the wire. Only one had made it, the man killed on the roof of the bunker. It had been a good night. Now Philips and the rest of us were going down to try to finish it off.

If it had been another sort of errand, it might have been a pleasant stroll. The ridge fell away gently, and a few hundred yards below the MLR we came into small pines that had a nice, familiar smell. I had expected the Orient to smell exotic. The snow after the night freeze crunched underfoot just like snow on a thousand sleigh-riding hills of childhood. The air was clear, dry, the whole east alight now, a pink glow spreading across the snow. Except for a point-fire team of four marines Philips had thrown out front, we moved in casual fashion, each man gauging his own speed, picking his own trail, but staying in sight. Once or twice I slipped, but it was only an easy glissade and not dangerous. A big marine named Keppler, a BAR man, trotted along nearest me. He paid me no mind but I watched him move, a big man but graceful. Keppler's weapon was a BAR, a superb weapon of long range and, with its bipod, extraordinary steadiness. The BAR weighed twenty pounds, and there was nearly that much more in the belt of maga-zines Keppler wore. I noticed the BAR was not enough for Keppler. Somewhere he had stolen or found an army grease gun, a rapid-fire weapon along the lines of the burp gun, very fast shooting and impressive at point-blank range, pathetic at any distance. Keppler fondled the grease gun in one big hand and lugged the BAR in the other. He was carrying forty pounds just in weapons and ammo, and he moved as fast as I did and easily, seemingly under no strain.

It was full light now and Philips had his hand up. They all stopped. I went over to Red.

"Looky here," the executive officer said. There was a confusion of footmarks in the snow, but Philips was point-ing down. You could pick out tracks that looked nothing like those of marines' thermal boots. Here and there, sprayed across the tracks or pressed into the crust by other feet, were drops of blood. Not much, but it was there.

"Like hunting deer in November," Philips said, looking pleased.

I was a city boy. I'd never hunted deer, had never hunted any game, had never shot anything but once a sparrow with a BB gun, for which I'd been chastised. I didn't mind going after the gooks, hunting them down, if necessary killing them. But the analogy with a sporting hunt bothered me. I needn't have worried. Philips didn't wait for me to say anything but was off again, galloping down the hill while I went off after him.

Out in front, about a hundred yards ahead, you got glimpses of the lead fire team scouting through the stunted pines, nosing this way and that, much, I imagined, like a pack of dogs running ahead of the shooters in a game drive. There it was again, the comparison to sport. It was contagious. Maybe I was thinking too much. I made a conscious effort to relax. Two or three times I saw, even without having the hunter's knack, where the gooks had halted, probably because one of their wounded had fallen, where they had propped him up, gotten him to his feet again, and gone on. Marines didn't leave their wounded, didn't leave their dead if it was possible not to. Those were the rules and the tradition, and in a bizarre way, they were comforting to remember when you went out in front of your own lines. Whatever happened, somehow they would get you back. The other side seemed to observe the same tradition. Well, why not? It was the proper thing to do and these, in all likelihood, were proper soldiers.

"Over here," Philips hissed at me. The exec had stopped and with three or four marines was looking down at the snow. I caught up to them. There was more blood, a lot of it this time, really a lot, and a bloody, twisted bandage tossed aside. Just beyond, a few feet away, there were several good-sized turds. Philips shed a glove and leaned down to touch the turds. He looked up at me, wiping his hand on his pants.

"Shit's cold, Brady. They've got a pretty fair lead."

"Oh," I said.

"Looky here. Poor bastard had piles too, with all his other problems." He pointed to streaks of blood running through the turds. "He's a cool one, though. Got to give him that. Shot through somewhere pretty bad, us after him, a long way from home, and when the call came he had to squat." Philips shook his head in admiration.

Jesus, I thought, just think of your life's blood leaking from you, people tracking you, wanting to kill you, and you absolutely have to shit, all at the same time.

Now at Philips's urging we were moving out again, but with less eagerness. The spoor was getting cold. The gooks, wounded and all, had moved too fast for us. Maybe thinking of that poor bastard with the piles, maybe that slowed us a bit.

Not Keppler. He stalked around on the flanks poking into bushes and under low pines, sniffing the air, mumbling to himself. Keppler was still eager.

"Sure, Keppler," Philips said, picking up his grousing, "sure. And if the skipper let us come booming down here without waiting first light you might be under those bushes yourself with burp-gun tattoos stitched into your belly."

Keppler kept poking in bushes, but he stopped mumbling.

Now we were near the bottom of the hill. The flat of the valley, broader than it looked from above, stretched in front of us, screened by a few pines and some bush. The valley wasn't nearly as flat as I'd thought, but terraced. Farmers might have worked this piece of land before the war. Now there was nothing but the smooth snow on the shelving ground.

"Mr. Philips." One of the scouts motioned Philips over. The gook tracks led out of the pines and onto the snow of the valley floor, in clear view all the way across to where they vanished into other pines on the facing hill. That was where Simonis had gone up, where Lissman feared he would have to go. It looked rather innocent at this hour. In the dark it would be a different quantity. Philips looked longingly at the tracks and then shook his head.

"Uh-uh," he said, "we go back."

The scouting fire team moved back from the edge of the clearing, walking slowly backwards in the snow, weapons at low port. I realized they were actually disappointed, that they would have crossed the little valley in daylight. Odder still, I was disappointed myself, not bitterly so, but we'd come a long way for nothing. Sympathy for the wounded gook had faded. I slung the carbine and started up the hill. As I climbed I was surprised at the height of our lines, how the ridgeline towered above us. It was really a long way up; coming down it seemed shorter. The gooks we killed had come all this way across the valley and up the hill in the dark, never making a sound, not until the crunch of their sneakers in the snow alerted Lissman's people. A long way to come just to get killed.

We climbed roughly in single file, only Keppler off rooting around to one side or the other, still beating the bushes as if he expected to find someone. About a third of the way up he called to the exec.

"Mr. Philips, something here."

Philips went over. I pushed uphill faster to see. It was an old bunker, roof caved in, sandbags rotted and split open. Keppler kicked around in the debris and old snow, then straightened.

"Well, he ain't feeling no pain."

There wasn't much left, just the thigh bones and the pelvic bones and some ribs. The head was missing, and the rest of him.

"How long do you suppose he's been here, Red?" I said.

"Oh, since summer maybe. Maybe even the year before. This ground's been fought over so many times, you can't tell. He's one of our side, anyway, in a bunker facing north."

"American?"

"Oh, I doubt it. No dog tags, for one, kind of runty for another. Course, he could of been, but I doubt it. Probably a gook, missing in one of the big retreats last year. We'll never know who he was. If there was something to bring back, a bit of uniform, insignia, or such, I'd do it. This way, well, the foxes and the birds and the worms must have worked him over."

We stood there a moment looking down and then Philips turned and resumed the slow climb and one by one we turned with him. Finally only Keppler and I were left. I wanted Keppler to leave but he didn't, and so I said to hell with it and blessed myself. I was surprised when Keppler did the same and then kicked a little snow over the nearest bone.

"Hell," he said, as if embarrassed, "doesn't cost nothing. Like someone to do the same for me if it came to it."

We turned and began to climb. Those bones were really dead, not the waxy dead of the gooks on the wire. I wondered again how long he'd been there, if he'd died fast or slow, who he was. It was a lonely place to end.

11

The next day Chafee gave me the platoon. And I got a nickname. I promptly lost the platoon and it wasn't for months I would know about the nickname.

Mack Allen and I were called up to the command post. Tex Lissman was to go down the hill the next morning to the rotation draft. That left the second platoon open. It was what we'd been waiting for, why we were here as replacements, Mack eager and I nervous. Chafee said he would flip a coin and Mack Allen call it.

Mack called heads and it came up tails. I watched the flight of the coin, glinting in the sun, went down to one knee to see it fall. I realized as it landed that Mack was standing there as erect as if at attention. The platoon meant a lot to Mack; he'd been dead serious about it at Basic School and he wasn't bending now.

"Well, it's your platoon now, Brady," Chafee said. "I won't worry about how you'll do. Both of you are ready to take platoons. You'll get yours soon, Allen, when Flynn goes home. The thing to remember is we were all platoon leaders once, a good job, the finest command a man can have. Nowhere, I don't care how long you live or what you do, will you ever have direct responsibility for so many men. You can command more men, you can be a general with a division, but it's no longer direct. Colonels and generals are knotted into the system, the whole military bureaucracy. You make your own system here. You run it. It's your platoon."

59

He told me to move in that day. When Lissman went down with the morning gook train, I would take over. Chafee shook hands with me; we saluted him and he went off. Mack tried being delighted for me, he tried hard and it came off. I was uneasy about it, knowing Mack was the better man, that Mack should have gotten the second platoon. He had experience in the war, he was older, he had VMI, he was genuinely hungry for command, for responsibility. I was a year out of college and my pleasure was shallow. Deep down Allen wanted the platoon and I wasn't sure I did. Of course, I didn't say that. You don't confess doubt.

The mortar sergeants seemed as relieved to be rid of me as I was glad to go. Porterfield made the gesture of a small joke, promising they would always reserve their best supporting fire for my platoon. Dodge was deep in calculations.

"I'm onto a way to add range, maybe another two, three hundred yards. But don't tell the captain. He might think it was dangerous or something."

I promised his secrets were safe after all the mortars and I meant to each other.

Lissman's bunker was pretty big, with room enough for an extra guest for a night. When I got there with my gear, Lissman was along the line saying good-bye. The platoon sergeant showed me around, a smart and smooth-looking young Italian from Hartford, a regular with a certain snap. He seemed genuinely glad to have me there. Perhaps it was that we were both young; perhaps it was Lissman's nerves the night of the aborted raid. Whatever, it was nice to see. When he asked if I wanted to meet the men that afternoon, I said no; let Tex leave in the morning and we'd do it then, from scratch. I didn't want to make false starts.

Lissman tried to make me part of things that evening, but it didn't really work. Lissman was leaving, and that was more important than getting a new officer. This platoon had been fighting nearly a year under Lissman. The other officers dropped by, all except Flynn, who never left the nose after sundown. Lissman had a bottle and a good crowd in the bunker, the bottle being passed around.

"Medicinal," Philips said, "strictly medicinal." There were rules about booze on the line.

Around ten I turned in, telling them I could sleep through

anything. With four men already sleeping in the bunker I was tucked away on a sort of shelf cut into the earthen wall, a handy place for storing canned goods and grenades and sex books and such, but less suited for sleeping. It was long enough and about four feet wide, but only about two feet high. I put the sleeping bag on the shelf and tried to squirm into it, but that didn't work, so I got into the bag standing up and then wormed my way feet first into the niche. When I was all the way in, the earth was only a foot or less above my face and I had the eerie notion of being buried. More frightening was the realization that a heavy shell landing near the bunker might bury me alive. I wasn't claustrophobic, but still.

Just after midnight I woke to an urgent pressure in my bowels. The bunker was dark and still, the party over, and when I tried to sit up my head thudded into the ceiling of the little crypt. As best I could maneuver I worked my way backwards out of the wall, slipped on my boots, and went outside. A more experienced man would have noted the location of the nearest head during daylight, but I hadn't. I climbed over the back wall of the trench, slid a dozen feet down the reverse slope, and squatted in the snow. Relieved, I clambered back up the hill and into the bunker to bed. I'd been inside only a few minutes when the rumbling resumed and I had to make the trip a second time.

Two hours and three descents of the slope later, I was feeling immensely sorry for myself. During one of my squirmings in and out of the crypt a voice in the dark asked if I were all right and I answered that I was fine. But now I was not so sure. My anus was getting raw, the toilet paper being what it was; I was tired, drained, and needing sleep. Light snow had begun to fall on the ridge, making the trips down the slope slippery, hazardous, and the squats each time colder and wetter. Snowflakes drifted down inside my two pairs of pants, the sweat-suit pants I wore as long johns, and my shorts, to land and melt on bare thighs as I squatted. There was no strain to shitting now. It just ran out of me. On my last trip firing began over on the left, probably Flynn's people trying to get wire out and being caught at it. As I struggled back into the sleeping bag, firing became general along the line, not really an engagement, but more likely nerves and sympathetic outbursts and the fatigue of after-midnight. I hoped, now I was praying, my bowels would tighten and I would not have to go out there again during a firefight. Sore and exhausted, I concentrated on stilling the rumbles below my waist. Someone in the bunker was up now, the platoon sergeant, working into boots and mittens and going out to see about the shooting. Lissman and the others snored on. His squad leaders would call Lissman if it was necessary. I thought about the wounded gook squatting in the snow during the retreat, no more able than I was to master this ridiculous, joke function of the body, whatever the risk. Now, oh God, now it came again. I wriggled out hurrying, bent over, through the bunker door and into the trench. As I came out, barely holding back the liquid pressure against my anus, there was machine-gun fire just above my head and rifle shots. Somewhere not far off a grenade exploded, and then there came the solid, metallic thunk of mortar shells leaving the tubes. I started to scramble again up the wall of the trench and then I stopped. What a grotesque stupidity if someone thought I was a gook infiltrating our lines. Suppose someone shot me, just because I had to take a crap. Empty and dehydrated, almost crying with frustration, and with intestinal pain, I stepped back into the trench, moved a dozen yards from the bunker, and dropped my pants. When I was through I tried to scrape snow from the trench lip and bury the feces, but the snow was crusted and worn and I couldn't get very much. Twenty minutes later, I was out again. This time, without hesitation, without attempting to camouflage the fact, I did what I had to do and crawled back to my hole. Blessedly, it was my last visitation. Carefully catering to tenderness, I fell asleep lying on my stomach.

Lissman and the sergeant and the runners were up when I woke. I got up quickly, thinking to clean the trench before anyone stumbled across my leavings, but from outside came voices, the usual early morning chat of the line, and I fell back, knowing it was too late. I considered playing dumb, letting it become a guessing game in the platoon, but I could not. Certainly my departures in the night had been noted. More important, Lissman was leaving, I was to take over, and I could not embarrass the whole platoon just to spare myself. Movement was agony, my ass burning, my whole body weak and tired. This platoon, the platoon I'd won from Mack Allen, that Chafee had put trustingly into my hands, deserved better than a leader who was less than fit his first day of command.

As I walked awkwardly, painfully toward the CP, passing the place where I'd fouled the trench, I saw that someone had shoveled snow and dirt and everything else out of the trench and heaved it down the forward slope, where it lay shameful and brown against the new fallen snow.

Telling Chafee I could not take over the platoon was as hard a thing as I'd ever done. Chafee listened and just nodded, and Mack was called on the phone and told. Now that it was over, now that I'd lost my command, I realized I wanted the platoon as much as Allen did, in as real a way. I wanted it so badly I knew I'd done right by surrendering it. Chafee tried to console me with tales of similar woes, telling me it was the water or the climate, but none of it helped much. An hour later when Mack and I met with Lissman and the platoon sergeant, they too were sympathetic. By now my ass was easing and I was feeling better. When Mack and I were alone, I tried a small joke, telling him we were a fine pair.

"What do you mean?" Mack demanded.

"Well, I come down with the runs and you tried to cut your ear off."

Mack laughed and I cheered up a bit.

It wasn't until February that Princeton, who was by then my platoon sergeant, told me about the nickname.

"You know, Mr. Brady, when you took over the third platoon some of the men were a little worried about it. I mean, after what happened with the second platoon and the nickname they gave you."

"What nickname?"

"You mean you never heard it?"

I said no.

Princeton wasn't abashed. I think he was enjoying this. "Why, after that first night you was with the platoon," he said, "after that night they was calling you 'Shit Trench' Brady."

"Oh."

12

Late in the second year of the war, whoever was running things in the Republic had worked out a system of sending agents through the lines to infiltrate the North Koreans and bring back intelligence, and to talk enemy soldiers into deserting, coming across to a welcome and a grilling. The men who went north to do this work were called Blue Boys.

When I gave up the platoon to Mack Allen, Chafee had the sensitivity not to send me back to the mortars, but named me machine-gun platoon leader. Since all the machine-gun sections were attached to rifle platoons under command of the rifle lieutenants, I had little to do, beyond the healing of my rear end. I lived in a bunker just off the CP with the gunnery sergeant and a runner, and hung around, trying to absorb everything, trying to learn. One morning Chafee said a Blue Boy, possibly with friends, was expected to pass through the company's lines by night, on his way south, on his way home. The Blue Boy had been given a special password so that the marines would not kill him as he came through. Chafee was very precise about this. He had an appreciation of good intelligence and the importance of these missions. Also, being Chafee, he did not want to risk the life of a brave man.

The following night, an hour before dawn, well down the forward slope, there was an explosion. In the dark the marines thought it might be an infiltrator who'd stepped on an old, uncharted mine. No one wanted to think it was our Blue Boy. It had been a quiet night, no firing before the explosion and only a few nervy shots after. One of the observation posts, situated at an angle to the MLR proper, reported at first light.

"Two men lying in the snow, couple hundred yards down the slope."

That was the general area of the explosion. Chafee hurried out to the OP with glasses to determine if this could be the Blue Boy with a deserter. That was the probability. Mack Allen was sent out with a patrol and interpreter and stretchers. It took him most of the morning to get down and back, and on one of the stretchers when he came in there was a body under a poncho. On the other there was a man still alive and moaning. Blood trailed off behind the stretcher, staining the snow. A corpsman had gone out with them; he'd been working over the wounded man, and he told Chafee he could do nothing more. They would have to send the man down by gook train to the battalion surgeon.

"He's most gone, sir," the corpsman said. "Both legs gone at the knee and lost a lot of blood. Only the cold kept him from bleeding to death out there." Chafee gave some orders and we went inside to hear Mack's report.

"It was the Blue Boy, all right, Skipper. He was coming in with a guy he'd talked into making the jump and they hit a mine. The Blue Boy lost his legs and the other one was hit all over, his eyes gone for one thing, but they were both conscious. Far as I can make out, they were both in terrific pain but afraid to call out for fear a gook patrol might be out. Soon as first light came, they figured they were finished. The one without the legs could see the other one was going fast, and of course he couldn't move himself. He told the interpreter he kept fainting and the other one was just whimpering and rolling around. Finally, they decided they were both going to die right there. They didn't know we'd seen them. And they decided not to wait, but to hurry it along."

Mack stopped talking and took a drink of water from his canteen. Even with the snow it was so dry up here, you were always thirsty. Chafee didn't hurry him, just waited.

Mack put down the canteen and ran a hand through his cropped hair, the big ears standing out.

"The Blue Boy worked out the scheme," Mack said. "He talked the blind one over to him and when they were in touch the Blue Boy somehow got up on the other's back and then they began to crawl back and forth over the ground where they hit the mine. They just crawled back and forth like that, the blind man carrying the other. They were trying to find another mine and kill themselves."

Toward evening Battalion phoned to tell Chafee the Blue Boy bled to death on the way down with the gook train. But they'd found some papers of interest on the deserter, so they were not writing off the operation as a total loss.

I was with Chafee when he took the call. The captain nodded. He told Battalion he was pleased they'd not been too disappointed.

A few days later we got word the regiment was to go into reserve, probably for a month. Chafee saw to it everyone heard promptly. It was good news to Mack and me, and we'd been on the line only ten days; everyone else had been there a month. People felt pretty fine about it. Another order came up which sounded so dumb I thought Chafee was jollying us. The order was to pick up all brass expended along the line and send it back for salvage. Brass is the military term for empty shell casings ejected from weapons when bullets are fired. In the States, on the firing range, you were supposed to pick up the brass, to police the area, keep it neat. But here? The following morning Chafee as usual was up and down the company front with his wolf's lope, moving fast without seeming to, seeing everything, knowing everyone. He called me into the CP when he got back.

"Your machine gunners aren't picking up the brass. It's piled up around the guns and down the slope. Didn't you give them the word?"

I said I hadn't considered it a serious order.

"All orders are serious," Chafee said and turned away.

I was ashamed and angry. It was a ridiculous order but Chafee was right; I should have carried it out. First I'd had to give up the rifle platoon and now he'd caught me doping off. This was a Chafee I hadn't seen before, a man with

whom you didn't play games. I would not again. I didn't
want that cold look coming down on me again. He didn't
shout or curse when he chewed you out, but he didn't have
to. You understood. I hustled down the line to give the
necessary orders to the gunners, who looked at me as if I
were mad. I said they were Chafee's orders and to be
obeyed. Shrugging, and sulky, they started gathering the
brass. It was not until later I learned that the order was
from Youngdahl and that Chafee, too, thought it was inane.
But in Dog Company he issued orders as if they were his
own idea, without passing the buck or permitting any re-
flection on higher authority. It would take time before I
learned to do the same.

Those last two nights on the line were clear with a good
moon. You came to love a full moon and the light it gave
off the snow. As if recognizing the company was tired, the
gooks stayed home, not even Flynn drawing fire to speak
of. Way off, far to the west, there was heavy artillery fire
most of one night, but it was only the army catching hell
and no one worried about that.

A last incident marked our stay on the line. I'd not yet
seen a plane, not since the transport that ferried us north.
Not a plane of either side had flown over, but on the last
night a flight of bombers, B-29s, magnificent ships that a
few years before had bombed Japan to ruins, now too old
for anything but night bombing, passed over on their way
home from a mission in the far north, up near China. It was
after midnight, but the roar brought us out of our bunkers
to look up, sufficient a novelty that even marines would
come out to see it. When the planes had gone I turned to go
back inside, feeling the cold. Then, off to the north, quite
far and very faint, came the sound of another plane, trailing
home after the rest. I scanned the sky and then I saw it, a
brilliant spark of light in the distance, just over the gook
lines, coming slowly, the sound not right. We knew then it
was in trouble. Everyone was out now, watching the sky,
rooting home the wounded bird. But it wasn't going to
make it. As the plane neared our lines we could see it was
aflame and gliding rather than flying, silent now and wob-
bling. Then there was an explosion that canceled out the
moon and blinded our night vision. When we could see

again the big plane was wheeling over and over, tumbling to earth like a leaf aflame, no longer a plane but only bits of fire in the night sky. It hit somewhere off to the left, on the forward slope, and burned for a long time.

Chafee phoned Battalion, but everyone along a ten-mile stretch of line, on both sides, had seen the B-29 go down. Chafee issued orders to watch for flyers coming in, not to fire unless we were sure it was gooks. I stayed up the rest of the night waiting, but no one came in. Toward dawn there was some firing off to the left and I thought I could hear burp guns, but at that distance you couldn't be sure.

We heard later one of the flyers had parachuted down, landed safe and gotten up the slope to within a hundred yards of the first battalion's wire. But a gook ambush was out in the snow, and they caught him there and shot him just before he reached the wire. Marines chased the gooks off and went out to bring in the body.

Of the nine others from the plane nothing was ever heard.

═══13═══

"Well," said Captain Chafee, "we've had worse tours."

"It'll be a bad reserve," the executive officer said.

"You're probably right," Chafee agreed.

"Of course I'm right," Red Philips said. "Tours can be good or they can be bad. Reserve areas are always bad."

I was puzzled by this exchange but too green to say anything. A month later, when we went back up to the line, I understood. By then the best thing about the month in reserve was that when it came to an end, I was in command of a rifle platoon.

The regimental reserve area was in a valley, ten miles behind the line. The camp stretched out along the bank of a stream running too fast to freeze, studded with smooth, rounded rocks. Where the rocks protruded into the clear mountain air, they were iced. Now in mid-December it was truly winter, the weather we'd all read about and feared after what happened to the marines a year before up at the Chosin Reservoir. The ground was completely white, the mountains heavy with snow. At night the temperature dropped easily below zero Fahrenheit. It was still autumn on the calendar but North Korea had a different calendar. On the west bank of the little stream was a gook camp, service corps personnel and kids teenaged and younger who slipped across the stream to work as number-one boys. It was all strictly against the rules, and Colonel Gregory let it be known it was against the rules. Then he picked out a sprightly youngster for himself.

That's how it is in the Marine Corps. There are rules and a subtle understanding some of them are to be broken. Colonels broke rules, I suppose generals did, enlisted men broke them, I broke them whenever I could with circumspection, but Chafee never. Captain Chafee kept the rules. Not that he was prissy. It simply did not seem to occur to Chafee to cut corners. Maybe it was his legal training. Take burp guns. Burp guns had an easily identifiable sound, and though they were not greatly accurate, they fired off lead in a hurry. As souvenirs, they were superb. Marines gathered burp guns as stoop labor picked beets. As we came off the line, half the marines seemed to have one; I saw one man with three. Then an order came down from Division, a new rule, an anti–burp gun rule. Chafee had the burp guns taken and tagged with the owner's name and sent to the rear. There was some nonsense about giving the men receipts, but even with Chafee regulations went only so far and then reason took over. He did not play out the farce of receipts but merely told people he doubted they would see their burp guns again. Yet in this the captain was not entirely correct, for within a week marines on various errands to rear areas reported that at Corps and at Army, burp guns were being peddled by army troops for twenty-five dollars apiece. It was enough to disillusion a man, Red Philips remarked, if a man were silly enough to have illusions.

Red and the captain had been right about reserve areas. Nearly five thousand men camped in tents had to be kept busy. Most days we trained and drilled and polished and oiled and held lectures. After dark, which was when most of the fighting took place now, in weather that came from Siberia down into the valley off the high hills, we ran night problems. They were as exhausting and only marginally less dangerous than the long patrol of Bob Simonis. Supper eaten, the cold night fastened down, a time when quiet, lazy talk under alcohol was what was wanted, they rooted us out into the company street and marched us into low hills drifted deep with snow, treacherous with iced footpaths, downed trees, and the occasional mine, to stage dummy assaults on empty bunkers. We lost men, one here to a mine, one there to a broken leg in the stream, another to an accidental discharge. There were too many of those.

Five thousand men under arms, people got hurt. Few nights passed without somewhere in the regiment a wild shot whipping harmless through the tent or sometimes into flesh and breaking bone. It was how we lost Dodge, the mortar sergeant, though as might be expected with Dodge, that story had a twist.

Sergeant Tallent, a machine-gun sergeant, had gotten a bottle, and he and Dodge, as sergeants will, made use of it. Some time after midnight, the ceremonial round went off. When people got there, Tallent lay across a bunk swamped with his own blood and Dodge was tidying the tent. Investigating officer put it down at first to an accidental discharge. Ten days later, Tallent recovering, the story came out. Stimulated by drink and good company, Dodge had proposed a round of Russian roulette. Other sergeants in the party demurred, suggesting since it was his idea, Dodge had all rights to it, and they left. Tallent, less sage or perhaps more drunk, stayed on. A quarrel developed, a struggle, with Dodge forcing the gun to Tallent's head. He probably meant just to frighten, but with Dodge you never knew. At the court-martial Dodge cheerfully admitted doing it, claiming to have been befuddled. Tallent got off with a reprimand and Dodge with six months' loss of pay and being broken to private. Private, Dodge sneered, he had been there before; the important thing was his mortars and those they couldn't take away from him.

For me, with no intention of playing Russian roulette, mines were the fear. This was ground that had been fought over before, and so there were mines, put down by both sides, no one knew quite where or what type. Battalion laid on a night problem that involved the scaling of a terrible cliff, a thousand feet nearly vertical with a frozen stream hanging down the height of it like a waterfall. I was assigned the point and got to the top first, climbing very fast, cursing my people steadily and forcing the pace. We got there so quickly we found the "enemy" troops, from Fox Company, still in their sleeping bags. I was pleased at what we'd done; I was toughening now and had barely felt the climb. But it was fear of mines that pushed me up the cliff, as if by going fast I might skim across the mines without exploding them. It was stupid and back in my tent I felt the drained sense of having done something well but for the wrong reason. I was going to have to do something about this phobia of mines. Easy to say. I kept seeing myself without legs.

Not everything about being in reserve was grim. We had showers, we slept on bunks in big tents, the oil stoves reeked but threw warmth, and when we weren't being chivvied and driven, there was something to it redolent of a boys' camp.

The number-one boy we had, Chang, was fine, an ugly little conniver about eleven with a deep scar over one eye. I romanticized it had been put there by a Japanese samurai sword during the Occupation. Chang fetched and carried and kept the stove going and once served us fried squid from the gook camp. We had movies in the big mess tent, and sometimes we sneaked in Chang. He did not believe what he saw, thinking everything was Hollywood make-believe, even the city of New York. It was touching, this ignorance of what it was like beyond Korea, and I wanted to do something for the boy. In the end, I did nothing; none of us did.

As Christmas neared there was a USO show. I felt about the USO the way Chang did about Technicolor movies. They were fine but they didn't really exist. Bob Hope might visit Europe but not here. Yet there it was, a USO troupe on a wooden platform in the middle of a drill field playing an act of *Born Yesterday*. Paul Douglas and his wife, Jan Sterling, and a Broadway juvenile named Keith Andes I'd once seen in a musical. Miss Sterling wore a short frilly dress with pink long johns under it, showing her legs and playing dumb for a few thousand marines while dry snow whipped in on a heavy, pushing wind. I was a New Yorker and I'd seen plenty of shows, but I'd never enjoyed theatre more than I did right there sitting cross-legged on the ground in the snow. I resolved that after the war I would go every week to see a play, if only from the balcony or standing room. I wanted to go up and thank Mr. Douglas and the others for coming, to say something polite. But they were hurried offstage to thaw out and I didn't have the chance.

Pierce Power came by to see me.

"I heard you were here," he said. "I saw your name on a replacement draft."

Pierce and I had been at college together. He'd been in the September push, on Hill 749, where Ed Flynn had all his troubles. Pierce was thin; he looked tired. I asked how he was.

"Okay," he said. "I got hit, you know."

"No, I didn't."

"On 749. I wasn't hit bad, but you think about it. We lost a lot of men there."

I said I knew. I told him about the marines who'd gone up the hill with me that first day with the gook train, the ones with the Purple Hearts and the pimply faces.

"I know," Pierce said. "It was your people tried to take it in the first place. They couldn't do it. Then they passed our regiment through and we took it. We nearly didn't, but we did."

Power didn't brag. At college he had been an admirable student, a fine athlete. Now he sat there gray-faced and hunched. He was twenty-three. I knew he wasn't bragging about the taking of 749. It was a statement of fact. I felt distant from him, uneasy.

But I wanted to know if he knew how Bradlee died, and I asked.

It was mortar fire, Pierce said, that killed Doug Bradlee his first week with Division. The fighting last summer had been brutal, when we last fought the Chinese and were pushing them back. The chinks would hold a ridgeline and hold it and hold it, and when the marines finally got up there the chinks were gone, falling back to the next ridge. All their mortars though were concentrated on this first ridge, and they'd hit it, before the marines had a chance to dig in. Then the next day the Division would jump off to take the next ridge and fight its way up, and the chink mortars would come crashing in again.

"That's where Doug died," Pierce said. I didn't say anything, and then he said, "Callan's dead, too, you know."

"No."

"He was killed in July. I don't have the details. It was a month after we got here."

"Callan. I didn't know."

Bradlee was a Harvard football player, a big, rangy red-head who'd gone out to Colorado to teach school and coach kids. His father sent me a wire at Quantico. "Regret to inform you Doug killed in action." Callan had been a cowboy, a rancher's son, actually. Nice, funny blond kid who wore western boots. I hadn't been able to see Bradlee dead; I couldn't imagine Callan dead.

Power was in the rear echelons now.

It wasn't much of a job, but he didn't worry about being a pogue. He'd gotten a Bronze Star for taking 749. It didn't excite him much. He talked for a bit about how it was up there, telling the story without feeling. Then he took a drink of my whisky and got up.

"Just take care of yourself," he said.

I said I would, and a little later Power left. We had been so close, but we didn't seem to have all that much to talk about anymore.

Christmas Eve at midnight, artillery all along the line fired up red and green flares and star clusters. The poor gooks thought it was a push, and they fired back with everything they had. It was a fine show for an hour or so. You could just barely see the flashes from the reserve area, but you could hear it, you could certainly hear it. That was the night Workman burned down his own tent. The fact Workman was also the battalion fire warden was especially galling to Colonel Youngdahl, who took Workman aside Christmas morning and spoke to him at length.

Christmas was gray and very cold, five below zero, thirty-seven degrees of frost Fahrenheit and marines in dungarees played tackle football without helmets or pads on the frozen dirt and snow of the drill field. My family sent me some gifts, sausage and canned sardines, things to give some taste to the rations. We decorated a runty pine and gave Chang some socks and canned goods and a few dollars in military scrip. He liked the tree, the first Christmas tree he'd ever seen. The rest of our replacement draft was there now, the men Mack and I had left behind when they flew us over in November. I was glad to see them, thinking without saying so that they had a green look, as if they were boots and I the old salt. That was pretty ridiculous thinking for someone who'd spent ten days on the line. One of the late arrivals, Spence, had made three landings in the war and was due to make captain any day now, but I enjoyed the feeling, hugging superiority to myself like a puppy that might squirm away if you didn't hold it tight.

The night problems went on and the inspections and drills and all the chickenshit of reserve area. The weather got colder and worse, but I began to feel wonderful. Suddenly I just stopped thinking about mines and about losing my legs. The hell with it; worrying and being afraid wasn't going to help. After that, I felt fine. One afternoon, coming back from a live firing problem, Mack Allen and I were in such high spirits we fell behind the party just to wrestle in the snow out of pure delight. I was easy for Mack, but we had a fine time and rolled halfway down the bank and nearly into a stream. Mack scrubbed my face with snow before we quit, and stuffed a handful down my shirt. It was boyish, it was silly and we knew it, but with another tour on the line coming up, you took pleasure where you could, whether it was Paul Douglas on a wooden stage or giving Christmas to a Korean kid or getting your face washed in the snow.

New Year's Day two marines stole a jeep, painted "War Correspondent" on the side, and were nearly to Wonju when they were caught. "We were looking for whores," they explained. "We heard there was whores in Wonju."

We were to go back on the line January 10. Chafee called me in and gave me the third platoon. Ed Flynn was finally going home, freed at last of the nose.

"No speeches this time," Chafee said.

I grinned at him. "No runs either, I hope, Skipper."

"You know," Chafee said, "we've all had 'em. The historians say Lee had them at Gettysburg and Napoleon at Waterloo. No one's immune; no one shits ice cream."

My new platoon sergeant was a big strawhead named Princeton, a regular. He and I flew up to the new position by helicopter with Chafee and the other officers and senior NCOs. The new stretch of line looked good, very long but high, and nowhere did we share a ridge with the gooks. Even Red Philips said it looked as if it might be a good tour. Someone whizzed a .76 shot at us up there out of sheer cussedness and frightened the chopper pilots, so we had to walk back down the mountain after our inspection. It took six hours to get back. I was glad we were going to have choppers with all the gear we'd be carrying when we went back up on the tenth to stay.

14

We were getting some incoming mortar fire when the helicopters brought us in on the reverse slopes of the new hill called 880. It was a brilliantly sunny day but cold, and with the trees and the snow and blue sky and everything but postcard villages and ski trails, the mortar fire didn't seem as much dangerous as out of place. Quite unreal. It hit nobody, and the battalion's three rifle companies were in place by midafternoon. We had been out before dawn, two battalions on the march, their tread across the fields of the camp like the beating of a slack drum. They had a long march, a long climb. Our battalion squatted on the parade ground waiting for the helicopters. Around us rolled the big trucks with their whining gears. They would truck the other battalions to the foot of the ridge from where the climb would begin. When the last truck ground off, the first choppers came in low over the camp, settled briefly like bees at field flowers, and rose again with four or six marines tumbled inside. As we waited our turn, the houseboy, Chang, nipped in to say good-bye to Mack and me and to get the expected tip.

"You behave now, hear?" Mack said.

"Yes, *scoshi* lieutenant."

Scoshi meant "little." Mack was short.

Chang said he hoped we would prosper and that he would see us in our next reserve the end of February.

"He isn't supposed to know that," I said.

76

"Hell," said Mack, "we don't know that." He turned to Chang. "Maybe you will and maybe you won't, son, but don't mouth it around."

"Yes?" Chang said, smiling.

I gave him something. "He's a good kid."

"I knew he'd get something out of you," Mack Allen said. He had given him ten dollars the evening before but didn't say anything. Now Red Philips went to the boy as if to chase him, shoving a bill into his breast pocket.

"Now get the hell out of here." The boy grinned and raced toward the gook camp.

The choppers were coming in every half minute now, bunching up, and then a wait of ten or twelve minutes and another bunch. This was pretty big stuff to us, only the second time an entire battalion had moved into the line by helicopter in a sector where theoretically we might be under fire. The fire was not theoretical, but it might as well have been. I got in about noon. Princeton was there before me, shoving men into bunkers and shouting hoarsely, manning every bunker before dark. Later on we could sort it out. By three the platoon was all in place and the relieved people were on their way down. Sergeant Hoops, the new platoon guide, was the last man in. He had a leathery, lopsided old face, and he nodded it at me as he reported in. He was a regular as well. I was lucky.

"This looks like a pretty good piece of line, Mr. Brady," Hoops said. He hadn't seen it before. Only Princeton and I had come up for the reconnaissance. I thought Hoops was right. The new line looked good, it looked tremendous.

Princeton was out leaning over the forward slope. It fell away steeply. You wanted that. There were a couple of aprons of wire. They looked redundant with that degree of slope and the deep snow. Ski troops would feel at home up here, the Tenth Mountain Division would like this. Below us to the north was the valley, nearly three thousand feet below. A stream wound off toward the northeast, called the Soyang-gang. I knew that from the maps and the tactical briefings. Off dead east was the Sea of Japan, perhaps five miles away, bright blue and very calm at this distance. A toy boat steamed over its surface, tiny and very slow. It might have been a cruiser, but from this far and this height it was nothing.

You couldn't see any North Koreans. You never did by day.

Princeton waved a big arm north.

"There she is, Lieutenant. There's the son of a gun."

Due north of us, about four or five miles, maybe more, stood the tallest of these modest North Korean mountains. The mountains ran north, hunched and white, each higher than the one before, until they ran up against this big one, Princeton's "son of a gun." It was 2,000 meters, twice as high as this fine ridgeline where Dog Company and the rest of the battalion had just dug in.

"We go north in springtime against that, Lieutenant," Princeton said, "we going to hold the First Marine Division reunion in a phone booth." He was casual in tone as if he did not want to upset anyone.

"Plenty of winter left, Princeton. Get the squad leaders up here and we talk." I didn't like thinking about spring or that 2,000-meter hill. But I wasn't going to have my platoon sergeant spooking the men. I could be casual, too.

Only six weeks in Korea but I had come a ways from those first nights in the mortars with Porterfield and Dodge. This was a new platoon for me, but it was new ground for all of us. I knew it as well as any and because of the recon, better than most. And I was beginning to pick up the little tricks, telling Princeton to call the squad leaders together rather than prolonging speculation about what might happen two months from now. In two months the war might be over. In two months we might be dead. I was still impressed by NCO regulars, but I wasn't going to be awed by them. Hoops and Princeton and the three sergeants came up, there was a little talk, I issued a few routine orders, and they moved out. Princeton and I would share a bunker, not actually in the trenchline but a few yards behind and above the forward slope bunkers, cut into the ridgeline. It was a snug bunker, small and clean, with a log roof covered with two layers of sandbags. I took the trouble to scoop away the snow to see. Around five, the sun nearly down but still daylight at this height, Chafee came bounding up. Hoops had seen him. Platoon guides were useful to young platoon leaders in such matters, and I was out and waiting when the captain arrived.

Dog Company was still understrength. Flynn and Lissman were gone, and instead of seven officers there were again only five, Chafee and the exec, Philips, and the three rifle platoon leaders, Simonis, Allen and me. My platoon had the company's right flank and held the highest ground. I tied in on the right with the Third Battalion. I had friends over there, Spence and Taffy Sceva, both from our Basic School class at Quantico. It was funny how small the Corps really was, how in the next outfit there was usually someone you knew. The middle of my platoon front had a nose, like Flynn's nose on 749, pointing due north as if it were sniffing out something that smelled bad up there. Difference was, we held the nose; we weren't sharing it with neighbors of another persuasion as Ed Flynn had done. That made it sweet. My bunker was toward the base of the nose, where it joined the main ridge. I showed Chafee over the ground, not going all the way to either flank. It was too late for that, the dark coming. But I gave him the gist of it.

"Keep a 50 percent watch tonight and until I tell you different. Half the men awake. Right?"

"Aye, aye, sir."

"This looks like a good line, Brady. Better than the last."

"Yes, sir, it does."

"We've got work to do, though. Get some more wire in, plot the mines. And don't get too relaxed just because it's high. Any hill marines can climb down the gooks can climb up. Get relaxed and you'll find trouble."

I said I wasn't too relaxed.

Chafee greeted that with a grin.

"I don't imagine you are, first night on the line with a new platoon."

I laughed. It was getting late, the sun gone now, but Chafee walked with me for a way, the two of us alone.

"Not much I want to say, Brady. You'll do a job for me. I'm not worried about that. But one thing they don't tell you at Quantico and maybe they should. Get to know your people as marines, as professionals. Learn their capacities, their strengths, their weaknesses. But don't get

to know them as men. None of this first-name stuff. Don't
ask about their families or their hometown, whether they're
married, if they've got kids. Do that and before you know it
you'll lose your judgment, you'll be sending a man out on
point because he's single and not because he's the best
pointman. There's something else. Get to know your men
too well, too personally, and when you lose one you'll be
losing a piece of yourself. A platoon leader can't afford
that. It's bad enough losing men without pieces of you
going, too. Remember that, Brady, it's hard learned and it's
right."

I said I would remember.

Chafee went off, bouncing along the icy path and down
the hacked-out steps of the reverse slope in the gloom, a
lean, tireless figure who did not look back, who told you
what to do and left you to do it. I looked around me,
enjoying the last half-light, the valley of the Soyang-gang
already pitch-black, darkness creeping up the forward slope.
The platoon runner, a young negro named Duke, passed the
captain. He came up the steps with two water cans strapped
to a packboard. He unloaded one of them in front of our
bunker.

"Yessir, fresh, real fresh water, right outa the spring."

I got down and crawled inside. Princeton had two candles
burning and on the Coleman stove was a can of pork and
beans. A can of peaches stood opened on my sleeping bag
roll.

"Thought you'd be hungry, Lieutenant."

I started to gush my thanks and then remembered Chafee's
counsel and just grunted. It seemed to satisfy the sergeant.

The first night on a new piece of line, even one that gave
promise of quiet, even with experienced troops, is always
hard. You are tired because the move up begins before
dawn. The choppers help, they are wonderful, but still,
you are packing a heavy load, you scramble from one
bunker to the next as the platoon moves in and the relieved
troops move out. Water has to be fetched; you can skip
meals, but you cannot live without water. Grenades are set
out, the machine guns laid, the telephone tested. You look
over the ground in front of you, memorizing it, the fields of
fire, the dead spaces; you check the mortar concentrations.

You do all this in the fading day, in the cold and the wind, trying to hold back the night, and then the night comes and you are as ready as you can be. But you are never really ready.

Now it was full night. Wind blew cold and heavy across the nose. I crawled out to look. No moon but a bowlful of stars shining off the snow so that only the deepest valley, the Soyang-gang, was truly dark. Wind eddied across the nose from west to east so that, huddled where I was in the doorway, I felt nothing. But I could hear it coming across above my head, heard it whistle as it came and saw a faint spume of snow picked up off the spine of the hill and driven east toward the sea. On the other side of the nose, on the windward slope, was the heavy machine-gun section. I put them there, knowing it was where they should be but also knowing the wind would be bad, warned it was bad by the outgoing platoon leader.

"The wind is a bitch. It never stops," he'd told me.

Now I had this machine-gun section attached to me, and I put them out there, in the wind, sparing my own men. Someone had to be there in the wind, and I did it and never worried about it again.

Inside the bunker, Princeton was crumbling a cocoa cake into boiled water, fussing and tidying as a bride tidies her little cottage with the roses and white picket fence. Here it was soot-caked sandbags and logs and earth and ponchos draped for warmth. I had thought about taking a watch and decided against it, needing the sleep and rationalizing that since Princeton and I were on call throughout the night if anything happened, we should not stand a watch. Anyway, from this bunker, you could see nothing. You had to cross over the footpath and drop down on the other side to the bunker where Hoops was, with Duke the runner and another man, the navy corpsman. They had a firing port down there, an aperture they could see through. Here, Princeton and I were blind. Having decided against standing a watch myself and not wanting to get started badly with the platoon sergeant, I told him neither of us would stand watch except by the phone. Princeton seemed neither pleased nor displeased but accepted this with a nod.

There were two phones in the bunker, one to Chafee at

the CP, the other tied in to my three squad leaders and to
the heavy machine-gun sergeant. I pulled off my thermal
boots and dug around in the rucksack to come up with the
Indian moccasins from Abercrombie's. I'd bought them and
shooting mittens in Manhattan before flying west to Camp
Pendleton. They felt good on feet wet with sweat, itching
and hot from the insulated boots. Princeton had all his gear
neatly stowed, close to hand. Regulars had this knack, like
good housewives, tidy and organized. The sergeant passed
the cocoa across the foot of space between the two bedrolls. We leaned back against the bunker's wall, sipping it
slowly, careful not to burn our tongues. I felt very relaxed.
Chafee and what Chafee said, that I shouldn't become too
relaxed, were very much with me. Maybe Princeton or I
should stay awake, should stand watch. After all, it was our
first night on a new piece of line.

I put down the canteen cup and drank some water to
wash down the cocoa. I looked over at Princeton.

"Go to sleep, Sergeant."

"Aye, aye, sir. Good night."

I blew out the candle and we arranged our bodies in
sleep. It was all right; that first night was a quiet one.

15

The morning came off clear on the ridges, but in the valley a thousand feet below us, there was fog, a blanket of fleece pierced through here and there by hills, then sloughed off entirely by the real hills to the north. The fog came off the sea. There was again no wind where we were on the eastern flank of the nose, but on the west, where the machine gunners were, it blew steadily and right at them. I climbed over the spine of the nose after coffee to see Kelso, the section leader. Kelso said it hadn't been too bad. He had complaints but did not pass them on. But when I left he kicked a big foot at the snow and muttered something to himself, or perhaps at the damned wind. Behind him an ammo carrier winced in the wind.

"Yes, Sergeant?"

"Shut your mouth and get them jerricans, unless you plan to live on melted snow up here."

"Aye, aye, Sergeant," the ammo carrier was saying as their voices faded.

The stretch of MLR my platoon held was simply too long to be held properly by a forty-five-man platoon, and although there had been replacements, and wounded men had come back, the third platoon was still understrength. Battalion in its wisdom, as Captain Chafee put it, would attach certain other units to me during this tour to beef up the line, fill in the gaps, "or just to be sociable." I was a second lieutenant thirteen weeks out of Quantico, six weeks in

Korea, and I now commanded a reinforced platoon of nearly a hundred men. I had the windblown heavy machine-gun section with two guns; a light machine-gun section split into two squads, each with a light gun. There were six engineers under a Cherokee Indian sergeant. They would begin today working over the mine fields. An artillery officer, a forward observer with four men, lived on the very tip of the nose. The 81mm mortars, the whole lot of them from Battalion, camped on my reverse slope. Two tankers were up nosing around to see whether tank fire on gook bunkers to the north might be effective from here. And there was a 75mm recoilless rifle team dug in just over the lip of the ridge to the south. Good thing I had no military ambitions; all this power could go to your head.

The ground was good. The nose on which I sat was really a minor hill projecting out of the main ridge. It was 880 meters high and it dominated that sector. I was realist enough to understand it was the dominating ground and not my leadership that brought these attached units to me. This was simply the best place to be if you were going to shoot gooks. It was my hill and these were, for the present, my hundred men. As the fog burned off the valley and the sun warmed the January air, I felt rather pleased about the whole business.

Colonel Gregory, the Battalion commander, had been promoted during our last days in reserve. Now he was executive officer of the Regiment. Chafee let it drop the colonel was not pleased with the move. When Colonel Youngdahl moved up to replace Gregory as Battalion commander, it was apparent this pleased nobody. I wasn't sophisticated enough to know why it mattered. Mack Allen made clear it did.

"Jim, a Battalion commander, he can screw things up generally, lose half the rifle platoons and then sit back there in his tent and blame the company commanders."

"He can't be all that bad," I said.

I was wrong.

Back in reserve Spence put his finger on it. Spence had fought right through the Pacific, island by island, as an enlisted man. Of all the officers in our replacement draft

Spence was the veteran. He had not yet been on the line in Korea, but we listened when he talked.

"They say there isn't a field grade officer in the Battalion worth shit."

"Well, Gregory was on the 'Canal,'" Mack Allen said.

"Hell with the 'Canal.' That was nine years ago. I'm talking today, up in these hills."

"Youngdahl looks the part," I said.

Spence just laughed. Looks didn't impress him.

"You know what I think," he said. "I think the reserve officers are carrying this battalion and probably some other battalions. These regulars, hustling for promotion, worrying about politics. Reserves don't give a damn about that stuff, just do the job and go home. Maybe I'll be wrong. I ain't been up there yet. But that's how I smell it right now. We'll see, we'll see."

The second day we were on the new line a two-seater bubble-domed helicopter floated in to drop on the landing platform behind my position. I got word who it was and hurried down, saluting as I saw the colonel's eagles. The Regimental commander and I exchanged pleasantries. He asked if it was a good position, and I said yes, and he asked if there'd been any action yet, and I said no.

"Show me around," the colonel said.

We climbed the slope. I slipped once on the ice, but the colonel, trim and dapper with a red silk scarf at the throat, moved lightly, easily. He must have been forty-five years old, and I marveled at how he moved. We went down the line, through the squads. We stopped at my bunker. It was all very polite and so good for morale. The colonel complimented me on the appearance of the men, how the area was policed. He suggested another apron of wire but being terribly nice about it. I wished we had a teabag; I would have offered him some. The colonel might have liked that. I was becoming cynical, like Spence. After six weeks.

Then the colonel said, "Where are your machine guns?"

I was sorry about being cynical, sorry about the teabag.

"Well, sir, the heavies are right over this nose. I've got attached heavies, two guns."

"And the lights?"

The answer was, I didn't know exactly. What I said was,

"They're down with the squads. The first squad has one, and the second, and . . ."

"Lieutenant, what bunkers are your machine guns in? Do you know their fields of fire? How they're laid? Do you have aiming stakes in?"

"No, sir."

"You should know, shouldn't you?"

"Yes, sir."

"Then find out."

"Aye, aye, sir."

The words still floated in the crisp cold of the hill as the colonel hopped jauntily into his chopper and left. I got on the phone to call Chafee. I told him. I thought I'd better since the colonel surely would. Chafee didn't say much over the phone.

"Well," he said, "I guess you had better go out and chart your guns, hadn't you?"

Chafee didn't say anything more. He didn't need to, but I knew there was plenty he would have said. There was plenty the colonel of the Regiment would say to the colonel of the Battalion who, in his turn and in the hallowed traditions of the Corps, would have a few words for Chafee. I felt pretty bad. It seemed unfair a fine officer like Chafee, a good man, should suffer because a green junior officer doped off. But it was the way things were and the way they had to be. Later in the day, when Chafee met with Philips and the three platoon leaders, he stressed, as might a teacher in kindergarten, the importance of basic things, the precise location of machine guns being only one of these fundamentals. He made no reference to the colonel, none to me. He simply reminded us of things he wanted done and said he expected them to be done. Then he and Philips loped off to look at something and the rest of us drifted back to our platoons. I wanted to tell the rest of them it was my fault we'd been lectured; I wanted to hug Chafee for not saying so. These were the mistakes and the decent instincts that came with still being an amateur in a professional's war.

We began patrolling the fourth day on the line.

In a static war it is a rule that you patrol, that you keep the enemy off balance. There are recon patrols, reconnaissance patrols that go out searching the ground and seeking information; there are patrols to bring in prisoners, the most valued coin of intelligence; there are ambushes to trap and kill enemy patrols; there are combat patrols simply to kill.

My first patrol order was simple. I was to send a recon squad out in daylight down the draw that separated the nose from the main ridge, to see if there was wire down there, whether the draw itself was a practical proposition for gooks to come up or marines to go down, how steep it was farther down, whether the snow was drifted deep, to see generally what was there and to come back to tell about it. We were not to go all the way to the valley, not to go near the enemy. For most of the route we would not even be under observation; that was why a rare daylight patrol had been laid on. It was a very simple patrol. I decided to take it out myself. I did not realize it at the time, but this was good judgment on my part. The patrol would be a fine experience, it would demonstrate to the men that I would not send them where I wouldn't go, it would be good for my confidence. I didn't rationalize all this. I went because I was curious.

At ten in the morning, January 13, another fine, cold day with sun, I led the dozen men to the lip of the ridge and stepped over the rusted apron of wire to begin the descent. Behind me was Fitzgerald, the first squad leader, then Duke, the negro runner, the rest of the squad and a corpsman last. Fitzgerald was a big Irish kid out of Flint, Michigan, a high school football star who joined the marines to play football so he could get to college on an athletic scholarship. Instead, they sent him to Key West, where the marine base did not field a team. Fitzgerald had been wounded on 749 in September and had rejoined the platoon during reserve. He had freckles and sand-colored hair. He was twenty years old and a buck sergeant.

I sank into snow that had drifted nearly a yard deep in the gully. But it was easy going downhill. The ground was frozen under the snow, and I did a sort of glissade down the steep slope with the others stretched out behind in single file. I looked back once to see the last man stepping gingerly over the wire, holding his generous windproof trousers so they wouldn't snag, like an old woman stepping over a garden fence, so daintily. I had just turned to resume my half-slide, half-step descent when my foot caught and I sprawled forward into the deep snow. Behind and below me there was a sudden, shocking upheaval of snow and earth, and as I threw my hands up toward my head, I heard the roar. Dirt and rock and ice rained down on my back, rattling on my helmet. I raised my head to see just behind me a blackened patch of snow. Fitzgerald was lying on his back, kicking his legs and waving an arm.

Up above someone shouted, "A mine, a goddamned mine. They hit a mine."

This was my nightmare come true. I couldn't feel anything. I had no idea what being wounded felt like, but I was sure it hurt, was sure it was worse than this. There was now a lot of shouting, but I shut it out and called to Fitzgerald.

"Fitz, is it bad? Did it get you bad? Fitz?"

Fitzgerald raised his head to look at me. He looked okay. I couldn't see any blood.

"Okay, Fitz? Is it okay?"

"I guess so, Lieutenant. I don't know. I can't get my other arm around. Do I look okay?"

I crawled up through the blackened snow toward Fitzgerald. Above us there was commotion, people moving in the gully, shouts. I waved a hand.

"Get the hell out of here. No one comes down here. There are mines down here. No one comes down, that's an order. That corpsman, stand by."

I was with Fitz now. The sergeant looked all right but pale under the freckles. He was tugging at the fouled arm with his good one. Then it came loose and his rifle came up out of the snow. There was blood on the arm. I pulled off Fitzgerald's glove and pushed at the sleeve. There were deep gashes in the wrist, maybe more higher up. Blood was leaking down. A lot of blood, but it wasn't pulsing; it didn't look that bad. I knew that much and I told Fitz.

"That's fine, Lieutenant. I appreciate it."

He sounded as if he meant it, wasn't just patronizing me.

"We'll get you out of here, Fitz. Right away. Don't worry."

This was a man who'd been shot before. Badly. "Well,

I'm not worrying, Mr. Brady. I guess I can just get up and walk back up there the way we came down. It's just the arm.''

"No, nobody's going to walk up or down through here until we get squared away. We tripped one mine, I did, I guess, and I'm sorry for that, Fitz. I really am sorry for that.''

"Forget it, Lieutenant. Could have happened to anyone. Could have got you instead of me.''

The runner, Duke, was only ten yards above us now and edging down.

"Duke, you stay up there. That's an order. You want to trip more mines, kill us all?''

"No sir, just want to get you both outa there.''

He was showing a lot of teeth and his eyes were huge and he wasn't afraid, as I was, of the mines.

"Okay,'' I said, "I'll tell you what.'' I wasn't afraid now but thinking clearly and fast. I'd tripped a mine and was alive, not even hurt, not that I knew of. If there was shock from the explosion, it hadn't lasted.

"Duke, you get a rope and toss one end down here. Tell them, get a rope or some com wire, something like that, and toss it to me.''

The order was passed back. There were a lot of people now on the ridge. I couldn't see Chafee. He must have been all the way at the other end of the company front or he'd have been here. Now a line came down, a long piece of communications wire. Duke tossed one end to me.

"Stay back there now, Duke. Stay back. How you doing, Fitz? Okay?''

"Just fine.''

For all I knew he was bleeding to death. But he said, "Just fine.'' I looked back up to the runner.

"When I tie this wire onto my carbine and Fitz's rifle, you play it all the way out and then drag it up through the snow to the ridge. That should trip any more mine wires down here. If there are any. Go ahead, now, get up topside and pull.''

I reached over to Fitzgerald and pushed down hard on his shoulder. "Put your head down, Fitz, in case they hook into another one.''

I lay down flat on the snow myself, my face in the snow, cool and soft. I felt very excited but not afraid. I hoped Fitz wasn't really hurt bad. Then I remembered to say a prayer, very brief. Now there was another shout from above.

"All clear, Mr. Brady, comin' down to help out."

Before I could speak again Duke was there with us, helping Fitzgerald to his feet, giving me a hand I didn't need. The three of us slipped and clambered up, the final yards helped by other hands. When we got across the apron Fitz sat down and the corpsman slit his sleeve and began to poke at the bloody arm. Fitzgerald sat there on the snow, looking tough, older than twenty.

"Okay, Fitz?"

"Just fine, Lieutenant, not bad at all."

"Hell, Fitz, that's two Purple Hearts," someone said. Fitzgerald shrugged.

Chafee was there now, not saying anything but smiling at me. I started to tell him what happened.

"Okay, Lieutenant," the CO said, "when you get your wounded taken care of come on down to the CP. You can tell Battalion over the phone just what happened. That way you'll only have to tell it once."

"Yes, sir."

I couldn't think what else there was to say. Marines stood around watching us. I felt in some vague but very real way that I belonged with them now. Fitz was on his feet, holding his arm and ragging the corpsman about his bedside manner. Men drifted away.

That night I worked hard at tidying my half of the bunker, ate very little but enjoyed what I had, and tried unsuccessfully to get Princeton to talk about the day's events. I gave that up and wrote a number of letters, separate ones to my mother and father, telling them what happened and that I was okay and I loved them, and another to a girl. The girl was tall and lean and very pretty and quite exciting, but we had never meant anything to each other. Now I wrote her, quite dramatically, that I'd nearly been killed, that my eyes had been opened, and as soon as I got back we should begin to consider the future.

"We've wasted an awful lot of time, you and I," the letter concluded.

It was a college boy's letter, and in the morning I tore up all three letters, chiding myself for being callow, and sent a three-paragraph letter home in which I discussed the weather in some detail.

Princeton, who wrote to his wife once a month, shook his head over all this correspondence.

But he hadn't been down the draw, didn't reflect as I did, each time I passed the little patch of blackened snow, how I might have lost a leg, might have killed Fitz. For a few days the draw haunted me, the blackened patch an obscene memory. Then a light snow fell in the night, a couple of inches, erasing the place where I'd tripped the mine. And there were other things to worry about, other fears and concerns, and gradually I forgot.

16

I started to get to know my men.

Like most people my age I'd been brought up on Hollywood's idea of a marine platoon: a demographically, ethnically balanced blend of WASPs and the rest of us. You know, a Brooklyn Jew streetwise but sensitive; a big-city Italian talking baseball and making obscene arm gestures behind your back; a dumb hayseed farmboy with a girl back home; a heroic black man; a Puerto Rican or a Mexican with a rosary muttering Spanish wisdom; a feisty little Jimmy Cagney Irishman with a chip on his shoulder. A goulash of stereotypes.

The reality in Korea was somewhat different.

My platoon had no Jews, one black, no Hispanics, one Indian, surly and sullen. There were Protestants and Catholics and a few who were nothing and that was it. Some Irish, some Poles, some Italians, a few French. You never saw a French enlisted man in a movie, did you? And the Irish were sober, and it was the Midwest rubes who got emotional while the Italians were being methodical and phlegmatic.

Nor were the battalion's officers what the Marine Corps had traditionally been, Southern gentlemen. Now we were Easterners, Ivy Leaguers, college kids, Californians, men from Detroit and Chicago and Seattle. The Corps's NCOs still favored the South; there was still a reek of Dixie, but less so. In 1951 and 1952 you never saw a negro officer. Maybe there weren't any.

I suppose that should have bothered me, aroused decent, liberal instincts. It didn't. I accepted the status quo as I accepted Sergeant Princeton's crude and vulgar ways. Was he a good platoon sergeant? That's what I cared about. It was what I cared about with the platoon: Would they do the job and not get anyone killed unnecessarily? Would I lead them well and not prove a fool or a coward?

In reserve area they were just forty men lined up on the parade ground, tall and short, mustachioed or smooth-faced, brisk or laconic. On the line, being with them one or two at a time in their bunkers or on patrol, you got to know them, you could tell them apart. At the same time, I was getting to know myself.

A marine rifle platoon in Korea was a superbly balanced tactical unit with enormous firepower and an eminently sensible fundamental premise: in combat no one man can reasonably be expected to control directly and effectively more than three other men. In a firefight, you can't keep tabs on more than three marines and still be aware of the enemy. A marine rifle platoon has three squads whose squad leaders are trained to maintain contact with the platoon leader. When he issues orders he issues them not to forty men, but only to these three sergeants. In their turn, they each control three fire teams, each of which is commanded by a corporal fire-team leader. They look to the squad leader for orders, he to them for action. In the fire team the corporal has three men, whom he controls and who look always to him during a firefight.

Army platoons also have three squads, but the squads aren't broken down into fire teams but remain an unwieldy straggle of ten or a dozen men. There is one other material distinction between marine and army rifle platoons: fire power and the Browning Automatic Rifle. The BAR is a wonderfully steady, fast-firing, very accurate weapon. Each marine fire team is built around the BAR. A marine platoon had nine BARs, the army platoon only three, one to each squad.

The BAR weighed twenty pounds even without ammo, and the ammo belts weighed that much again, yet it seemed that a stunted little guy weighing about 130 pounds was always lugging it. At Quantico we bitched about being chosen as BAR men during field problems. Out here you couldn't pry one away from a BAR man. It was the finest one-man weapon employed in the infantry, a great weapon. It had a range with a certain type of ball cartridge of 5,500 yards— more than three miles. BAR men were forever arguing over that, whether you could hit a man at three miles, or if at that distance he had disappeared below the curvature of the earth and you couldn't even see him. Marines delighted in intellectual debates like that, loud and obscene.

But those nine automatic rifles gave young marine officers like Simonis and Allen and me one of our two big advantages over our army counterparts. We had more firepower. The other advantage was the marine rifle platoon's organization, easier to command in a firefight, when even the coolest of men can become confused. Add to this the fact that marines, enlisted marines, take orders without question, and you understand why it is simpler to command troops as a marine officer and that it has little to do with courage or brains. Marines are no better or worse than soldiers as men. What the marine has is better training, a more maneuverable unit, more actual firing practice, often better noncommissioned officers, and an intangible spirit founded on tradition.

He also has more BARs, which may be more important than anything else.

I had good NCOs. Fitzgerald, whom I had nearly gotten killed, was outstanding, both as a marine and as a man. Fitzgerald genuinely liked combat. He had the true killer instinct, liked going out at night to set ambushes. I'd seen marines like him in movies. Now I was seeing one up close and for real. The second squad leader, Nelson, was a cowboy and claimed to have been a rodeo rider, a lean and nasty man who had enlisted in the Corps for a four-year hitch while dead drunk after a rodeo in some forgotten Wyoming or Montana town. One night in the reserve area three of Nelson's men cornered him, angry over some real or imagined injustice. Two of them held Nelson while the third punched his face, breaking his nose, blacking both eyes, and knocking loose a tooth. Princeton found out about it in that way platoon sergeants have, but Nelson told him to forget it. He wanted Princeton to do nothing, say nothing. It was explained to me that Nelson had fallen down. It appeared marvelous that a rodeo rider could fall down on level ground and so damage himself, but I took the story, not believing it, just tucked it away and said nothing. Nelson was strong and not afraid and worked hard at his job. He was just one of those unpleasant people with a sour personality who find it difficult to get others on their side. No matter what Nelson did, or how well, it was easy to dislike him and that was his problem. You understood why he might well have been a rodeo rider, where it was just the man and the horse, and you didn't need friends. But I wasn't going to start replacing squad leaders because they weren't popular. Nelson told Princeton he would handle the three malcontents in his own time and in his own way. The platoon sergeant accepted this and had confidence Nelson would see justice done.

The third squad leader was a Pole, a swarthy, stunted man from Dayton. He lacked style, but Princeton said he was a good man and tough, that on 749 he had done good work as a fire-team leader. Now he was a buck sergeant and rated a crack at the squad. Flynn promoted him and then left the country. With me, the Pole lasted three weeks. There was work to do, chipping out ice steps, as mountaineers do, on the reverse slope, laying wire, reinforcing bunkers. The Pole evaded it. Once he had to see the chaplain, to confess. Another time he wanted some favor from the Red Cross. When Princeton remonstrated, the Pole gave him lip. When I summoned him up he was humble, respectful, devious. I broke him back to fire-team leader.

"Give it to Dils," Princeton suggested. We gave it to Dils. Dils was quiet, solid, out of the state of Maine, unpretentious as a potato, lean and mild looking, but he had worked in lumber camps. That was enough for me; Jack London was always a good reference. Dils had no personality, but he got the ice steps chipped, the wire laid, a good sergeant.

Hoops was the platoon guide. The guide is the second-ranking NCO in a platoon. He deals with supplies and he chivvies people from the rear while the platoon sergeant and the lieutenant are up front. You want an old salt as platoon guide. Hoops was old and he was salty. He was thirty-five and had been in the Corps eighteen years, had been three times a sergeant, once a staff sergeant. He was also a drinker. Four times he had fallen back, the victim of his thirst and an insensitive court. Now he was a sergeant again. It was difficult, though not impossible, to get liquor on the line. If you had a bottle, you had humped it up yourself, and when you were carrying sixty pounds, you didn't add to the load. I took a chance on Hoops. Princeton's word carried weight and he wanted Hoops as guide. It was a good gamble. Hoops stayed sober and did the job. A few bottles made their way to the line that winter and presumably some of it got to Hoops, but not much; there was no trouble, and he never let the platoon down, or Princeton, who had argued for him. Or me, who bought the argument.

In those early days of January, while I was getting the feel of the platoon and the platoon in turn was taking my measure, the line, our sector of it, was abnormally quiet. There was occasional shelling by gook 105s, guns they'd captured from the ROKs or from the army, but it was nothing serious and not at all accurate, more searching fire than anything. We were too high for 61mm mortars to reach us, and the gooks seemed to have better things to do with their 82s. Up and down the line on both flanks there were nightly firefights on the lower ridgelines, where it was easier for the two armies to extend probing fingers, to touch and grapple. Here in front of my position, in front of all Dog Company, the reach was too great. We had, if not peace, tranquility. In war, any abnormal condition creates problems, vacuums demand to be filled, and it was no exception with us. Kelso, the heavy machine-gun sergeant whose men faced the wind on the northwest flank of the nose, reported one morning he was having trouble maintaining security among his men.

"These nights are just too damned quiet, Lieutenant. I haven't caught any of them, but some of my gunners are doping off. They sneak inside away from the wind. Then one night them gooks is going to climb up here and my men going to be inside and people going to get hurt."

Kelso was a sensible man who had come to me with a

serious problem and asked for help. I thought of telling
Chafee. But I disliked the notion of running to Papa.
Princeton sat there with us, not saying much beyond the
muttered suggestion the machine gunner "boot a few of
them sea lawyers in the ass."

I started to ask Princeton for advice and decided against
it.

"Tell you what, Kelso. If you want to try it, tonight if
everything's quiet, say at eleven o'clock, you toss a couple
of grenades down the hill in front of your position. That
ought to wake up your people. If the gooks won't do it for
us, we'll do it ourselves."

Kelso nodded his head, concentrating on the order of
events. He was not quick but he wanted to be thorough.

"Should I fire off a burst from the gun, too?"

I started to say, hell, yes, when I saw Princeton's mournful face. I said no, we would leave it at that and see how it
went. We agreed on eleven o'clock and we left. Kelso was
talking to himself, memorizing everything.

"You don't like it, do you, Prince?"

"Begging the lieutenant's pardon but I don't."

I asked why.

"No hard reason I can show you in my hand. I just don't
like firing live rounds on the line 'less you've got something
out there you might hit. Course, the way people shoot these
days there's little enough danger. But you're the platoon
leader and you gave the order. So we might as well try it."

It was as if he wanted to talk his objections out, and
having done so he was ready for whatever happened.

Princeton came out of a dry county in Texas. When he
was seventeen, eighteen, he was driving a bootlegger truck.
He didn't apologize for what was apparently a quite honor-
able profession in a part of the state where both Baptists
and bootleggers were against Repeal. Princeton was only
twenty-eight now, a ten-year man who seemed older, married to a former Wave. She sent him erotic photos of
herself, nude or half draped in a robe, or fondling her
breasts. He showed me the photos neither proudly nor with
embarrassment, but matter-of-factly, the way men pass
around snapshots of children. Chafee had warned me against
learning too much about the men's personal lives. I re-

treated behind a polite "She's very pretty, isn't she?" Princeton would nod, justified, and put the pictures away.

"It's her girlfriend takes the pictures," he said, as if to allay suspicion.

Kelso remembered the timetable and had a good watch. We were awake, waiting, Princeton cleaning his M-1 rifle like most marines contemptuous of the carbine. Then the first grenade exploded. Followed by a second and a third. The phone sounded at my ear. It was Chafee. The man never slept.

"What have you got up there, Brady? Is that your area where we're getting grenades?"

"Yes, sir. Over by the heavy machine-gun section." I gave him the closest mortar concentration as we were trained to do. Then I tried to cool down the affair. "But there's nothing else. Maybe someone's a little shook over there, throwing at shadows. No firing anywhere."

"Well, they're not supposed to throw grenades at shadows," Chafee said. "Tell them to hold their fire until they see something. Want me to come up there?"

"No, sir."

Chafee asked to be kept informed. As I hung up the CP phone there was a whistle in the platoon phone.

"It's me, Dils."

"What have you got?"

"Gooks, I think," the squad leader said, whispering into the phone. "There's movement out there on my right front, over near the machine gunners, where those grenades went off. I think they're working their way toward me now."

"Jesus," I said. I hadn't figured on this.

"Lieutenant, there's a dead space fifty yards down the slope below me. I think they're making for it. I'd like to call in some mortar. We have a concentration right there, right on that dead space."

A dead space was a dip in the ground machine guns couldn't hit. You had to use high trajectory weapons. Mortars.

"Jesus," I said again. I looked over at Princeton. He still had the M-1 on his lap. Chances were Dils was imagining things, that there wasn't a gook this side of the Soyang-

98

gang, that Kelso's phony grenades had created imaginary terrors.

But Dils was cool; suppose he wasn't imagining things. It was now I wished I knew my men better, that I wasn't so goddamned green, that Ed Flynn were still here to give me a quick assessment of Dils. But there are no reference libraries in combat. You have to make up your mind fast.

I wanted to tell Dils it was all a joke, a stunt Kelso and I pulled to wake up those dope-offs of his. I couldn't do that over an open wire with the other squad leaders listening in. I wished Kelso were in Parris Island and I anywhere but here.

"Are you *sure* there are gooks out there, Dils?" I asked, desperate for help. "It's just those shook gunners, tossing grenades. No one else reported anything."

"Lieutenant," Dils said, his voice a croak, "I hear them. I fucking hear them! There's gooks out there. Call in that mortar concentration, for God's sake."

I didn't say anything. I looked toward Prince, but he was suddenly busy again with his rifle. NCOs let officers hang themselves.

"Mr. Brady, they're out there!"

The concentration Dils was calling for was practically on the MLR, right in front of his position.

"Okay, Dils, I'll call in the mortars. Keep your head down."

I took the other phone and rang Chafee. The captain listened and got me to repeat the concentration. "Okay, three rounds on the way."

"Dils," I shouted into the platoon phone, "three rounds. On the way."

The squad leader might be excited but he wasn't scared. "I'm going up to try to see the gooks in the flash when the rounds hit."

I picked up the thunk-thunk-thunk of the mortar tubes. I knew that sound better than anyone here. They were firing at minimum range. Dodge taught me the sound. And I hoped Dodge was there with Porterfield. It was the first time I thought of Dodge since he was court-martialed.

The mortars crunched in, one, two, three. Then, over the phone, there was a sort of cry. "Dils, you okay?" I asked.

There was a pause. Then, weakly, "Sure, sure. Mortar. Short round. Hit me in the head . . . the helmet, bleeding a little. Don't think it's bad . . . maybe you better get up here, Lieutenant."

He sounded scared, sounded hurt.

I was out of the bunker and on the way, bounding over the ridgeline as if it were full day and this wasn't gook country. The night was fiercely cold but still, the usual wind down, so very still after the blasphemy of the mortars crashing through the silence, fouling the night, tearing at Dils. I ran along the path, down the icy steps past the 81s, stage-whispering the password at each bunker, hoping I wouldn't be shot, hoping Dils would be okay, hoping there weren't any gooks out there coming toward the wire and then hoping there were so that my stupidity might be less monstrous. Chafee and a runner were at Dils before me. The squad leader sat propped against the wall of the bunker. His helmet was dented and there was a purpling bruise on his forehead and a shallow cut he was patting with a dirty handkerchief. He looked up to see me and grinned.

"Damn me, Lieutenant, but you was right. I got a good look out there in the flash of the first round and it wasn't nothing. Nothing out there at all. Just my imagination. Then that short round came in and knocked me on my ass. Served me right, I guess, for getting shook." He looked sheepish. Chafee leaned over to pat his shoulder.

"You're not shook, Dils. You're a good man, a good man. It can happen to anyone. I'd rather spend a few rounds than let them get through the wire. Just check it next time; maybe call in a flare for a look-see instead of H.E."

"H.E." was high explosive. I didn't say anything, couldn't. I opened my first aid kit and began to dress the cut. Dils winced from the iodine. Chafee talked to him some more, wanting to see if the wound had dulled him, watching his eyes.

"I'll leave my runner here with you tonight, Dils. Get some sleep and let him stand watch. Send him back when you wake up. You'll have a headache, I'd guess. If it's any worse than that let us know and we'll send you down to the surgeon at Battalion. And Brady, tell your people maybe they can relax, just a little, whatever I said before. We don't want any more of these one-sided firefights."

"Aye, aye, sir."

In the morning Dils was fine. I was at his bunker before seven. The head felt okay, no ache of concussion, just the sting of the cut, a little soreness. One of his eyes had gone black. Dils was still berating himself for his imagination.

"Your imagination's fine, Dils, I'm the one who's cock-eyed." I told him how Kelso complained about his men and about my subtle scheme to get their attention. Dils just sat there looking sore. Then he must have seen how hard I was taking it, the look on my face, my hands working one against the other.

"Hell, Lieutenant, forget it. One thing sure, them machine gunners will be standing watches like marines from here out."

I don't think he really meant it. I think he thought I was an asshole. Probably he respected my frankness if not my judgment, and of course he had himself to blame for the mortars. More importantly, he had to live with me for the next six months, maybe more, take my orders, follow me. There was no point getting an officer down on you; you couldn't win. It was one fight a sergeant surely couldn't win.

17

Now the snow came, heavy on an onshore wind from the Sea of Japan, burying the land. The peaks and the valley and everything but the closest apron of wire, the nearest bunker, the yellowed ammo-tube urinal stuck in the snow, everything but those and the war itself were blotted out. I was a skier, I had always loved snow, but all of us in the second winter of the war were haunted, whether we said so or not, by what had happened that first year, when MacArthur split his forces and drove them north and the Chinese came down across the frozen Yalu and caught the Division at the Chosin Reservoir and very nearly bagged them.

This now was lovely snow, the first real snow there had been since we came back into the line, blanketing debris that remained from the last tour, debris that so irritated Colonel Youngdahl, inspiring daily messages to the rifle companies ordering its policing. The colonel had not yet visited the line; nor to my knowledge did he know the location of the Battalion machine guns, but somehow he knew about the debris. All along the front the snow fell, deep here in the real hills and on the high ridges, and the battle fell into halfhearted feints and jabs with no hard fighting. Even the North Koreans, whose land this was, huddled against the snow and sheltered out of the wind. On the third day of the storm, the snow thinned and stopped. More than three feet had fallen, and now a colder, dryer wind swept down from the north, ignoring the line of battle on its cruel neutral passage from Siberia to the sea.

I was having bowel trouble again. Not as severe this time, only frequent, and five or six times a day, I slid down the slope to the holed ammo box set into the hill, to sit there and empty myself while I tried to keep the snow from drifting down into my furled trousers. Even Chafee was grounded by the snow. He held his daily company meeting by telephone, transmitting the password, giving a brief account of the fighting elsewhere, checking on the condition of the men and irregularities in supply. There were no patrols. But Chafee urged us over and over not to be lulled, not to relax, to be alert when everyone else might nod, to scout out the ground each day whatever the weather, to see to it the weapons were clean and lightly oiled. Oil froze in this cold; you couldn't use much. Princeton and I alternated visiting each flank of the platoon once a day. In this snow it was easier to duck into the bunkers to talk, to inspect weapons, to question men at the firing ports. They brewed cocoa or coffee, and I took it. Odd, I'd never liked coffee, not even coffee ice cream, and now I was sluicing it down black and strong, cup after cup. Fitzgerald's arm, poor Dils's forehead, Nelson's broken nose and smashed mouth, all were healing. It was curious our only casualties so far were the three squad leaders. The Pole, when I visited his fire team, was quite genial. Perhaps he sensed there was some sort of hex working among the squad leaders and he was relieved to be free of it.

I wrote letters, read the one book I had a second time (Budd Schulberg's novel about Fitzgerald), learned from Princeton how to roll cigarettes and taught myself to blow smoke rings in the still, stale air of the bunker. I was not a smoker; it was something to do. I cleaned my .38 and that damned silly carbine over and over, shaved every other day, ate canned peaches and pears, drinking the sweet juice from the can, tolerated the rest of the ration and feasted on a salami and a small wheel of cheese my mother sent. One evening, after Princeton and I crawled into the bunker for the night, the fragile sound of a harmonica hung in the unnatural still, muffled by the snow. It came from the bunker just below, Hoops or the runner, Duke, I supposed.

I'd been writing a letter and I put the pen down to listen. The tune came clearer now, "The Minstrel Boy." I sat back and listened, remembering the words, words that had application to me, to every boy who had gone to the wars. The song ended, the player went on to other tunes, good ones, too, but the spell was broken.

I wanted to talk to someone about the war, about my having gone to it, or the irony that found me here while other, surely better, men were aground at Camp Lejeune or "Dago" or on ships in the Med. But there was only Princeton to talk to, and the platoon sergeant was asleep, mouth open, his bristly blond mustache faintly moving with his breath. There were men I knew who would have understood how I felt, who might have reacted as I did to the lonely, sad tune of the Irish soldier gone to war. I was lonely myself and sad, sad because I was lonely. Princeton was a good NCO but we had so little to talk about, so little common ground. And then, shaking myself out of the mood, I thought of all the men awake and asleep on that same ridge above the valley of the Soyang-gang, all of us so far from home, all of us gone to the wars, and how they were with me and dependent, in a very real way, on my strength and judgment and courage. Thinking about them, of the bonds we had, made it better, and I slept.

We were all sleeping pretty well. It seemed this high ground was in every sense above the battle, that maybe there wouldn't be any real fighting during this tour. "Cushy," men began to say of our piece of line. Then, on a bright, cold afternoon the nearly forgotten war reached again to touch us in a particularly hideous fashion. Someone had been lulled, someone had relaxed.

It was a vivid afternoon, cold and bright under a high blue sky, after the big snow. Two marines from Fox Company, on the left flank of my platoon, went down the forward slope to fetch water. They carried jerricans, two each, but no arms. It was unusual to go forward of the MLR unarmed, everyone knew that, but all the time we had been on these high ridges there had been no enemy ground activity. Still, had an NCO or an officer seen them go, he would have stopped them, chewed them out and insisted they make the carry to a more distant watering point on the reverse slope. But no NCO saw them, no officer.

The marines crossed the two aprons of wire and ploughed through deep snow down to a good flowing spring a patrol had discovered a day before. The spring rose in a grove of stunted pine three hundred yards, no more, down the forward slope. How the enemy soldiers got there before them was impossible to say. They must have come up the hill in the night and lain there all day buried in the snow, shivering and waiting. You had to admire them. A BAR man on the ridge saw the two marines enter the wood, and then he heard a yell and the clank of jerrican on jerrican, the metallic sound carrying clear. When the BAR man stood up for a better view of what was happening a burst of burp-gun fire sent him tumbling back into the trench. He fired a quick burst of his own high over the grove of trees, fearing to hit the marines but wanting to give the alarm. But the gooks were already away, the two marines with them, hands tied behind them, their legs free to move fast, prodded along by the burp guns. There were six Koreans. Now they were 200 yards below the grove of pine and moving fast.

A new lieutenant had just joined Fox Company, an Annapolis graduate, a trade school man, a matter of understandable pride already in the Battalion, our very own Academy graduate. He had four years of Annapolis behind him, all those parades, all that tradition, all those Army-Navy games, and another four months at the Basic School at Quantico. Fox Company was very excited having him; it made everything so official, so grand. But beyond that he seemed a good man, a cool and professional young officer who would do his job. His name was Folger and his nickname was Lucky and he was twenty-two, twenty-three years old.

When the BAR man squeezed off the burst, marines came out of every bunker along the Fox Company line and on my flank. A dozen men with rifles and BARs started down the hill after the raiders, hoping they could move faster than the gooks with their prisoners, hoping to catch them before they crossed the Soyang-gang and disappeared into their own lines. Folger, who had not yet been out in front of the line, because of the five-day rule, was one of the first men to reach the grove of trees. As he and the others ran through the low pines, hurdling over the spring, the deep thunk of mortars drifted up to us from across the valley. All around Folger marines threw themselves flat in the snow, pulling helmets down tight over their ears, legs pulled in close, cupping their bodies against what they knew was coming. Folger had never heard an incoming mortar before. One of the first shells hit Lucky Folger. A marine who lay nearby said Folger made no sound, could not have known he was hit.

The 82mm mortars, which the gooks had carefully registered on the little grove of trees as cover for their raiders, stopped our people. No one else was hit, only Folger, but they were pinned down, unable to do more than squeeze off a few despairing ranging shots after the Koreans. You couldn't move in the open under those mortars. Fox Company's commander, a Mormon who owned trucks in Utah, called in his own mortars to shell the raiding party. He knew he was risking the captured marines. Marine captains are paid to make decisions. He hoped if the shells landed close, his two men might slip away in the confusion. Observers reported some near misses. They hadn't seen any hits. A sniper unshipped an old Springfield '03 with a scope. He wanted to pick off the Koreans as they skidded and slipped down the hill, now far below. The shot, if he could make it, would be a thousand yards. He lay very still in the snow at the lip of the ridge, the stock of the old rifle smooth against his cheek, trying to decide through the scope which were the gooks, which the marines. His finger tightened on the trigger, then eased off. He turned to the company commander and shook his head. At this range . . .

They fetched more powerful glasses and swept the lower slopes of the hill and then the valley of the Soyang-gang itself. There was nothing there. The raiders were across. They'd slipped away and now night was coming on. As the blue shadows crept out of the valley and climbed the forward slope, a marine with an artillery observer's scope thought he saw something. A bundle of old clothes, it looked like. Or a man. Down there where our mortars had hit.

In the morning, even before dawn, Fox Company had a

106

patrol low on the slope. They found the bundle of clothes. There was a marine inside the clothes, one of the men the gooks had grabbed, his hands tied behind him, his body ripped by mortar fragments. They couldn't tell more because the body was frozen into the ice of a small feeder stream that ran into the Soyang-gang, a stream that at this point ran slow and shallow so that overnight it had closed in about the body and sealed it in. They radioed for help. They needed a demolitions man to come down and blow the body out of the ice.

Hoops had served as a demolitions instructor; he knew how to handle the stuff and he had the nerve. When the call for a demo man came over the wire from Chafee, I told him I had him.

"This is a volunteer's job, Brady. Don't order him to go. But we bring out the dead. We want that body back. Let him decide, but hurry it. Fox can't keep that patrol down there all day."

Chafee never sounded urgent about anything. This morning he did.

I told Hoops what they wanted. The platoon guide stood there for a moment looking as if he wanted very badly not to be on the wagon. Then he nodded and went swinging off to Fox Company, where they had the stuff. The day drifted on quietly, no shelling, everyone waiting, knowing what was happening down there, and on 100 percent alert to support the patrol if the gooks came out. Toward two o'clock came the muffled boom-boom of explosives. Three hours later they came back in through the lines with the long green sleeping-bag cover slung heavily and sagging, with four men at the corners.

I'd gone down the line to be there when Hoops came in. He looked bad, as bad as a man who'd been drinking all night and throwing up all morning.

"I got him out, Lieutenant," he told me. "Took two charges. But we got him out. In two damned pieces. I puked when I was finished."

He didn't say anything more, not to me. Maybe to Princeton, or to Duke.

The marine had been shot through the back of the head. They figured the gooks did that. Princeton said he didn't like losing a marine, but it was the sensible thing to do if he was so badly hit by the mortars that they couldn't take him with them.

"He would've bled to death anyway, or froze."

"Maybe they shot him first, when the mortars began, and then a round hit him later."

Princeton brightened. That hadn't occurred to him.

"Jesus, Prince, that was a marine we killed or they killed. Anyway, he's dead. Doesn't that get to you?"

I was sore and the platoon sergeant knew it. He was unsentimental, thick, but he wasn't stupid. There was no pity in him, only a homespun contempt for amateurism.

"Well, Mr. Brady, I get your point. I don't like marines getting killed no way, not drunk in cars or shot by jealous husbands or murdered by gooks. But dammit, Lieutenant, the son of a bitch deserved it out there in front of the MLR without his damned weapon."

I thought of asking him if Folger, our Annapolis man, had been guilty of amateurism. But it would have been a wiseass, college-boy question. And I didn't ask it.

We never knew what happened to the other marine they caught down by the spring. He was out of a town I never heard of in Florida. Chafee said he supposed he'd end up in some prison camp near the Yalu. It was no place for a boy from Florida, but he wouldn't have anything to say about it, would he? For a month or so I asked if his name showed up on prisoner lists. Hoops wanted to know. I guess I did, too.

In the end I stopped looking at the lists, and by spring I'd forgotten his name, even if it had been on one of those damned sorry lists.

═══ **18** ═══

We were out patrolling now every night. Youngdahl must have caught hell for the raid. It wasn't smart letting those gooks get that high up the hill by dark. Each night it was the turn of one of the three rifle platoons in each company to go out. You put out a squad to cover a stretch of ground and set up an ambush along one of the likely routes of approach. The patrols went out, night after night, but they came back in each time without having made contact. Now it was the cold, rather than the enemy, that hurt us.

I took out the first patrol for Dog Company, Nelson's squad. It wasn't required that the platoon lieutenant go out, but it was sensible, showing you wouldn't send a patrol where you wouldn't go yourself. The ridge fell away very sharply in front of Nelson's position, and we went down the face using a rope anchored to a barbed-wire stake pounded into the frozen ground just beyond the wire. We made a lot of noise going down, slipping and sliding, and I whispered hoarsely at Nelson to shut them the hell up. The squad leader moved quietly along the line of men, punching each on the arm and hissing at him, and it went more quietly after that. As long as we were on the move the cold wasn't too bad. Working with compass and by moonlight we covered a W-shaped route assigned by Battalion across the face of the hill, halting at each point of the W to report back by telephone. I carried a field phone and one of the riflemen a long spool of wire as well as a radio for backup. The phone connection was very clear, and it made me feel good to have a link with the line, an umbilical cord. It was nearly midnight when we reached the ambush point and the dozen men melted into the shadows of rocks and stunted pine along the uphill side of a shallow draw.

I was wearing a knee-length parka, something I hadn't done since we came up the hill. Under the parka I wore a field jacket with a wool lining, two woolen sweaters, a wool shirt, a sweat shirt and an undershirt. I wore sweat pants over my shorts, enlisted men's green wool trousers over those, and windproof pants that buttoned at the ankle. On my hands were wool mittens, over them the Abercrombie & Fitch shooting mittens with the slit right palm and, underneath both layers of mittens, light wool gloves. But after thirty minutes, only my feet in the thermal boots were still warm.

I lay in the snow, propped up on one arm, the telephone warmed under my parka, the carbine outside and ready but cradled against my chest. Around me the men were very still. There was no wind; we should be able to hear gooks coming. It was a good ambush, what we called a "duck blind." I phoned Chafee at twelve thirty and then at one. We were to stay there until four and then come in before the dawn caught us. By two o'clock I was shivering, not badly, but I was not able to stop. Around me came the first low noises, men shifting body position in the snow, the light slither of a mittened hand on a gun barrel. By two thirty the men were moving more, changing position, rubbing hands against their thighs or jamming them into their crotches to revive feeling. I was now actually shuddering with cold, sudden, involuntary lurches of my whole body interspersed with the steady, tiring shivering that would not stop. My face was stiff. I rubbed a mitten hard against my cheeks and nose and tried to sink my chin deeper into the neck of the parka. My shoulders were tired from hunching against the chill. Around me men started to cough. I hissed to Nelson and he crawled from one to another. It was no good; we were losing effectiveness. I could hear them too clearly, could hear myself. So could any gook. I knew some really had coughs, but a few of them were putting it on, cadging sympathy and trying to convince me to take them in. I called the CP and got Philips. Chafee was finally asleep. I asked permission to come in, telling Philips about the coughing, about the cold.

"Hell, I know it's cold. I'll call you back. I've got to ask the skipper and then he'll have to get Battalion to okay."

But we'd woken Chafee and now he came on the line. I told him the same thing. My teeth chattered as I spoke. My lips were cracked and sore and I was afraid one cheek had begun to frost.

"Skipper, it's no good, we're not effective anymore. Any gook out here could hear us."

Chafee said he'd call back.

"Battalion says cut it by an hour. Stay out till three. Then come in by the designated route."

"Aye, aye, sir." It was two fifty. At five minutes to three Nelson crawled back to me, his eyebrows frosted white like a department store Santa Claus.

"Lieutenant, this ain't no use."

"Okay, Nelson, we'll move. Tell them to get ready. We go in five minutes and we go quiet."

"Yessir."

By three thirty we were back to the bottom of the climbing rope. There had been no gooks. In the bunker I woke Princeton. The sergeant crumpled a cocoa cake into a canteen cup and made some. I huddled inside my sleeping bag, still shivering but less badly.

"It's the damned coughing. That's smart. They know you've got to bring them in when they start coughing. You could hear it down in the valley."

Prince nodded. There was no limit to the ingenuity of the enlisted marine. As a former enlisted man, he was rather pleased. As a staff NCO he was outraged.

"Them sons of bitches," he said.

Out of curiosity I asked Red Philips in the morning just how cold it had been. Red didn't know but he said he'd try to find out. That afternoon he called.

"Battalion says as far as they can figure, about thirty below."

"Jesus." In a perverse way I was very pleased. Had Philips told me it was only zero or something like that I would have been terribly let down.

"Battalion didn't want you to come in, you know. Skipper had to do some talking."

"I'd like to get Youngdahl out there one night."

"Shit, Brady, the man needs his beauty sleep."

It was beginning then that I started to lose men. One of Dils's squad had rheumatism, picked up during the summer and fall sleeping on wet ground while the division was on the jump. He lost his air mattress and the chill got into his bones. He was a good man and tried hard, but you could see it, how every day he moved slower and stiffer, as people do in their sixties and seventies. I talked to Dils about him, and the squad leader said it was so, the man wasn't shamming. He was sick. I sent him down to Battalion for an examination and he didn't come back. There was no question: he was twenty-one years old, and rheumatic.

There was another Pole in the platoon, Koski, a huge, burly man, older than most of us. He was twenty-nine. I didn't know much about him, but Nelson came to me and said Koski couldn't do the job, his legs were going.

"He jes cain't cut the hills, Mr. Brady."

Koski had been an auto mechanic in Chicago. I told Philips about him, and when a request came in for technicians to work on helicopters back at Division, I sent in Koski's name, lying about his expertise, building it up. Koski was sent back. At twenty-nine he was just too old and he couldn't cut the hills.

I lost two more men. One of them, Danker, had a fire team in the third squad. Danker was one of the men wounded in September on 749. His wounds were cured, but he was only a month away from rotation and he was shook. That's what they called combat fatigue. Danker did everything he was told to do, but he was afraid. He begged Princeton to do something. Then one of Chafee's runners broke a leg on the ice steps, and I sent Danker to the CP as a runner. He came to thank me.

"Lieutenant, I haven't shirked on you. But if I have to go out on another ambush, I'm scared I'll do something bad and get people hurt. I don't know, I just can't no more control the way I am, the way I feel. I used to be a good man."

He began to cry, and I turned away and told Prince to get him saddled up, that the captain was waiting.

We had an Indian in the platoon, Evans. Naturally, he was known as "Chief." Princeton and Hoops found him a chore. Every other marine in the platoon was to a greater or lesser degree sensitive to curses, rewards, threats of court-martial or beating. Chief took all of them in phlegmatic style. When I was called into it the Chief had been put to work chipping ice from the steps on the reverse slope, making a two-day affair out of a couple of hours' work. I sat down in the snow next to the path, confident I could reason with him.

"Chief, the platoon sergeant isn't happy."

Evans nodded solemnly and leaned on his shovel.

"You know you're letting yourself in for trouble acting like this."

The Chief grunted.

"I don't want to have to run you up before the captain. You don't want that, do you?"

He grunted again. It was difficult to say if it was a negative or a positive grunt, all the Chief's grunts sounding pretty much alike.

I suspected I wasn't appearing very authoritative. "Well, unless you shape up and start doing some work around here, that's just what's going to happen. I'll run you up."

The Chief grunted.

When the sun slipped behind the western ridges, he had chipped out maybe a dozen steps. I shook my head and Princeton cursed.

"I'm taking his ass down behind this hill, and I'm going to whip his ass."

"Prince, he's as big as you."

"Yessir, and he's mean as me, too. But I ain't going to let him dog it this way. Won't do much good, even if I whup him. Them Indians back home, you can beat up on 'em all day and half the night and they just grunts at you."

"They why whip him?"

"Well, it ain't going to help him, but it's going to sure make me feel better."

In the end I had to run the Chief up before Chafee. The captain looked at him sadly and shook his head. Then came a request for marines to fill out military police billets, and Chafee shipped him out to division, with a magnificent recommendation as a model marine. It was a good joke on those rear-echelon pogues and it was wonderful getting rid of the Chief.

Kelso, the machine-gun sergeant, lost a man. This was less amusing than the Chief. It wasn't the gooks that did it but the wind. We'd been on the line three weeks and the wind never stopped. One night Kelso's corporal went berserk, firing off a heavy machine gun inside the bunker, trying to kill rats no one else saw. They carried him off in the morning, cursing the wind and the rats, drooling and trying to tear off his clothes. Princeton looked at him thoughtfully. I was shaken by the sounds coming from a good marine, a solid NCO.

"Never knew a machine gunner yet worth shit," Prince said, spitting in the direction of the corporal and the two gunners leading him down the ridges to Battalion.

We lost other men. Only Fitzgerald's squad did not lose anyone. Fitz would not permit himself to be evacuated the morning I tripped the mine, and he would not permit his men to quit. He was tough, but he was more than that. He was the best we had and his men knew it, and they refused to weaken even when weakness closed on them. Fitzgerald drove them and they drove themselves.

Mack Allen lost men. His platoon sergeant took out a typical patrol, terrible cold but no fighting. They came in about 2 A.M. using a fixed rope to help them scramble up nearly sheer ice below the wire, came in half-frozen and tired. Mack was there to meet them, to check in each man. As he questioned the platoon sergeant about the patrol, the sergeant remembered:

"Damn me, Mr. Allen, we left that rope out there, hanging down from just below the wire."

The sergeant yelled for another marine to give him a hand and disappeared over the lip of the ridge with a husky blond marine in tow. Mack was back in his bunker taking off his boots when a burst of machine-gun fire, then another, ripped through the mountain stillness.

Outside, marines were running. Mack pulled on the boots and crawled out, grabbing a man running by.

"Where's the platoon sergeant? Where's the sergeant and Wingate?"

In the confusion it took a few minutes to find them. They both lay dead on the forward slope, big Wingate draped over the wire, the sergeant curled up, looking like a man taking a nap, on a reddened patch of snow. One of Allen's machine gunners knew the patrol was in, but no one had thought to tell him about the two men going back out to retrieve the rope. As they came back he took them for gooks trailing the patrol home, trying for a straggler, and he fired off the two short, effective bursts. He was a very good gunner and he caught both men in the face. The rope was coiled neatly over the sergeant's shoulder.

Wingate was in my machine-gun platoon on 749 before being transferred to Mack's platoon, not a terribly good marine, a brooder. Most men disliked him. One of the few friends he had was the gunner who killed him.

Knowing what losing the sergeant and Wingate would mean to Mack, I called him on the company phone to talk about it. He wondered if he should just have left the damned rope out there dangling. No matter that the sergeant should have passed the word they were going back out, this was Mack's platoon and these his men and their deaths his deaths.

They carried the bodies to the supply tent just below the company CP and laid them out. The cold would take care of them through the night, and in the morning the gook train would come through. But when the gooks got there and eight stretcher bearers fell out to approach the supply tent to pick up the dead and carry them down the hill, a marine stopped them, the gunner who'd killed Wingate and the sergeant. He had sat crying all night in the tent, sitting over the bodies, and now he stood just outside the tent flap dry-eyed but holding a .45 automatic.

"You're not taking them," he said. The gooks dropped the two stretchers and scattered along the path in both directions. Crazy marines. The stretchers lay on the ice. Chafee walked up to the gunner.

"Give it here, Corporal," he said, "you know Wingate wouldn't want you doing that."

"Stay back, Skipper," the corporal said. He waved the gun, crying again now and shaking his head. I was down there by now, with all the excitement, and to me it was pretty clear a fast man, standing this close, could jump him. And I knew Chafee was very fast. But the captain just stood there, easily, hands on his hips.

"Phil," he said, "Phil, you know Johnny wouldn't want anyone hurt over him." The New England nasal accent was very evident.

The corporal didn't move for an instant, and then he shook his head and his right arm relaxed, then fell, the pistol hanging loose in his hand. Chafee reached out to take it. Then he did something I would not have done. He slipped the .45 back into the corporal's holster, patted him on the shoulder, and waved the gooks back to the tent. Then Chafee and Philips and I, with the corporal's help, lay the two bodies very gently on the stretchers. They were frozen solid and handled like cordwood. The corporal sat in the snow crying until Red Philips got him to drink some coffee and go back to his bunker.

I realized it was the first time I'd heard Chafee call a marine by his Christian name.

The ranking sergeant in Mack Allen's platoon now was a negro named Keefe, the platoon guide. Mack had two Southerners as squad leaders and another dozen in the ranks. There was some of the usual talk about a "nigger" taking over. Mack called the platoon together that afternoon, his soft Virginia voice carrying on the air. It was the only sound.

"Sergeant Keefe is the new platoon sergeant. He runs the platoon. I don't care about anything else. To me, and to Keefe, you're all just marines. And to me, and to you, he's the platoon sergeant of this platoon. Dismissed."

So the gooks were not the only danger. We were killing ourselves and breaking our legs and falling sick and cracking up and being carried away. It was how it was in a mountain war in deep winter. But the gooks were to have their chances. Both Mack Allen and I had lost men and now it came Simonis's turn.

=== 19 ===

I heard the firing before I was really awake, part reality, part nightmare. I sat up suddenly in the bag. Princeton was up and dressed, and he handed me a canteen cup, hot with coffee, very strong and black the way he made it. Prince went on fussing with domestic chores, keeping a tidy bunker.

"Mr. Simonis is catching it," he said.

Simonis had taken a patrol down the mountain the night before, an ambitious affair, all the way to the valley. He should have been back in to the line by this time. It was almost six. I tried to call the CP but nobody answered. They must all be out trying to do something about Simonis. Then I remembered that Chafee wasn't there. He'd torn his hand helping men lay barbed wire; it had become infected and he was down at Battalion getting it repaired. Chafee had no business out muscling wire, but try telling Chafee not to do things. Red Philips had the company. It was a bad time for Chafee to be away with Simonis out there and his patrol caught by daylight in front of the line. That would be it; they must have been caught.

It was usually quiet this early in the morning with the night ambushes pulled back and the artillerymen not yet awake. Poor Simonis. The coffee was too hot, and I wriggled out of the bag fully dressed and tugged on my boots. The firing was mostly mortars punctuated by small arms. It seemed I should be doing something about it. I pulled the field jacket from beneath the bag where it played pillow and told Princeton I was going down the line to see what was happening.

"Now don't you go get yourself in no firefight, Lieutenant."

It was a fine winter's day with the low sun already bright and the Sea looking closer than it was, the usual painted destroyer out there patrolling our flank and looking like one of Teddy Roosevelt's Great White Fleet. I couldn't see anything happening in the valley, but the firing went on. Holding the rope where it was icy I went down the trail to the command post, passing a marine here and there, each of them staring down at the valley, trying to see something, to see the violence that shattered the morning calm.

It was Simonis, all right. He had radio contact with Company. He'd been caught at first light as they crossed the little stream. He had some dead and nearly all of them had been hit. Simonis was okay, so far. Philips was on the radio with him and looking nervous about it all. They were a long way out; somehow we were going to have to get them back, and without the cover of night. Red hadn't commanded a company before. Now he was on the phone to Battalion, asking for artillery, and having no time for me. Then the radio operator quoting Simonis on the other headset said the firing was coming from 462, the small hill between the lines just the other side of the stream. It was 462 Simonis was down there reconnoitering. Philips couldn't get artillery yet, but he ordered his own mortars to start hitting 462 and keep hitting it. "Keep them busy down there," he said. The Company gunny was passing out rifles with scopes attached. Just to be doing something I took one and lay down along the ridge in a line of men and began squeezing off single shots, carefully aimed and laid, at likely-looking knobs that might be bunkers on 462. It was like being back on the rifle range at Quantico, the smell and the noise and the solid, comfortable prone position. I was a good shot because of my eyes, but I knew it probably wasn't very effective. Still, it might keep their heads down.

A stack of brass mounted beside me, sizzling as it hit the snow, dully gleaming. "This is stupid," I said aloud. Anyone could be doing this. I got up and handed the scoped rifle to someone else. "Good hunting," I said. Philips was standing in front of the CP looking solemn.

"Look, Red, I'll take some people down there if you want, with stretchers, and help Simonis get out of there."

Philips looked at me for the first time in what seemed to be focus.

"Yeah, yeah," he said, "that's a good idea. I sent a fire team down already with a corpsman and some blood. but they're going to need more than that. Good idea. Get a squad of people together."

It was simple rounding them up, with everyone ready to go, some even eager. I didn't fall them in, just counted heads to be sure I came back with the same number I took out, and we all just started simultaneously, picking our way carefully through the wire, then moving faster as we hit the powder snow below. You couldn't get lost; it was straight down the draw and into the trees. Philips's voice sailed after us, nervy.

"I appreciate this. Get them back. I appreciate it."

It came to me he was afraid maybe they wouldn't get back.

From the wire it was easy going, like skiing, and I found myself going too fast at first, the deep, light powder giving easily, flowing out to the sides, slipping over the frozen pack underneath. I took giant steps down through the draw, leaping eight or ten feet at a time, the way you did as a boy running downhill, moving so fast you couldn't stop with your legs pumping to stay up with you, until you ran out on the flat and came to a standstill, winded and excited. But the valley was too far for that, and every hundred yards or so I grabbed at a tree, swinging around the trunk first on the right, then on the left, like a slalom, trying to keep momentum under control. Ahead of me another marine was doing the same; behind I heard a whoop. It was kid stuff but it was good to be moving, to be going down to get Simonis, better than playing grabass topside with nothing to do but squeeze off rounds at people you couldn't see. The mortars, from both sides, had died. The pop-pop-pop of a burp gun came very fast, the pops so close it was really more like the sound of canvas ripping, and the heavier, spaced reply of rifles cracked the wooded silence. Now we were too deep in pine to see the valley, so we only had the sound and Simonis's tracks going down. I followed the chewed-up snow the way you'd follow ski tracks on unfamiliar ground. I kept thinking how much it was like skiing, like the first time I'd ever taken a serious ski trail from the top, at Mount Mansfield, starting with the Seven Turns, knowing that my competence was only pose, my legs and stomach not sufficient for it. But on Mansfield, as here, there were people watching, pushing you into doing what you did not really want to do, until the climactic instant when shame balanced fear, then overbalanced it, and you pushed off toward the first of the Seven Turns, and then it was all right and you knew it was.

That was the point of what I was doing: afraid, I went anyway.

I was at the bottom before I expected it. A dozen or more marines lay around in the snow under some pines at the edge of the flat ground. The frozen stream, the Soyang-gang, was a few hundred yards out, and I walked over to where Simonis sat cross-legged working the radio. I stood there waiting for him to finish. Simonis looked up at me, his face tight, but he threw me a grin.

"Take that goddamned thing off!" someone shouted at me. "Can't you see it shining?"

It was the corpsman, standing face to face with me, snarling and jabbing a finger at my cap. I reached up. The gold bar on the cap. I didn't like taking orders from a sailor, but I pulled the cap off while I thought about it. The corpsman shuffled away and I looked around. Nearly everyone seemed to have something shiny, a Marine Corps emblem or those Korean army insignia marines collected. I looked down at my own cap with its gold bar. Shit, the corpsman was nervy and working it off by shouting. Feeling rebellious, I put my cap back on and tugged it down tight. The hell with you, pal!

There were two dead, Simonis told me, and seven wounded out of twelve. Only one of the wounded was really bad and he might not make it. The others were walking wounded. It was the mortars that caught them on the open ground at first light.

"They must have had a concentration registered," he said, "because there were no ranging shots. Just silence one moment and shells whirring in the next."

There was no firing at all now, from either side.

The badly hit marine was called Caulfield. He lay quietly on a poncho in the snow. Close by, too close for propriety, I thought, were the two even quieter figures, rolled tight in their ponchos, shrouded, anonymous. I wondered which of the faces I'd come to recognize these past couple months were hidden there, but I did not go near them. Caulfield was a big negro, six six or so, maybe taller, and I'd seen him bobbing lankily around camp. He looked as if he'd played basketball, and several times I'd nearly asked. Pointless, now.

They had the stretchers out and rolled the bodies aboard, strapping them on with their own belts, and then four men lifted Caulfield and slid a stretcher under him. He groaned softly, and I turned away to look at the open ground. Across the stream looming above us was 462, that little pimple of topography on which I looked down contemptuously every day. Now it dominated us, dangerously close, hostile and towering. Huge patches of snow on its flanks were browned and blackened from the shelling, from the napalm. From 462 the gooks really had that valley taped. How did anyone figure Simonis could cross the valley and get away with it in daylight? But he was supposed to be out of there before the night ended. Simonis had been lucky that first time on 749, lucky and at night. This time was different, this time dawn caught him, the gooks caught him.

Simonis got on the radio and asked for fire on 462 while we moved out. He was very cool, very much in command of himself and of the situation. I was still pretty new at it all and self-conscious about standing around, so I moved in at a corner of Caulfield's stretcher and took a handle. Lord, the man was heavy. We heaved him up and started off up the trodden snow, slowly, as it had to be with this weight and on this hill. I glanced at my watch as we moved off. It was eight o'clock in the morning. Behind us our shells began to hit 462, a good sound.

We'd been climbing through loose snow up the steep trail for an hour when I began to look around for some way to free myself from this damnable corner of stretcher. Despite the cold, sweat ran from under my cap, salty, hot, into my eyes. I could taste it as it crossed my lips and ran down my chin. I found myself hating Caulfield for putting us through this, then was sorry, took it back, and then resented him again. The gook mortars and a few ranging rifle shots followed us for the first few minutes, but blindly because of the trees, off to one side or another, cracking through frozen branches as they smashed into the forest. Odd, but the firing didn't frighten me. Now even that distraction was gone. It was as quiet behind us as in front. The hill reached endlessly upward. I'd read about Mallory on Everest, and I wondered what real mountaineering was like, why men did this for fun. The climbing sun sparkled on the snow. The snow itself debated every step with us, slipping backward, sliding out from under us. Coming down had been sport; climbing back was forced labor. Twice we fell and dropped the stretcher, Caulfield moaning as we rolled him back onto it. There was a lot of blood on his trousers. He was slippery, difficult to grasp, and on the steep pitch of the slope we could not lift him cleanly. There were no cross braces on the stretcher and it had a will of its own, seemingly intent on rolling itself away out of sight. What a rotten design. Caulfield was tremendous. His weight slipped him down the stretcher on the steeper places so we had to push his body up again or lose him entirely. I thought we should tie him the way they had with the dead, but with his wounds this was impractical. He was hit too many places. The corpsman who'd yelled at me, a violent little man, came back intermittently to look down at him and mutter depressing noises. He did not seem to do anything, only mutter.

I was no good at this. I was a sprinter. I knew that before the morning was half spent. I lacked endurance for the marathon. Maybe I'd always known this, had seen my proper event, the quick, dramatic splash through surf, the pounding up a beach somewhere, adrenaline pumping in an assault, the whole affair over, dead or a hero, in a few hours. That was the marine role, not this endless, static war, two months already, maybe a year of it receding ahead, a patrol like this every few nights. I was near to crying in frustration, knowing I was not holding up my corner of the bargain. I raised my head to look around, afraid they were all looking at me, ashamed they knew how I felt.

The other three men looked as bad as I felt. We were all tired, the four of us, and among us there wasn't a damned shred of sympathy anymore for Caulfield, the cause of our exhaustion, of our misery. We all hated poor Caulfield. When I realized this, some pride seeped back into me. We were all in the same fix. I didn't want to be the first to give up. I was, after all, an officer, the biggest joke of all. Was there one among us who wasn't stronger, braver? My mind wandered. Five characters on a hill in search of some flat ground. Props: one lousy stretcher, bandages, blood and all the snow on or off Broadway. If I didn't give up soon I would die there, with Caulfield, there in the snow, broken by the impossible load we carried. I was climbing now with my eyes shut, not wanting to see how much hill remained, my mouth wide open and gasping. We all fell again, the third time, like Christ under the cross. This time I didn't get to my feet but crouched there, gulping in air. Around me the others were still down. Then Simonis was at my side.

"Time to change over. We'll take him for a stretch."

I got up and handed over my corner of the stretcher to an anonymous, furred figure. I told him to watch the tendency of the stretcher to collapse and stood there resting for a moment as they moved off, quite briskly, ahead of me. I followed.

Climbing alone was another world. Soon I was moving surely, even easily, able to plant my feet sideways to the slope where it steepened, breathing deeply, slowly, again taking note of the country, and once looking back to the valley, now far below, through gaps in the trees. I could not yet see the ridge above. I was thirsty but my canteen was frozen solid. Princeton was always warning me about that, but I hadn't wanted to add whisky the way Prince did. I regretted that now and scooped up smooth snow from just off the trail and let it melt in my mouth. It was flat but cold, and what little of it trickled down my gullet was good. I wasn't going to die after all at the corner of Caulfield's stretcher. Well, I would have quit before that, anyway. Or would I?

We lunched on the march, sharing out the dry biscuit and

tinned fruit and beans and sugar Simonis's men carried. The rest of us had gone down the hill without. I wasn't hungry but I kept eating snow. Simonis was on the radio to Red Philips. They were going to try getting a helicopter to us if they could get a pilot to come down in front of the MLR and if we could find a flat space, a clearing in the trees. Then it was my turn again at the stretcher, but this time it wasn't as bad, because we were all tired and moving slower. Caulfield was awake again and moaning. I busied my mind with designs for a new stretcher, one that wouldn't fold up so infuriatingly, maybe with runners so it could be pulled like a toboggan. I thought about skis, short ones you could slip off, that you could wear in this country. I thought about a lot of things, about Princeton up there in the bunker, with plenty of drinking water, about why I'd come down here when no one asked me to, where we were and what I was carrying, trying not to see the blood Caulfield trailed in the snow. Toward two o'clock the corpsman wandered back and bent over Caulfield. He seemed to be listening more than muttering. After a moment he drifted back to my corner, not scowling now.

"Listen, Lieutenant," he whispered, "this guy isn't going to make it."

I didn't say anything.

"And another thing, Lieutenant . . ." He dropped his voice even lower, as if embarrassed. ". . . he's been talking funny, the nigger. Lieutenant, he thinks he's Jesus."

When he left us to rejoin the walking wounded up ahead, I still heard his words. Now I couldn't stop watching Caulfield's face, watching his lips to see if they formed anything comprehensible, anything important. But the big black face was still. If he were Jesus, what were the rest of us? A bloody lot of Simons of Cyrene helping him climb the hill of Calvary? My corner of the damned stretcher assumed a new significance. Perhaps the going was a little easier now, or maybe the pace was slower, but Caulfield didn't seem as heavy. When it was someone else's turn to carry, I relinquished my corner with a real reluctance and for a time walked along beside them, squelching an irrational urge to reach out and hold Caulfield's dangling hand as we climbed. The corpsman didn't come back again, and I had the sense he knew there was nothing he could do, realized he was out of his depth. The big black face was still.

Simonis drifted back to talk to me.

"If we're going to get through the lines before dark, we'll need some help," he said. "Some of the walking wounded are stiffening up. You lose blood when it's this cold, you freeze."

The sun fell toward the ridges.

I was getting restless again, spooked by Caulfield and what the corpsman had said and wanting to get away from him. I told Simonis I'd scout ahead for a clear place where the chopper might put down, and I left the column, moving fast through the trees, soon losing them behind me. I liked being on my own like this, with no one else to worry about, but still doing a job. Now even the sound of their climbing, slipping and crunching and cursing, receded behind me. I was alone on the big hill. I looked at the sun, trying now to will it to slow, but it was way down, nearly sitting on the ridges. Hill 462 had resumed its proper role, no longer towering above us, threatening and dangerous. I was feeling pretty good. I'd gone down there, all the way to the valley, and I was helping get them out. I hadn't quit on the stretcher when I'd wanted to. There wasn't even any residual guilt that I was off alone and unburdened while the others were still at it, lifting themselves and the wounded up the steepness of the hill. I was out there trying to find a landing area, and now ahead of me and slightly to the left there seemed to be a clearing. It looked good, smooth but gently shelving toward a cornice. I stood there trying to gauge whether a chopper could get in here, how close in the trees were. Perhaps it would go. It was . . .

A single shot cracked through the still cold across the face of the mountain and echoed dying in the trees. I lay facedown in the mothering snow below the cornice. I'd moved quickly, instinctively, faster than I knew I could move, expecting all the while to feel rather than hear the second shot. It did not come. The forest was silent. We'd been followed, the gooks had come after us and gotten in ahead of us, were off there now in the trees, waiting for me, waiting for the others. I stayed under the cornice, eyes shut, the snow smooth and cool against my face. Just over this little cornice of snow was the war. Here there was peace. I lay there, not wanting to return to the war, not wanting to go where someone with a rifle had just tried to kill me. Why? I'd never really wanted to hurt anyone, nor had I. Even when I'd lain up there on the ridge pumping clips into the chamber and squinting through the scope to see the brown dust spurts on 462, that was only to keep their heads down, not really to hit anyone. I'd had no target. Now I was the target. Hadn't I been glad back in November when that gook got away from us, the wounded gook who stopped to shit in the snow? I'd been glad we didn't catch him. And now they were shooting at me and I wanted to explain to them how I felt.

Whether it was the cold or shame that drove me, I got to my knees, crouching and half crawling over the cornice lip. The woods were quiet. No shot, no movement, nothing, no one. I hustled across the clearing, bent double, and dove back into the trees. Simonis came up to meet me, his eyebrows raised, questioning. He'd heard the shot but they hadn't seen anyone. I told him about the clearing, that it just might go.

"No," Simonis said, "the copter people decided against landing in front of the line. They'll be waiting on the reverse slope after dark, to carry out the wounded."

Anyway, he said, there was one less now. Caulfield had died.

"He would of made it," the corpsman said, sulky and not really addressing anyone. "He wasn't that bad hit. It was shock and the cold. And all that damned dropping him."

In a way I was relieved. I never believed we would get Caulfield out alive. Now there was a third shrouded figure and the rest were moving pretty well. We would get out, unless there were more gooks up ahead. Simonis and I had another talk about dusk. There was still another hour or more of climbing, and for the first time Simonis sounded nervous about it. He didn't want to be caught this close to home. He wasn't so much worried about the one gook that might be ahead of us but about being taken from behind. Again, there was no direct request, but I found myself saying I would drop back with a couple men and cover the march. Simonis seemed grateful. We swapped weapons around until all three of us had BARs, and we sat down in the deepening gray of the forest while the rest of them moved up the trail.

For the rest of the way I had the feeling I was a child again, pursued up some weird and menacing corridor of imagination, as happens in dreams, chased by something just behind, just about to catch up, with my legs not moving fast enough to escape. We walked slowly uphill, one man always walking backwards, peering into the gloom of the trail behind us, watching for whatever might come after us. I had visions of muffled, quilted figures flitting silently across our tracks, picking up the spoor the way we did when it was our turn to pursue, tracking us by the blood we left behind. I became angry at the wounded for bleeding so much, and when I came across a pool of frozen blood in the snow I scuffed it away righteously with a boot and smoothed down the place. The BAR was heavy and cold through the mittens, but it felt good, solid and comforting. The phantoms were still behind us, always just behind, and then, toward nine o'clock, we were at the fixed rope that led upward the last hundred icy feet to the wire. I shoved the two marines ahead of me and they scrambled noisily uphill. I cursed them silently, the sons of bitches. Couldn't they be quiet about it, with me still at the bottom? Then it was my turn and I slung the BAR and climbed, concentrating on keeping the climb slow and smooth and not falling, concentrating on the rope and not what might be following. Then I was at the wire. The gate was open. I turned my back to it and sat down in the snow, tired and with my leg muscles pulsing, the BAR in my lap, sweeping my eyes back and forth over the blackness below, listening carefully, half hoping someone would come now and I could kill him, wanting to kill someone for what they'd put us through. But I heard nothing, saw nothing. Then I shouldered the BAR again and moved through the wire to where Red Philips waited.

The climb was over, thirteen hours after it began, over for today. Tomorrow could be the same. Or worse. It really wasn't fair that having done so much, there was still so much to do. You never really mastered war, never got on top of it. It was always too big, there was too much to it ever to finish the job.

On the reverse slope the wounded were being loaded into choppers, the bad ones laid out in coffinlike boxes slung alongside the cabin, the choppers taking off into the night sky as if it were the blaze of noon. They'd refused to come out in front of the line for us, and I guess they were good at what they did. But they couldn't do what we did, the "airedales." Men stood around, talking. One marine was swearing hard and steadily. I recognized him, a husky PFC who'd carried one of the wounded piggyback the last couple of hours. He'd gone down into the valley with me, and I knew him but not his name. I asked what was the matter.

"That son of a bitch."

"Who?"

"Lieutenant, you saw it. I carried that bastard maybe three, four hours. He's big as me. I carry the guy because he says he can't climb no more and he's afraid we'll leave him or he'll fall behind and the gooks will get him. So I put the bastard on my back, on my goddamned back. I carry him maybe the last thousand feet up the hill. You seen me."

"Yes, I saw you."

"And we get to the damn bob wire, the wire, mind you, and he bounces off my back like the Easter bunny and goes vaulting over the bob wire and into the first chopper, shaking hands and handing out cigars. The son of a bitch. I won't be able to walk upright for a week, and I probably got a rupture. I bust my chops lugging the bastard, and he's in better shape than me and shaking hands."

"Well," I said and could think of nothing more to say.

The wounded were all loaded down and the copters gone. The dead would go down in the morning with the gook train, silent lumps being carried down the hill to Battalion and the morgue. You didn't waste chopper space on the dead.

Philips was very relieved and wanting to talk about it. But Simonis was there and he had more of a story to tell than I did, and I was glad of it. It was behind me now, and I didn't want, not right now, to mouth it over. Later, maybe I would. I stood there for a few minutes in the cold night by the supply tent, where three long bundles lay stiffening in the night, and then I left, climbing again the last few hundred feet and the quarter mile to my ridgeline. It was a familiar climb, the path worn and dirty, steps cut in the steep places treacherous with ice. The nearest tangle of barbed wire was almost to hand off there on the left, the occasional empty, yellowed ammo tube stuck rakishly in the snow to the right, unsmelling in the cold despite the icicles of urine, milestones in an alien landscape.

I climbed past bunkers too widely spaced. And how could they be otherwise along a front of this length? There should be more machine guns, for one thing, more mines out there in the dead spaces, more wire everywhere. I was thinking like an officer now, like a professional. As I passed, from the bunkers—smoky, murmuring, dim candlelight shining through the ponchos—came the creak of leather, the rasp of unoiled metal parts sliding over each other, a cough, a brief snatch of talk—familiar, comforting sounds. The bunkers all faced north, toward the enemy. It was there death held the mortgage, where the gooks lived, where I had so recently been and returned from. I knew the bunkers that I passed, which were liable to be alert, which not, which filthy and slovenly, which kitchen-tidy. My mind catalogued the men who lived in them, my dependents, my children, my supporting struts, the men who made me what I was, the men I led, the hundred professionals, the hundred marines.

Princeton looked up when I crawled into the bunker.

"So you went and got in a firefight," he said.

"Yes," I said.

=== 20 ===

When you weren't fighting, the war was pretty good.

Mornings were the best time, the terror of night ended, the patrols and ambushes and duck blinds. Men slept late. When there was snow in the night, it lay smooth and untracked, no industrial smokestack or city's soot turning it dour and gray, no vehicles to churn it into slush. It hung, glistening, on the pine branches until the sun, warming as it rose, thawed it into tiny, shining icicles, glistening, melting, drop, drop, drop. Men crawled out of the bunkers into the morning calm, the industrious using entrenching tools to dig away the snow, tidying the trench. One imaginative fellow after each snow crafted a small snowman on the reverse slope a few yards from his bunker. Eventually there was a formation of them, a foot tall or so, some hunched gnomelike by earlier thaws, each with a cigar butt rakishly affixed in the center of a gargoyle's face. I passed them as I went down the slope for the morning dump. It was odd how you became hardened to almost anything, even that holed ammo box perched over its mingled scents of shit and creosote. You had lived through another night, you were healthy, your bowels were moving, the snowy hills stretched peacefully toward a horizon, the morning sun had begun to soften the hard chill of night. These were times of contemplation, ease, tranquility, with no decisions to be made or action to be taken. You just sat there and let it happen, totally passive, not having to work at it. Times like that were rare and wonderful, and even the stench became familiar and nearly welcomed.

Princeton, like most regulars, made a fetish of shaving daily. Water was always short. We melted snow in canteen cups over Coleman stoves and parceled it out from five-gallon jerricans. Maybe water is the heaviest thing marines ever have to carry. Do you know what five gallons of water weigh? Leftover coffee, just an ounce or two in the bottom of a cup, did for shaving. I was lucky, with a barely noticeable beard that an every-other-day shave kept clean. We never washed. There wasn't the water for that. I suppose we smelled pretty bad, but you stopped noticing. The air in the bunkers, lighted by candles and warmed by Coleman stoves, was so foul that you spit soot, and body odor didn't really register. You never changed clothes except for socks. I had two pairs of heavy wool socks and I tried to change every day. The socks you put on were filthy but after twenty-four hours they were dry, the sweat evaporated. Frozen feet were a continual fear; we all knew horror stories from the winter before; men who had lost toes or an entire foot, sometimes both feet. If you could somehow keep your feet dry, the cold wasn't as dangerous. You might, if the Koreans didn't get you, or a mine or an accidental discharge or a short round, survive the winter with limbs intact. How the socks smelled didn't matter, only that they were dry.

Mornings were coffee or cocoa, as hot as you could stand it, the ration cans of fruit, the syrup heavy and sugared. Unless there was serious shelling or heavy snow, after breakfast I walked the half mile along the ridgeline to the company command post to see Chafee and Red Philips. The other platoon leaders came by, and Chafee gave us the orders and the situation and listened to complaints. Then we sat around gossiping, the way men do. By now it was maybe ten in the morning, and if the wind wasn't too bad we sat outside on the lip of the trench, smoking and talking, men easy with one another and relaxed. Night wouldn't fall for another six hours.

If there was mail from the gook train I carried it back to the platoon stuffed inside my field jacket. Some men got a lot of mail; there were some who never got anything. You didn't ask. It was a man's own business; marines don't want people being sorry for them. That didn't mean I never wondered about it. By noon Princeton would have visited every bunker, inspecting weapons. The men could get dirty; the weapons had to be clean. If Chafee had ordered a patrol Prince and the fortunate squad leader and I would lie in the snow with field glasses and a map and go over the route in daylight. It was funny, no matter what the weather, I was never cold by day. The nights were different; the nights were fierce.

When Princeton went off again on any of the thousand things a platoon sergeant did, busying himself, chivvying and prying, sometimes I just stayed out there somewhere sheltered from the wind and looked at the country, those serried rows of mountains, treed heavily lower down, sparser at top where granite pushed up through the earth, gray and cold, flinty looking and edged. If I had one, I smoked a cigar, chewing the stub into pulp, spitting juice onto the snow at my feet, onto my thermal boots. It didn't matter which; there were no inspections up here, none of the garrison chickenshit you lived with at Quantico or Pendleton or even in reserve. These were good times too, afternoons looking at the mountains and the snow, and smoking and spitting with no one to complain, scratching yourself where you itched, your groin or your belly or wherever. In a country this lovely, unless someone was shooting at you or sending you out on patrol, if you could stay dry and warm, and you knew there was one more little can of sweet peaches or pears back in the bunker, the war wasn't so bad.

Then, by two thirty or two forty-five in the afternoon the sun would start to fall toward the ridgeline and the wind out of Siberia would pick up and I would begin to shiver, not just from cold but knowing that the good time was nearing its end, that darkness was coming, the dark and the night and the terrible cold and, unless we were lucky, the fighting. I hated to see the dusk come. In combat there are no beautiful sunsets; a falling sun is a warning of the night. The shadows lengthen and the temperature falls and the wind seeks you out. Men began to move around more now, restless, nervy, busying themselves with chores to take their minds off the night, breaking down weapons one more time for cleaning, rearranging the grenades and bringing in the sleeping bags left out for a day's airing, heating a supper of lima beans and ham before dark. Once the night comes there may not be time; once the darkness falls the good times are past; the pleasant indolence, the contemplation of day is gone.

By four thirty there is no more sun and then only a swift dusk and then the real night, cold and frightening and, too often, deadly.

I wondered what this country, these mountains and narrow valleys, was like in summer, without the snow and the killing wind. The pines and the spruce would be the same, of course, ever green and unchanged. But would other trees bloom and flowers grow on the ridges and the hillsides, would farmers work the river bottoms and the lower slopes, terracing the land into paddies, fertilizing the crop, as we were told they did, with human waste? And would the smell of shit float upward to the ridges from the rice fields below?

But there were no abandoned farmhouses here, no barns or silos, no huts or roads or telephone poles or fences and gates, no man-made structures of any kind. Despite snow cover, there should have been something; not even war flattened everything. There should have been ruins, a brick piled upon a brick, the remnant of a chimney, a lonely fence post. There were only the hills and the slim valleys and the evergreens and the snow, nothing else. This was simply not a country where anyone lived unless it was the wanderer passing through or a lone hunter carrying his tent and goods, his shotgun or his snares. But what would draw a hunter? We saw no game, not even a rabbit or a fox, nothing. Could the war have done that? Or had this always been a barren place?

Woodsmen might have come here. It was forest land, perhaps to be winnowed and harvested, the thunk of the woodsman's axe echoing against the hills. But there were no stumps, no patterned clearing that lumbering might have left. Amid the evergreens were other trees, and I wondered if they bloomed and grew leafy when the snow melted, sprouted lush green foliage and buds and flowers and maybe even fruit. Would we still be able to see that terrible 2,000-meter mountain that loomed so frighteningly just a few miles to our north? Or would the death that waited there be veiled by blossoms?

I hoped I would live until spring to see.

We were not to keep diaries. That was a rule. If you were killed or captured, a diary could provide military intelligence to the enemy. But I kept a few notes in the little spiral notebook in my breast pocket, writing very small to conserve pages, and in pencil. If you got wet, and we were always getting wet, ink ran. And I composed my letters home very carefully, describing as accurately as I could the land and the weather and the sense of place, on the cheap airmail flimsy they parceled out to us and which we could send without a stamp. There was supposed to be censorship, but I don't believe there ever was. Maybe in the rear echelons. Up here no one ever slit open a letter that I knew of. And so I wrote about Korea and the war and the men, self-censoring things that might frighten my family or friends, and sent off little essays and brief reports of war, knowing one day I might see those letters again and remember.

It was not difficult to fill a letter without giving alarm. If you have never been to war you cannot realize that some of it—not all, of course—is such sheer, boyish fun. You lived outdoors, you were physically active, you shared the boisterous camaraderie of other young men, you shed fat and put on sinew and muscle. Except for those nagging, minor hurts, you were clear-eyed and generally healthy, and your body responded, instantly and instinctively, whenever called upon. You slept like the dead; not even the dull menu of the ration box killed appetite. You saw the dawn and the night stars and came to calculate time and date by the phases of the moon, and on those rare days of thaw you heard the gurgle of running water under the snow, heading toward the valleys and the sea. You smelled the pines and listened to the wind and could sense when snow was coming and knew to the instant when the sun would rise, when the sun would set.

A city boy, I was falling in love with country those first months in the hills.

If only I would get home to tell about it.

=== 21 ===

A year or so before, I was just out of school and sharing my room with my brother on the second floor of a small row house in Sheepshead Bay, going to work on the subway and writing furniture and household appliance ads for Macy's, starting to learn the writer's trade. Now I was living on a mountaintop in Asia with a hundred other men and learning a very different trade.

You learned from men like Chafee, a Yalie with a law degree from Harvard, who came from money, a handsome, patrician man, physically courageous and tireless. From all that could have come arrogance, snobbery. He possessed neither of those traits, he was only calm and vigorous and efficient, usually cheerful, decent and humane, a good man, a fine officer. And you learned from men like Corporal Geist, whom I heard one day expounding on what was wrong with war movies.

"Ya notice in the movies," Geist said, "marines never shit? John Wayne or none of them. They never have to take a crap, never! How can ya believe the rest of a movie where no one ever takes a shit?"

Regulars like Princeton and Hoops, despite the dirt, somehow were able to stay neat. They carried little sewing kits, what they called "housewives," and they were forever darning and sewing on buttons, and I learned from them, too.

You associate thirst with desert warfare, Rommel at To-

135

bruk or T. E. Lawrence in the Empty Quarter. But here in the winter mountains we were always thirsty. Most men carried two canteens hooked to their web belts, but the problem was getting them filled. The gook train carried up jerricans, and you connived and hustled to get one for your platoon. Melting snow was tedious and not very efficient, and it used up the fuel in the Coleman stoves. Yet in this cold, dry air your throat was always parched, your canteen might be frozen and you longed for drink. I vowed once the war was over never again to pass a faucet without pausing to slake my thirst with a glass of cold water.

Sometimes, there was hot food. The gook trains carried it up, and the company commander, if he were a good one like Chafee, would manage to get it heated, and men would come in from all the way along the company front, a half mile or more, to queue up with their mess kits in front of the tent or the bunker where they did the cooking. It didn't really matter what the food was, or how it tasted. It was hot and it was different and you didn't have to use a can opener to get at it. We rarely had bread. Fresh bread, you learned the value of bread, and promised yourself you would never again take it for granted.

Hoops was full of wisdom. On shrapnel he could go on for fifteen or twenty minutes. "Shrapnails, now," Hoops would say, counselor and teacher, "less'n they big chunks, they ain't gonna kill ya. They's like splinters, nasty little things. The medium ones you can pluck out okay. But the teeny ones get in there and fester and the corpsmen ain't got the time to tweeze them free. So you try to get them out yourself, you know, working with a good knife or a sewing needle just like you do with wood splinters. Otherways, they stay in there and fester, until they work they way out, gradual, coming right up through the skin so you can lift them out with your fingertips. Shrapnails is pesty, but usual they won't break bone like a bullet does. Unless they kill you, all in all, I'd rather have shrapnails."

At Quantico they taught us to field-strip cigarettes. When a cigarette burned down to where you couldn't smoke it anymore, you tore it in half lengthwise, letting the burning embers and the ash and residual tobacco fall to the ground. Then you balled up the cigarette paper between your thumb and middle finger, and you dropped that. Then you ground what little was left into the earth with the sole of your shoe. It says something about the way they teach you in the marines that we were still field-stripping cigarettes here, rather than litter the snow.

Halfway through winter they sent up some new field jackets, lighter and warmer than anything we had, and lined with fiberglass. At first men fought to get one and there weren't enough to go around, but then the rumor got out that if you were shot the bullet would carry tiny fragments of glass into your body. And because the fragments were glass and not metal, the aid stations and even the hospital ship had no way of tracing them inside you and you'd never get rid of the slivers; they would cut and tear at you and work into your intestines and cause infections and hemorrhaging the rest of your life. After that, men refused to wear the new jackets. I never knew if the rumor was true.

There were other rumors.

Except for the odd bird, and very rarely a track of some sort in the snow, there was no animal life in the hills that winter. But there was talk that this far north, and this high up, a few Korean tigers still roamed. We never saw one, or heard one roaring at night the way you did in safari movies, but there was a thrill just thinking about them, coming across a tiger one of these nights on patrol. Everyone agreed that would be something to tell them about back home.

You didn't brood about rumors, even about tigers. Reality was too much with us to waste much time on imagining things.

We were beginning to learn a new word for someone who'd had a bad scare or was losing his nerve. We said he was "shook." English majors such as me wondered why it wasn't "shaky" or "shaken" or something grammatical, but it was always "shook," and you knew what it meant. It had little to do with the old World War "shell-shocked." That was another, very precisely defined thing that came from being too close to an incoming shell. "Shook" was nerves in general, and once you had a man who was really "shook" you tried to get rid of him because he was no good to you anymore, as I'd done with that man I sent up to be company runner. Later on that year we had an outdoor movie, and we were all lying around on a hillside watching when a big snake crawled right over a marine and he jumped up and started yelling and stamping the ground. Everyone moved away from him because they thought he might start shooting at the damned thing. They said he was "shook," but that wasn't the real thing, that was just a snake. Snakes could scare anyone, but they couldn't make you "shook," any more than that machine gunner who fired off a burst at the rats in his bunker and nearly killed himself. It was 76s coming in flat and fast or mortars dropping on you or fear of mines or maybe too many duck blinds and night ambushes or a wind that never stopped blowing. Those were what made you "shook," everyone agreed, and no fooling.

Men who had been out here for a long time reacted in different ways to stress. And when they knew there was a rotation draft coming up and they were due to go home, you couldn't predict how it would take them. Some men became sloppy at their work, others terribly cautious, a few reckless as if nothing could touch them now. Most got worse, odder, the nearer rotation came.

The most bizarre was an enlisted man in Dog Company who'd been out a long time and had been in a lot of fighting, a fine marine, a good, solid man. But now with the rotation draft beckoning, he began to act funny, refusing to wash or shave. And he would not get out of his sleeping bag. That was the strangest part. He didn't refuse to muster or go on duty, but he went everywhere in his sleeping bag. He cut out the bottom of it so he could walk, taking mincing little steps, his arms and body completely inside the bag and the hood of the bag over his head, only his bristly face showing. He lined up for meals that way. I don't know just how he handled going to the head. Mack said it was a psychological return to the womb. I didn't know what to make of it. He only had a few days left, and no one wanted to run him up for it or bring charges, because he'd been a very good man. But people moved away when they saw him coming, because they knew he was spooked and because he had begun to smell, much worse than the rest of us. Maybe he was shitting in the bag; some people insisted he did. He didn't seem to mind being snubbed as he hopped around

Battalion, with those little steps, content just to be in his bag.

Later, after he'd gone home, men talked and wondered, giddily, if this might be permanent and if when he got to San Francisco he might still be in his bag, hopping along Market Street to the St. Francis bar.

He was "shook," "gone mental," some people said. But there were other things happened to us.

Men were always getting hurt. I don't mean wounds. Take hands: your knuckles were always chapped and sore and red, cracking and dry. Outdoors the cold worked at your hands, and in the bunkers it was the dry heat from the Coleman stoves. Some men got the idea of asking their families to send Jergens Lotion—which the wags called "Jerkoff Lotion"—and that was a pretty good idea, lubricating your hands and making the skin more pliable, especially across the knuckles. When your hands were always sore and bleeding you weren't as good or as efficient at doing anything. It didn't matter what, firing a weapon or opening a can of fruit or wiping your ass with toilet paper, you didn't do it as well with sore hands. They didn't issue us Jergens Lotion, but we had a sort of lipstick in a little olive-drab tin casing. In this cold, dry air with wind, your lips were always chapped and sore, sometimes so cracked they bled, and the lipstick helped. It put a coating on, a sort of lubricant. If a man lost his lipstick, he borrowed one. They were passed around the way men shared a canteen cup of steaming coffee in the lee of the wind during a break, the way two men smoked a single cigarette, passing it back and forth. There was no privacy anywhere; hygiene was a derisory concern. You couldn't wash, you couldn't get clean, so why worry about dirt? Maybe that's why when the flu hit the Division so many of us came down with it. But the flu hit us only once that winter; getting hurt was something that happened to us every day: twisting an ankle on the ice or smashing a thumb in the bolt of a weapon or cutting your hand on a ration can or chipping a tooth or tearing off a fingernail trying to shore up the ceiling logs or dropping a jerrican of water on your foot or bruising your knees or your elbows or your hips just moving around in the dark on a big snow-covered hill laced with wire and pitted with holes and veiny with trenches. There were men with rheumatism from the wet months and sleeping on the ground. And men who coughed and spit up blood. And men who'd been frostbitten early and had to keep those parts covered the best they could because the tissue was damaged and would always be susceptible afterward. That happened to my ears, both of them, the lobes.

None of these things qualified you for medical evacuation. You tried to heal them yourself or asked the corpsman, and you stayed on the line.

When I had first gotten to Korea I hadn't known about the accidents, the little hurts and pains that made life hard. My nightmares had been about the winter and the cold. Now three months had passed, and I hadn't frozen to death or lost any toes; I'd even stopped sweating about mines. What had happened was that I'd learned about war, from Chafee and Hoops and Fitz and the others, and without becoming cocky or careless, I'd begun to relax.

Which didn't mean you never had a bad dream.

This is the country in which the First Marine Division fought during the winter of 1951–52, in the corner of North Korea we still held, a cold and savage place. The wind came out of Siberia and Manchuria to the north, and the snow and sleet came in off the Sea of Japan a few miles to the east. When I got there Thanksgiving weekend of 1951 the country was already deep in snow, and we lived under the ground, like animals, both the North Korean enemy and ourselves. You couldn't live outside; if the mortars and the artillery didn't kill you, the winter would.

Capt. John Chafee commanded Dog Company, to which I was sent as a replacement platoon leader. Here in December 1951 in a reserve area in North Korea, Chafee kneels in front, right, with his executive officer, Red Philips, whom I would eventually replace. Behind them are officers and senior NCOs of the company. Chafee later would become governor of Rhode Island, would be named secretary of the navy and would be elected a United States senator, an office he still holds today. Nowhere, at any time, did John Chafee serve more nobly than he did as a marine officer commanding a rifle company in the mountains of North Korea.

Chang, at left, appointed himself houseboy to Dog Company's officers in December 1951. He was perhaps eleven, an orphan, a scar-faced child clothed in oversized marine hand-me-downs, an energetic, honest, delightful kid who mysteriously reappeared each time we came off the line to rest and refit in a reserve area. Chang would be nearly fifty now. I wonder what became of him.

In January and February 1952 a stream called the Soyang-gang divided the marine line from that of the North Koreans. To get at them we had to cross the valley of the Soyang-gang; to get at us they had to cross it. It was a sort of no man's land, burned by napalm, pitted by shells. I went down there only once, to help Bob Simonis get out when his patrol was caught by daylight on the Soyang-gang.

Lt. Maurice J. (Mack) Allen of Lynchburg, Virginia, of the Virginia Military Institute, of the Harvard Business School, was second platoon leader of Dog Company. Mack and I had trained at Quantico together, had flown together to Korea, joined Dog Company together. Here, in a typical pose, on Hill 880 in North Korea, early in 1952, Mack grins his *Henry V* grin: how fortunate we are to be here at Agincourt while men abed in England, etc. Easy for Mack to grin; he'd been to war before.

There were occasional days of thaw even in February when you could stroll about Hill 880 in a wool shirt without a parka. In my left-hand breast pocket is a "gook spoon," the universal eating utensil of Korea, hammered out of a brass shell casing; on my right hip is the Smith & Wesson .38 I bought in Oceanside, California. At this time in February 1952 I was Dog Company executive officer.

The Dog Company command post on Hill 880, North Korea, January and February 1952. I lived here, briefly. Neither *House & Garden* nor *Architectural Digest* would have been impressed by the decor. But the log and sandbag roof would sustain even a direct hit by enemy mortars. Or so we hoped.

The reverse slope of Hill 880 in January or February 1952. Here were the supply tents, the mortar emplacements; here men could move about in daylight. On the forward slope, just over the ridgeline at the top, to show yourself by day was to tempt the North Korean gunners. This hill was once a forest of evergreens. All its trees were chopped down for the construction of bunkers or for firewood, leaving the hill ugly, bare, and scarred.

The reverse slope of Hill 880, early 1952. The trail along which we moved and over which the "gook train" carrying supplies and ammunition passed twice each day was shoveled clear of snow after every storm. Young marines who joined up in part to evade such juvenile chores at home found themselves wielding snow shovels in the mountains of North Korea.

Casualties were evacuated by chopper, if we could get a chopper, the wounded laid out in these coffinlike affairs on either side of the bubble. Here one of our people is going out from the landing pad on Hill 880. I enjoyed helicopter rides; I had no desire to make them in one of these airborne coffins.

After forty-six days on the line, the Battalion was relieved, and Dog Company was helicoptered out on February 26, 1952. Here, in helmet and with rucksack, left, I waited my turn on the chopper pad of Hill 880. When we reached the reserve camp we were herded into showers, peeling off clothes we hadn't changed for nearly seven weeks, and were deloused. I can't ever recall being happier or feeling healthier.

With the snow finally melted in the spring of 1952 we came across all manner of things long hidden. Here, near Panmunjom, a man had died. The marines called dead men "stiffs" and might pause for a moment to look down, perhaps kick a little dirt in the vague direction of the bones and pass on. No one knew how many men died or, as here, how they died and who they might have been in life.

By spring 1952 I considered myself a reasonably salty character and affected cigars. I suspect I still looked like a schoolboy. This photo was taken in May or June in the tent where I lived behind the line near the truce corridor of Panmunjom.

In the spring of 1952 our air officer, Capt. Ramon Gibson, took me up in this O. Y. observation plane to fly to Kimpo Airfield for ice. On the way back Gibson flew over the Chinese lines as a courtesy to me, the Battalion intelligence officer. When the Chinese ack-ack fired at us, the joy of the occasion rather oozed away. Here, I'm wearing one of the new flak jackets, which would not stop a bullet but, it was said, might shed shrapnel.

22

In three months of war we hadn't seen an enemy plane or a tank. It was not the sort of country where you could use tanks, except as artillery, dug in hull-down on the ridges with their guns nosing out. One night we were alerted, someone thinking he'd heard the sound of tank motors way off to the north, up near the 2,000-meter hill. I went outside to listen and just hearing their motors, as they ground up some distant slope way off and out of sight, sent a thrill through me. I thought of what it would be like to see tanks coming up this slope, rolling over and flattening our wire, crushing the trenches and the bunkers. But of course tanks could go nowhere in country like this in winter, and we heard no more of them, not even as artillery.

We saw our own planes more often now. The small, slow observation planes droned overhead any day there was flying weather, plotting the enemy lines, calling in artillery, mapping out terrain for air strikes or naval gunfire. Marine and navy fighter bombers came in twice during February to strafe the gook lines and to drop 500-pound bombs that sent brown earth in plumes up through the snow like fountains of filthy sewer water. Once, they dropped napalm, the slim, streamlined tanks of jellied fuel hitting into the flanks of Hill 462, bursting into flame as they turned over and over, leaping and bouncing, spewing fire, until in their wake there was only flame, and afterward, a field of blackened snow and earth. The gooks were dug in so deep in their hills, or so intelligence said, with great tunnel and gallery arrangements, that it was hard to believe any of this was effective. Probably it was not good for enemy morale to be bombed and burned like this, but it seemed to do little harm. The marines enjoyed it, much as we might a stage show.

The navy played its spectacular, and equally impotent, role, cruising north and south along the eastern shoreline, occasionally firing off a vast salvo of eight-inch shells from the cruisers, creating sound waves that washed again and again against the ridgelines before echoing away into silence. I wondered what battleship fire sounded like, with their 16-inch guns. To most marines, naval gunfire was just useless noise.

Then one afternoon, by some fundamental error whereby one ridgeline was unaccountably mistaken for the next, a cruiser salvoed three eight-inch shells into the Dog Company positions. It was a clear and very cold day, and I'd been amusing myself watching the toy boat cruising slowly past the extreme right flank where it met the Sea. It was so clear, and windless, it seemed impossible to make a mistake. But they did. The shells screamed in, louder than any artillery I'd ever heard, smashing into the reverse slope just below Mack Allen's platoon.

"Jesus Christ!" Princeton said, even his celebrated calm disturbed.

There were frantic messages from the naval gunfire officer attached to Battalion, and later, quite a bit later considering, the ship signaled a rather petulant apology. Mack showed me where one of the shells had torn through the branches of a spindly tree.

"If they'd hit a decent tree we would have had an air burst and you would have been collecting my people for days."

"And you, too, Mack, let's not neglect you."

"It's okay with me if the navy neglects me from now on."

An hour later the cruiser was shelling the North Korean ridges with the same equanimity. Not for the first time I thought of myself as closer to the enemy infantrymen, huddled in their bunkers, filthy and cold, than to my own navy, all starched and clean and warm, shelling those poor bastards as they had shelled Mack Allen. Marines are contemptuous of soldiers, simply because they do not consider soldiers very good at their trade, but they hate sailors, a hatred tinged with envy for the creature comforts in which navies everywhere specialize: dry bunks, hot food, showers, clean clothes. Something like this only confirmed what we thought about sailors.

The first weeks on the line, I'd been afraid of the night. It was night when they came, night when diarrhea seized me, night when men died. Now, unless there was a patrol or an ambush out, I was even coming to enjoy the night. Sometimes I would crawl out of the bunker past the snoring Princeton into the dark. The trail would be quiet, except for the dry crunch of snow under my boots, the weird, gentle tinkle of tin cans hung on the barbed wire, rustled by the breeze as it flowed south, whispering softly, conspiratorially across the packed corrugations of the snow. This wind came out of Siberia, a couple of hundred miles north of the little toehold of a country we were fighting over. I thought about Siberia, and hostile Russia, wondering if we would have to go there before this damned war was finished, if we would fight in Siberia, where the north wind lived. I hoped not. I hoped we would not even have to climb 462, yet again reduced to a pale pimple in the darkness below, or that 2,000-meter mountain beyond where once we had seen men skiing at twice the height of our own ridge. No, it was too far to go, too high, and I was too young, too often afraid. Too far, Siberia, oh, much too far.

The stars were far off, too. And in a strange way, very close. Overhead they shone, my lone companions, frosted diamonds incredibly near in the black night, incredibly far their fire. Cold, the night was always cold, and that had frightened me too, reaching for me through the scientifically blended layers of cloth, as if the cold were already within, dangerous cold. How could you ever get warm if the cold were inside you? Even the snow at first was sinister, the snow I had always loved, lying in a warm bed with the blinds open so I could watch it drifting slowly down through the yellow cone of the lamppost light. The snow at home was warm, friendly. This snow had seemed hostile and different.

But I had lived with that snow and in that cold in these mountains since November. I walked carefully along the trench hacked out of the ridgeline to a small, cleared space on the reverse slope, to the wooden ammo box where we sat to shit. It was quiet there, peaceful. I sat on the box, trousers down just far enough. Around me my hundred men slept or kept watch. Off to the left, far off, you could hear the dull rumble of the big guns. They didn't bother me. If the guns were not firing at you, they were of no account. Off to the right was the Sea of Japan. I could not see it now, but it was there, with its warships, the swabbies sleeping warm and dry with their candy bars and movies, their hot coffee and showers and dinner on neatly compartmented little cafeteria trays, and their lousy gunnery. I sat there thinking about the gooks on 462, sleeping huddled together, burrowing in the straw for heat in those massive underground galleries they were supposed to have. I understood them as I didn't understand sailors. Yet I had tried to kill them and they had tried to kill me and tomorrow, with any luck, they would try again, if I didn't kill them first.

I pulled some toilet paper from my pocket. I was cold now, but it was from outside, this cold, from the north wind freshening. My body was stiffening with cold but inside I was warm. I stood up, buttoning and fastening the elaborate arrangement of trousers, looking out toward where the serried ridges ran endlessly north, and I stood there for a time, looking at them by starlight. Well, I guessed, I could go anywhere the rest of them went, if I had to. They would expect it of me and you could not disappoint them. I turned then and strolled back to the bunker, a city boy on a winter's night in strange mountains, a boy once filled with the fear and wonder of it all. But now no longer so young, having lost something of the fear if not of the wonder.

We had more snow, a lot of it, night after night as February filled, and when the snow stopped it came off very cold again, well below zero, and both snow and cold discouraged fighting and kept both armies calm if not actually peaceful. This was fine with most of the marines, who believed fighting was something you did and might even occasionally enjoy, but not in this weather and in these hills. Here, survival was difficult under normal circumstances. It tipped the scales to have to battle men as well as the elements. The generals, as was their nature, did not always agree. They ignored trivial incidents like the Simonis patrol that loomed so large for us, and came to the conclusion, in their well-tended quarters behind both lines, that the sum total of actions along the mountain front had been distressingly low. Retail merchants spoke of making their figures. This winter the generals had not made their figures.

Chafee went down to Battalion for a briefing by the Regimental commander, glad of the opportunity to speak to them down there, because the company, all the line companies, had been badly hit by a sort of three-day flu. Had we been in a reserve area about a third of Dog Company at the moment would have been certified unfit to serve. Another third were coughing hard and the rest were just over the flu or about to get it. Dog Company was in a weak condition, and if this had been an active stretch of line, Chafee in conscience would have asked for replacements or a full relief, knowing he could not hold a line of this length with sick men. There was, fortunately, no substantial enemy pressure, but Chafee wanted to know what might be done: were there serums, how long would it be before we came off the line, what prospect was there of sending down the sicker men? He got no chance to ask the questions. What he got instead at the briefing was something called Operation Clam Up.

Clam Up was a splendid plan, the sort of exercise they would probably be discussing at staff colleges for years, bragging up its genesis, lying about its actual accomplishment. It was, first of all, an Army plan. The Eighth Army put it out, and the First Marine Division got its orders as did the other divisions, and we carried them out. Chafee called an officers' meeting to brief us on Clam Up. Red Philips was coughing; I had a sore throat and Allen a fever. Chafee handed around coffee and aspirin tablets.

"There's this new plan," he said.

Philips coughed and Mack sneezed and I started to say, "God bless you," but my throat was too sore and I said nothing.

"They call it 'Clam Up.' The idea is that day after tomorrow, toward sunset, it will be made to seem that the entire

Division, and divisions all along the line, are pulling back to new, and better, positions for after the snow melts and the fighting resumes. We will seem to have pulled back several miles, maybe more."

Red coughed again, but he tried to silence it, turning it into a heaving wheeze. Chafee went on.

"They're going to bring trucks up as close as they can get to the reverse slope, gun the motors and run them back and forth over the roads. At the same time our artillery will hit enemy batteries to cover our withdrawal. Our planes will be up, too. And the navy. As for us we will shoulder full field packs and leave our position to march down the reverse slope."

"Going where, Skipper?"

"Going nowhere. We'll sit there on the reverse slope until dark and then climb right back to our bunkers. This will be in total silence, of course, no lights, no talk, no grabass, the smoking lamp out, and so on. I'll give you all this in detail."

"Then what happens, Skipper?" Allen asked. He looked confused, but that might be the fever and not necessarily implied criticism of this fine plan.

"Then for five days we sit in our bunkers, not going out at all by day, as little as possible by night. No patrols. No firing. No nothing. And wait for the gooks to take the bait and come marching up the hill."

"Like 'the King of France,' " I rasped, immediately sorry I had said anything with my throat like this.

"Well, Brady, that's generally the idea. But we hope they won't all go marching back down again. We hope some of them will stay here." He paused. "Now let's look at the order in detail."

It was all bullshit, a silly, flamboyant scenario and not a real operation. That was how we felt, and Chafee must have known, but he didn't curry favor with subordinates by criticizing the brass. He had argued down below, at Battalion, and lost. Here he passed on the orders and said he expected Dog Company would carry them out impeccably.

When I told the squad leaders, there were only two questions. They wanted to know, as we had wanted to know of Chafee, whether we could burn fires in the bunkers. If not, we would have cold meals and cold nights. The answer, Chafee said, was no. The second question was put rather indelicately by Sergeant Nelson.

"Where do we shit?"

"In a Dixie cup," Prince said sourly. Nelson nodded, and jotted a line in his spiral notebook.

Fitzgerald liked the whole thing; he was full of ideas on how we could profit if the gooks really did come up the hill, how close he wanted them to get, whether he would hit them first with grenades or automatic weapon fire. This was Fitz's kind of war, laying traps and killing people.

Clam Up covered such questions. Enemy troops were to be fired on when they began to cut through the barbed wire, not before, not later. Rifles were to be used, and grenades, including concussion grenades, so prisoners could be taken. No machine guns, no BARs unless the position was being overrun. This firepower restriction was another layer of camouflage, intended to convince the gooks that if anyone still manned our line, it was only a thin screen of rear guards.

Toward mid-afternoon of the day set for Clam Up to begin, it started to snow. Princeton found nothing abnormal about this; Providence always made things difficult in order to test the steel in us. Only Prince put it somewhat differently:

"They always shit on you so you know the smell."

"Oh," I said, continuing to fill out my rucksack to look as bulky and weigh as little as possible. Empty ration boxes, crumpled toilet paper, and the rarely worn parka filled it out. We bundled up and went out into the snow. The artillery was already firing, and in among the rounds passing overhead we could hear heavy trucks grinding uphill somewhere to the south of us.

The operation, bizarre as it was, went smoothly. Everyone got wet and cold and our flu worsened and a mortarman sprained an ankle climbing in the dark, but we went down the hill, sat miserably in the drifting snow as the shells clattered overhead, then climbed back to the bunkers to stand watch or go to bed. Fifty percent watch was stipulated, but that was nothing new, that was what we were standing already. There was one positive: no patrols. Only Fitzgerald, peering through the firing port of his bunker as if the gooks were coming up now through the snow, refusing to let his bunker mate smoke because it blunted his sense of smell ("I can smell gooks, Mr. Brady," he told me once, "I can *smell* 'em!"), was restive under the new rules. He was forever crafting magnificent patrols that slipped out silently, waited motionless, and slew by the horde. No one else missed patrolling.

The five days of Clam Up passed. Prince and I sat in our bunker without even the luxury of a firing port to give light, coughing up lampblack from the candles we had to burn to see, reading again the one book and two magazines we had between us. My throat was still bad, but I was smoking. It was something to do. In the dead air of the bunker I became proficient, when not coughing, at blowing series of near perfect smoke rings. On the second morning, Chafee put through a conference call, reporting that the Division front had been quiet but an army outfit had fired off some rounds at a phantom infiltrator and pretty much blown the game in that sector.

"Whaddya expect of dogfaces?" was Princeton's only reaction.

Each night we went out in turn to defecate and to empty the tin cans of urine from the day. Fortunately, my bowels were tranquil and I was able to wait for the evening stroll to the ammo box. Chafee kept us informed. Apparently here and there Clam Up was actually working, with gooks coming out of their holes, some of them venturing surprisingly high up our forward slope, reconnoitering, and going back. It was expected they would return in greater numbers, probably by night. I'd given the North Koreans credit for more sense. Except for a few isolated incidents there was no shooting and troops were behaving with unexpected discipline. The gooks shelled us several times a day, trying to draw a response, and in the next regiment a direct hit crushed a bunker and buried three men alive. They got one out. On the fourth day, Operation Clam Up fetched the first gooks to Dog Company.

Mack Allen's people saw them first, six tiny figures like alpinists at the end of a Swiss telescope making their way slowly uphill through deep snow. The marine who spied them did not have a telephone in his bunker, but by tugging

148

at a wire, he attracted the squad leader, who phoned Allen. Chafee got Simonis and me on the wire when he was told. For the next two hours we waited, Simonis masked by the ground from seeing the six gooks, I frustrated and blind in my portless hole. Their progress uphill seemed incredibly slow, with Mack reporting frequently on their pauses, their searches of terrain and probing for mines, their forward movement past the various landmarks and mortar concentrations we all knew. I followed it on a large-scale map, as you might fill in the box score in a baseball program, and with the home fan's rooting interest. Princeton passed the time dusting hand grenades and warming them over candles so they'd be ready. He had no faith in Clam Up, no expectation the gooks might come to us, but he was a platoon sergeant and a regular, and platoon sergeants are not supposed to be caught unaware, whatever their private doubts. Toward noon the six North Koreans reached the aprons of barbed wire protecting the second platoon. They deployed belly down in the snow, and one of them fired bursts of burp-gun fire at the nearest bunkers. The marines made no reply. I could hear Allen whispering over the platoon phones, "Hold your fire, hold it."

Then they cut through the first strands of wire and began to come in. Mack reported this to Chafee, finishing by asking hoarsely, "Now?"

The one word came back, and I could hear Mack shout into his phone, "Hit them now! Grenades. Give them the grenades!"

The crack of bursting grenades rolled up the hill to us, dulled by distance and by the bunker, but after four days of relative silence they sounded like Niagara Falls. Then a burp gun ripped through the explosions, followed by the heavier, slower firing of M-1s. It was over in maybe a half minute.

"Secure, secure, secure!" shouted Mack. Then to Chafee, "They're all dead, Skipper, two of them inside the wire, the rest hanging on it. Can we go out and bring them in?"

"Negative, Allen. Let me get Battalion on the line."

There was a long pause. I kept the phone to my ear. It was like eavesdropping on a radio drama. Then Chafee came on. "Leave them out there until dark and then bring them in. Battalion wants the bodies sent down after Clam Up is secured. They're pretty excited. This is about the biggest bag anyone's gotten.''

They secured Clam Up the next afternoon about four. By now Mack Allen's six gooks, neatly lined up on their backs on the reverse slope near where the gook train could pick them up, were frozen stiff. Marines drifted down to look at them. Clam Up hadn't been much of an operation, all that bullshit and planning, and less than a dozen enemy killed all the way along the Division line. Three marines were dead, shelling. Two more were killed around seven o'clock when, apparently in anger, the North Korean artillery slammed our lines for ten minutes and tore up some wire, holed a supply tent, and hit two bunkers. That was the kind of war it was that winter, casualties counted on your fingers, both sides halfhearted about really starting anything, the generals assigning busywork rather than doing anything that might achieve real results. To kill a lot of people you had to lose a lot of people. I supposed some pogues believed that's precisely what we should have been doing that January and February. But the hills and the snow and the cold stopped them.

To most people's surprise, Chafee named me executive officer. Red Philips, who'd been with a rifle company eight months and wanted out, was being transferred to one of those prisoner-of-war islands off the coast, where the gooks were always rioting and going on hunger strikes and killing other prisoners for collaborating. Those islands, they said, were zoos. But compared to a rifle company on the line, they were a sinecure. I expected Simonis to get Red's job on combat experience, or Mack simply because he was older than I was, more mature. Chafee made no explanations, simply told me I was the new exec, and that same day I moved my goods into the Command Post, a big bunker where you could actually stand up straight. A couple of new lieutenants had come in on the last replacement draft; they joined Dog now, and one of them got my platoon.

Being executive officer is a rotten job. You have no direct command, you are dominated by the Company commander, patronized by the platoon leaders, and your main work is logistic. This brings you into communion with the first sergeant, the gunnery sergeant, the supply sergeants at Battalion, the company clerks and sundry runners. These are not the most stimulating people in military society, most of them devoted to creating postage-stamp empires within which they rule and do no work. Philips had been an older man, which helped, and a booming extrovert, which helped more. In civilian life, I believe, he sold automobiles. Chafee was a fine Company commander who expected his executive officer to follow through on everything with no excuses and a minimum of friction. Even Philips had not totally satisfied the captain, and I was no Red Philips.

Still, I was flattered at having been chosen over the other two platoon leaders to be the Company's second in command. And I was relieved, though I would not admit this even to Mack, not to have any more patrols. Mostly I was pleased to be leaving the platoon in good shape, having commanded it well, without serious blunder, without having embarrassed myself before Princeton or anyone. I'd not lost a man. That was important. I knew I'd not been a great platoon leader, but in all honesty, the circumstance for greatness had not been offered. I'd been competent, and that was sufficient, and pleased as I was to become the exec, there was a sense of loss on leaving the platoon. I made a little speech and told them so, and they seemed to react to it. Only Fitzgerald, who would soon be going home, and Princeton, who seemed to have been there always and was never going home, spoke to me after.

"I just want the lieutenant to know that the lieutenant was the best platoon leader we ever had," said Fitzgerald in his proper and earnest way. Just what he meant by the "best" platoon leader was not precisely clear, but I was inordinately pleased by it. Fitzgerald was a superb marine and only Chafee's opinion meant more.

Princeton's notion of farewell was to tell me how I became known as "Shit Trench." And then he went on to say something rather puzzling.

"You know, Mr. Brady, when you come up to us I was afraid. I thought you was gonna try to win medals with this platoon. That scared me. But you didn't, and that was a good thing. We liked having you as platoon leader."

That was all, but I worried about it for a few days. Had I

given a first impression of boyish recklessness and then gone overcautious? I did not know and would not ask, but merely tucked Prince's comment away and eventually forgot about it.

The big concern was my replacement as platoon leader. There was a slew of new officers in the Battalion, straight out of Quantico. Now we had the requisite seven officers in Dog Company, several of whom looked even more young and green than I had. Chafee told me to stop worrying about it, and he gave my platoon to one of the new men. The inference was clear, that Mack and I and even Simonis had been just as innocent when we arrived and we'd been given platoons and it worked out all right. I realized I was taking a proprietary view, that the responsibility for the third platoon was no longer mine, that this new lieutenant might be a very superior officer. Still, I fretted. It was partly that I would have worried anyway and partly the nature of the new man.

He was a Finn named Maki out of a Michigan iron-mining town, a big blond brute with stupid eyes. He was pretty stupid. He was also very funny, his entire conversation consisting of anecdotes about the people of his town, iron-mining Finns, all of whom apparently were drunk most of the time. That was why, Maki explained, Finland had sauna baths, to sober people up.

"There was this guy," he would begin, "who used to be drunk by 9 A.M. and roaring around the street in high boots waving a bottle and singing dirty songs in Finnish. One night he collapsed on the floor of a gin mill. Nothing new about that. But there he is flat out on the floor, and a couple of the boys thought they would play a trick, and they got some fresh dog turds from somewhere and loosened his belt and slid them down between his shorts and his trousers. Then they dumped him in the cellar.

"A couple hours later everyone's drunk and he comes up out of the cellar. He's sober now, for him, but he's shaky. He goes up to the bar and orders a drink and he says to the man next to him, 'Did you ever hear of a man who shit his pants and don't dirty his underwear?' "

That was Maki's pal, with dog shit in his pants, and as far as I was concerned, that was Lieutenant Maki. I thought of my platoon and of our weeks on the line, not a man lost, and I hoped to hell this big stupid Finn wasn't going to screw up and get people killed.

A week later we were relieved and the Regiment came down off the line, Dog Company again going down by helicopter. I stood there at the landing pad waiting my turn, maybe sixty pounds on my back and a helmet on my head, and never more pleased to be going anywhere in my entire life. We had been forty-six days on the line, living in holes. I'd not taken off my underwear in forty-six days, and my hands were so dirty that if I·rubbed them on bare ground, they became cleaner, since the skin couldn't absorb any more dirt but only shucked it off under friction. My sore throat was gone and I felt wonderful. I was not the same man who had gone up the hill January 10. No better, or any worse, just different. In a month and a half of fighting we had not moved an inch, forward or back. A few men had died on both sides. That 2,000-meter hill still brooded in the north, with none of us having planted a boot on even its lower slopes, waiting for spring for that. And in the valley the Soyang-gang still ran sluggish through ice to the Sea, where a painted ship patrolled a painted seascape.

The men changed but the war did not.

23

I was naked for the first time in forty-six days. Steam came out of my underwear. The issue shorts had once been green, but now they were yellow in front and brown in back, and we threw them into a big, stinking pile. I wondered whether they would try to launder them. If it were up to me, I'd burn the lot. We hadn't gotten lousy, which was a break, but after the showers they were going to delouse us anyway with white powder sprayed from a sort of Flit gun down our pants and up our sleeves. I don't know why we weren't lousy. It must have been the cold. I looked at the growing pile of clothes, skivvies antiqued yellow tossed every which way.

Two big squad-sized tents were erected over a boulder-strewn dry stream bed where hoses with shower nozzles hung down from the cross beams. Outside the temperature may have been zero. Inside, icicles dripped from the corners of the tents farthest from the oil stoves and the steaming showers. We lined up outside like cattle, shivering, filthy men with faces dotted with blackheads, and itchy, chafed crotches, in clothes that had been clean seven weeks before. An enlisted man with a runny nose frozen into a snotty icicle herded us into the tents. I was at the end of the line. You sent the enlisted men first if it was something pleasant, chow or a shower; you went first yourself if it wasn't. The rules were so simple once you learned them. I felt totally naked without the weight of the Smith & Wesson

.38 and the holster on my hip, the web belt sagging to the right. The water was very hot and we stood under it, steam rising, men shouting and laughing and playing grabass, faces very brown under the long matted hair, bodies fish-belly white with purple bruises and mottled red places and scars and festering pimples. It was funny how few marines had really good builds. Hollywood wouldn't have cast many of us in a Duke Wayne war movie. There were thin ones and fat ones, swaybacks, bowlegs, rounded shoulders, bony rib cages, big, scabby buttocks. I didn't feel so bad anymore about being skinny. There were big bars of soap, yellow laundry soap, industrial strength. I rubbed the soap into my hair and face and under my arms and in my crotch and then, for a long time, in the cleft of my buttocks, where the dingleberries hung.

They are not the most delicate of subjects, dingleberries, shit matted in anal hair curled into hard little balls. But they obsess some men and interest us all. Small, hard balls composed of feces and scraps of toilet paper and lint and dust and sweat. They gather and grow down there in the dark, unknown to you, uncultivated and unwelcome, gathering and growing in the anal hair, becoming hard and crusted and hanging there between the cheeks of your buttocks. They cause no pain, nor even great discomfort, and no one ever died of dingleberries that is recorded anywhere. But like Everest, they are there, and you cannot deny their reality by not talking about them. The only way really to rid yourself of dingleberries is to sit overlong in a very hot tub and soak them soft so they can be gently pulled away. Since there were no tubs, but only this wonderful shower, we failed to get entirely rid of them and later men borrowed scalpels from corpsmen or used razor blades to slice them off. This was awkward, and occasionally painful, and marines sometimes cut into their buttocks with the razor and sent up terrible cries and oaths.

Still, a shower after so long was not to be snubbed. It felt marvelous in there in the water and the steam and the heat, and I toweled myself until I was red and glistening and sore, trying to get the soot out of the pores, sandpapering away the tops of whiteheads and the pimples. It would take a dozen showers like this really to be clean again.

They issued clothing out of big cardboard boxes, all used stuff but laundered clean, feeling stiff and smelling of strong soap and bleach. I pulled on the underwear and a sweat shirt and some nice kersey pants and two pairs of sweat socks. I had a good wool shirt back in my rucksack, and a nearly clean sweater. The others were dressed when I got through, looking younger, innocent, less formidable in their clean clothes, like neighborhood roughnecks stuffed into Sunday suits. We picked up our boots and weapons and web belts and packs at the end of the tent, where we'd left them.

"Fall them in, Sergeant," the platoon leaders called, and I watched Princeton march my old platoon back to its tents. I trailed along, feeling left out, watching them swing along with good, measured strides, Prince grunting the cadence just every so often. They looked good, and I permitted myself to swagger just slightly as we reached the Company area.

Chang, the little Korean houseboy, was waiting for us when we got to the reserve camp. The old bush telegraph was working. But this time it was Youngdahl and not Colonel Gregory who had the Battalion, and when the usual rules prohibiting civilians were posted, they were actually policed. Chang went off with stage tears and forty bucks in scrip tucked into his boot, and we went back to fetching our own oil and firing up the stove in the morning and airing our own sleeping bags. There were other changes, too. Chafee was being rotated home. I valued him with what was very near hero worship. But there was no chance to talk, just a handshake. The truck was waiting; Chafee was a married man and, I believe, with kids. He'd kept that to himself, faithful to his own strictures. Don't get to know your men personally, he'd warned. Don't ask about their kids or their gray-haired mothers. Captain Chafee had been in Korea a year, during the bad fighting, and now he was going home, and I didn't blame him for hurrying off. There was so much I wanted to say: what his confidence meant to me, how I admired him, how much he'd taught all of us. He was the only truly great man I'd yet met in my life, and all I had time to do was say thanks. Maybe he understood.

He climbed, with the usual Chafee grace, over the tailgate of the truck, looked back once at the bunch of us, and then he was gone.

A big, redheaded captain named Charley Logan replaced him. Logan was old, maybe thirty-three or thirty-four. A nice fellow, but he brushed his teeth with a lot of toothpaste and insisted on talking to me while he brushed, so he sort of foamed at the mouth and some of it ran down his chin all the while, and I found that disgusting. Otherwise, except that he wasn't John Chafee, we got on, and if he hadn't brushed his teeth so much it would have been okay.

Red Philips was still hanging around, waiting for a ride out to that prison island he was going to govern with a company of Korean marines and a couple of NCOs. He made no secret about being pleased not to be going back on line, and even though there was no fighting on the island except prisoners killing each other, you wondered about being out there with a couple of thousand pissed-off gooks and a radio. "Suppose something happens and they make a break?" Hell, Red laughed, he figured he and the gooks would get along fine. He had the capacity for selling himself, or anyone else, on just about anything. He had enthusiasm; it was what made him good at selling cars.

As I got into the business of being executive officer and seeing tents didn't burn down and keeping track of the rolls of barbed wire and the toilet paper supply, the third platoon faded from me, coming back only occasionally when someone from the platoon swam into focus and I was once again, for a moment, a platoon leader and not a counter of tent pegs and sleeping bags.

Duke came to me first, run up as an early victim of Lieutenant Maki. Logan was still settling in and I heard the case. Duke had sassed the platoon sergeant, and Princeton turned him in. I cared about Duke, remembering he'd come down the draw when Fitz and I lay in the bloody snow.

"What's eating you, Duke? Why'd you sass Sergeant Princeton?"

"Nothing eating me, Mr. Brady. Jes' nothing going right."

"How so?"

"They always on me. Do this, do that, go here, come back."

"Well, that's a runner's job."

He wasn't like the Chief; he wasn't sullen. "Well?" I said.

"Mr. Brady, you know what's wrong with me, what I needs?"

"What do you need, Duke?"

"Mr. Brady, I needs a bout."

Duke fancied himself a boxer, and I arranged some fights for the weekend with Duke in the light heavies. Some machine gunner, a mean kid from Boston, broke Duke's nose and split his lips, even with big twelve-ounce gloves, and Duke waved an arm and quit right there, vomiting on his own blood. I saw him a few days later breezing past on some errand.

"How's it going, Duke?"

"Jes' fine, Lieutenant, jes' fine. I needs a bout ever so often. Sergeant and me getting along jes' fine now."

Fitzgerald came to the tent one evening. He was leaving next morning in the rotation draft for home. I told him, meaning it, that I was sorry to see him go and wished him well.

"What are you going to do with your life, Fitz? I mean, if you decide to get out? Go to college and play ball?"

"No, sir, football's over now. My legs are tired. I thought I'd go up to the Ford Motor Company and maybe get me a job. They got a plant up near Flint, and they say they need plant police around there, you know, security and so on."

"Fitz, you could go to college on the G.I. Bill, you know."

"Lieutenant, I don't think I could cut the books no more. All that reading and stuff. And I kind of got used to wearing a uniform, carrying a gun, got pretty good at it. It won't be the same as the marines, but it's something I can do, do pretty well. No, I think I'll go up to Ford."

Hoops fell early out of grace with Maki. He'd gotten a bottle somewhere and was found urinating on the officers' tent. He grinned sheepishly at me, the old battered face ashamed and amused at the same time.

"Well, Mr. Brady, it was a stupid thing to do, but when I start I just never did learn when to stop. It was different when you was there, you was always a character yourself, if you understand what I mean. You knew what I was, and you didn't much care long as I did a job for you, and I always did. But the lieutenant, he's surely right to bust me like this, no doubt of it, but he ain't the same as you or Mr. Flynn, and the platoon ain't the same, and that's no fooling."

I felt sorry for them, Duke a negro and Hoops a drunk and now Fitz, the best of us, just wanting to carry a gun the rest of his life, breaking heads for Ford. None of them could change, wanted to change. I couldn't change them. I worried about them and wallowed in brief regret, and then they drifted out of my life and I gradually stopped worrying and took on new worries. That's how it was in the war when someone close to you was out of sight, even for a few weeks; he misted over and grew vague in your mind. Chafee, that magnificent officer, was gone and I was thinking about Charley Logan with his goddamned toothpaste foaming up his mouth. Maybe later on, when we were back in the States, they would all come back to me as vividly as they had stood there on the hill or lain in the snow on a night ambush or blown frozen bodies out of the ice for me. I hoped so, and that I hadn't lost them forever.

There were other changes. For a second time old Colonel Gregory came back to us as Battalion commander and Youngdahl ascended to someplace near Eden with a big staff job at Division. Youngdahl was there one day all pink and bright with his creased trousers and polished boots and hair slicked down, and the next day he was gone and Colonel Gregory was back, cackling and twisting his turkey neck to see what we were up to. Then, after having it only a couple of weeks, I lost my job and got a new one.

One of the new officers in the Battalion was a regular, not a trade school man out of Annapolis like that Lucky Folger, who was mortared the day the gooks took the two marines on the water run. This new lieutenant was called McCarty, and he was a first lieutenant and paint smart. He was assigned to Dog Company, and Charley Logan said he was glad to have him and then gave me the bad news.

"You see, Jim, he outranks you, so I can't very well give him a platoon and have you exec over him. That wouldn't be right for either of you. You see that, don't you?"

I said I did. I'd been exec twelve or fourteen days and that was enough for me. There was just too much paperwork and not enough real soldiering about it. I'd been flattered by the promotion, but these mornings when the platoons marched out to their field problems, the platoon leaders hustling along, pushing the men and shouting orders, everyone swinging along fast on the packed snow, leather slapping and web gear creaking and NCOs counting cadence and boots smartly hitting the snow, I missed it.

"You won't be taking a platoon again," Logan said. "The colonel has some ideas. He wants to see you."

That didn't sound good. "Okay, Skipper," I said.

"And Allen, too. Go get Mack, and the two of you go up there and report to the Old Man."

I knew then we would both be leaving Dog Company. When a company commander starts using your Christian name, you know you'll no longer be serving under him. I got Mack and we went up to the Battalion CP.

Colonel Gregory cackled at us for a few minutes and then sat us down real friendly in his tent and began to talk. I thought back, uneasily, to that first night in Gregory's place when Mack and I joined the Battalion and Youngdahl gave us that pep talk and we thought it was so wonderful. Later we knew better.

"Well, now," Gregory said, "you know we've got this new batch of shiny young lieutenants on board, just like you were a few months ago. Quantico is turning them out so fast officers will be rotated quicker, much quicker. Some will be going south for rear-echelon jobs. I could send you two south easy enough, a good job back there, drink some whisky, maybe look over the native girls. But I'm not going to do that." He cackled a little and sat back, enjoying toying with us.

"No, sir," he said more firmly, "I'm not going to send you two back. I'm keeping you with the Battalion. And you know why? Because spring is coming."

It was now March and I guessed the colonel was right on that. The calendar said so.

"Yes, Colonel?" Mack said uncertainly.

"Well, this is it. We had a pretty quiet winter. I know maybe up on the line it didn't seem so, but it was pretty quiet. We haven't had a big action since 749 last September. The gooks have been most gentlemanly while the snow flew. Why, I don't know. They fought plenty that first winer. Ask them. But what I do know is in a couple or three weeks, a month at most, the snow is going to melt and the mud to dry and then we're going to have spring, and spring is the time for the big offensives.

"I'm not telling any military secrets when I say I don't expect this Division to start a push from the positions we hold now. You've seen the terrain ahead of us. We practically smashed this Battalion on 749. You've seen that 2,000-meter hill dead ahead. There are bigger hills behind it, up north, and the gooks hold them in depth. We know because we fly over them and sometimes get a prisoner, and occasionally a Blue Boy wanders in with some real dope. No, sir, we're not going to assault those hills. That's my thought."

I tried not to exhale too noticeably in relief.

"But what maybe is going to happen," and the colonel was seized by a fit of cackling, perhaps at the audacity of a mere Battalion commander venturing a military prediction, "is that just maybe the North Korean army of liberation might decide to come south. If they do that, we're going to have a merry time holding a line stretched as thin as this one, and we're going to take losses. You lose platoon leaders fast, company commanders fast, awful fast. That's why I'm keeping you two in the Battalion. I want a few young fellows around who've been in a firefight, who know what it's like. I want people like that around me if it gets rough, and I think it might get rough."

Mack rubbed one hand against another.

"That's mighty fine of you, Colonel."

"Yessir," I said, just to be in harmony. I wasn't as enthusiastic about all this as Mack, whom you'd think had just been promoted to major.

The colonel was so pleased at our gratitude he was beyond cackling, and a kind of strangled noise issued from his throat, and his bony frame shook with inner laughter.

"Then again," he went on, "this Division might start being marines again. You never know. These army gentlemen who run this war might recall we have a blushing acquaintance with amphibious warfare. They might just send us up the coast a piece to drop in and surprise a few people.

And if they do, gentlemen, we're going to need a few folks around who can run a platoon or a company in a pinch."

A big flat grin spread over Mack's face. I said, "Fine, that's just fine, sir."

In the meantime we would join his staff, Mack as adjutant, me as intelligence officer.

"Jesus," Mack said when we left, "think of that, maybe a landing, maybe getting a company!"

I *was* thinking.

"Mack," I asked him, "what does an intelligence officer do?"

24

This reserve camp was closer to the line than the last, a blocking position behind the MLR more than a true rest area.

A battery of 105mm guns was dug in just to our rear, and they fired regularly through the day and the night, keeping the gooks from relaxing. For some reason the gooks never directed any counter-battery fire at these guns, so the Battalion wasn't disturbed by incoming mail. I wished we could have said the same about outgoing. Days it didn't bother me at all; you could ignore it. Nights were different, lying there on a cot in a canvas tent, our shells roaring out very low and directly overhead. Some shells had proximity fuses, a sort of timing device which exploded them while still in the air, so they could spray shrapnel over a large area rather than muffle the effect by exploding deep under the snow. These fuses were good, the shells blowing up fifty or a hundred feet over the target. But a few went off prematurely. I worried about premature air bursts and thought seriously of sleeping with my helmet over my face.

Mack Allen and I settled down to learn the new jobs. He was now S-1, the personnel officer or adjutant of the Battalion. A lot of paper shuffling and record keeping, and he hated it. Only his dream of taking over a rifle company in combat kept him going. I was S-2, a job much more satisfying. I had access to maps and information that showed the entire line, with the Marine Division sector larger scale and in full detail. For the first time I could see the war as something more than the draws and defilades and barbed-wire aprons in front of my own few hundred yards of line. Now I saw where the other allied Divisions were, I read the daily intelligence reports on action along the whole front, what prisoners had to say, what aerial photos could tell. I felt like that fellow Krebs in the Hemingway story who came home from fighting in the First War and started reading up on it and thought that for the first time he was really learning about the war.

But mostly, and this was my job, I learned about the enemy.

When the North Korean Army came down over the 38th Parallel the summer of 1950, they had nearly forty divisions to smash right through the rotten South Koreans and the soft garrison troops MacArthur had rushed into battle from Japanese occupation billets. Now after twenty-one months of war there were only nine North Korean divisions left. The rest had just melted away in bloody fights up and down the country. All nine North Korean divisions now faced the single American Marine Division and one South Korean division on its flank. Now the nine North Korean divisions were there in front of me, neatly circled in red grease pencil on a transparent overlay atop a big map. On paper they looked pretty formidable. But they were no longer full divisions, numbering only eight or nine thousand men, shrunken by casualties to less than half the size of the Marine Division even without its extra rifle regiment of Korean marines. They were small divisions, but I knew they could fight. Chafee put it best one time before he left:

"They're more like the Japs in the islands than like anyone else. You have to dig them out of the caves, you have to kill them. They don't surrender, not very often and not in bunches."

The Chinese army was different. That's what the intelligence reports told me. Marines hadn't fought the Chinese since the previous year. The chinks were better equipped than the North Koreans, their communications were better, their artillery, too, very soldierlike. But they did surrender. They had more sense than the gooks, and if you could prove to them they were finished, well, they gave up. Of course it wasn't their country they were fighting in, and that may have made the difference.

The other thing about the Chinese, and this was impressive, there were more than a million of them.

I began to read up on the Chinese. Stuck in my head was Gregory's remark about an amphibious landing. Maybe it would be the chinks who'd be facing us. I wanted to know what they were like, how they fought, how they thought, everything. The intelligence reports didn't supply it all, but they were a start. The third day I was in intelligence, the new Regimental commander swooped down on us for a surprise inspection. I was summoned up to Gregory's tent, and the maps were carried in and set up on an easel.

"Tell me about the enemy, Lieutenant," the Regimental commander said. He sat back in a camp chair and waited. I was nervous about experting something I didn't fully understand, but grateful this was not the same man who caught me without my machine guns sited. I raced through a brief exposition of the enemy forces facing us.

"How do we know that?" the Regimental commander said.

"Prisoner interrogation and aerial recon," I snapped back, entirely without foundation. He nodded and lighted his cigar. He was a small, blocky-looking man with short legs and a big head that sat on his shoulders seemingly without an intervening neck. His name was Krulak and he was known as "the Brute." I talked on, pointing to the map.

"How long have you been S-2, Lieutenant?"

"Three days, sir."

"Ha! And before that, another staff job?"

"No, sir. I was rifle platoon leader and then company exec, Dog Company."

The Brute turned to Gregory.

"Good stuff, Colonel. I like to have men around me who've been out there, who know what it's like on the line." He puffed cigar smoke at Gregory, who cackled happily. Wasn't that exactly what he'd been saying himself?

Later Mack asked how it went. "Nothing to it," I said, "you memorize the numbers of the divisions opposite, estimate their morale and condition, and use the pointer a lot."

"You really fell into it," Mack said. "The Brute was all

over me because I didn't know how many men short we were."

The weather broke and we had rain, the first I'd ever seen in Korea, and then a real thaw that sent the snow melting into ditches and dry streambeds toward the Sea. Brown patches began to show on the southern faces of the hills, and men went around in wool shirts and boondockers instead of parkas and thermal boots. Green sprouts struggled up through the earth, and drunk and disorderly charges rose commensurately. Someone produced a softball and a facsimile of a bat, and when we weren't running problems there were games on a rough parade ground.

I was getting to know my new intelligence section. There should have been a staff sergeant in charge, but as usual we were short of staff NCOs and a corporal was running the section. His name was Jay Scott, and he'd been two years at Yale and was related to the DuPonts. He wasn't like anything I'd yet come across in the Battalion. He got letters from stockbrokers and had a subscription to *Fortune* magazine and wore Brooks Brothers shirts, button-downs, under his issue sweater. He got packages from Abercrombie & Fitch and food parcels from S. S. Pierce. His mother sent him new linen handkerchiefs every week. I wondered what Hoops would have made of him.

Scott, though, was very good. His eight scouts considered him an oddity but the sort of oddity they talked about with a certain pride. Yale gave him cachet. Most of my scouts were city boys, which puzzled me, but later on, when I saw them in action, I knew they were the right men. The accepted wisdom that farm boys or country kids from out west were superior in the field did not prove out. The best man I had was from Jersey City, the second best from Hartford. They were good scouts and good marines and I had no complaints about the section. It was pleasant having Scott there, with a deprecating wit about himself and the world. When he was promoted to buck sergeant, he pointedly showed off his third stripe.

"The gap is narrowing, Lieutenant," Scott said.

Later, when I became a first lieutenant, I took delight in telling him, "The gap just widened again, Sergeant."

A half dozen Korean interpreters were assigned to the

section. Five of them were good men. The sixth was a conniver and eventually discovered to be a sneak thief. It was the Jersey man who caught the thief.

"You want I should kick the shit out of him, Mr. Brady?"

"No, that's not too good an idea."

"I mean, just a little bit, nothing fatalistic or anything."

I said no. I'd been told what happened to interpreters who screwed up. They were immediately drafted into the ROK Army or, if not fit, into the Korean Service Corps, where they would end up carrying loads in the gook trains. The interpreter knew this, and when I sacked him there were tears and much emotion. When he was gone I had perhaps thirty seconds of guilt, and then, as I was learning to do, I said to hell with him and opened another bottle of Asahi beer.

We had beer regularly in reserve, and whisky too. I'd never been a drinker, not even beer, but I was learning that as well. It came our Battalion's turn to send an officer to Japan to buy booze. We drew lots and I won. I'd thought about it, about a booze run and about that smooth little girl in the geisha house, and I decided that if I got the chance, I'd go. Then my number came up and I shook my head.

"Hell, let someone else go. I'm a lousy con artist anyway. I'd never talk anyone into flying the stuff back."

And so I stayed with the Battalion. The thought of that girl, of any girl, was immense within me. But that was another world, those things didn't belong here. After five months this Battalion, these hills, these men were what mattered. There was a purity about life on the line, a crude priesthood of combat, that I didn't want to soil for a few days of pleasure. You didn't get laid up here, you didn't masturbate, you tried not to muddle your mind even by thinking about it. I had no religious scruples about it, not this time. It was as if a trip to Japan would have spoiled something, betrayed the Battalion and my men. And myself. I couldn't imagine John Chafee on a booze run. And for me, Chafee was the model.

The thaw brought up green buds and turned roads to mud here in the valleys. On the hills there were snowslides, and at the briefing Gregory told us that along the line bunkers were collapsing under the weight of layers of sandbags. In one regiment two men were suffocated in one bunker. Another marine's back was broken when his bunker slipped sideways and slid down the hill. Fox Company lost a man when he stepped on a mine during a night problem. Both legs were blown off at the knee, and by the time they got him back to camp and a surgeon, he was dead. A machine gunner shot his bunkmate with a .45. Then one night there was an alert and the Battalion moved out fast in trucks to a support position. The alert was nothing, the gooks never came, but a marine fell out of one truck and was run over by the truck behind. So the war went on, no fighting to speak of, the daily communiqués banal in their sameness, and marines continued to die. The mountains killed them, and the cold, and now even the thaw conspired to kill them. And they killed themselves and each other, and sometimes the gooks had another turn at it.

=== 25 ===

March 22, the first day of spring, we moved, the whole damned Division moving west, battalion by battalion, regiment by regiment, to the low, red-dirt country just north of Seoul. We were crossing the whole country from one coast to the other, 20,000 men and their guns and their goods. The First Marine Division would straddle the north-south corridor that had been for centuries the traditional invasion route of people coming out of Manchuria in the north to take Seoul and flow south through the good rice country, the granaries, to the south coast and the ice-free ports. Now it was the Chinese who lurked north of Seoul and whom the Division would be facing, the million Chinese who had not moved since the previous summer, who now, when the mud dried and firmed, might come south again. Eighth Army decided the Marine Division should be there to break the Chinese, if they came, before they reached Seoul and the valleys. In preparation for the move west, the Battalion struck its tents the afternoon before and slept out. Jay Scott woke me about 3 A.M., shaking me in the sleeping bag.

"Wake up, Lieutenant. It's snowing."

Shit. And we thought winter had forgiven us.

It was a true spring snow, the flakes falling straight, heavy and wet. By first light there were four inches on the ground, but the Battalion was ready to move. Striking the tents had been smart; muscling heavy wet canvas was some work. Men dug out ponchos against the wet, but it was awkward hefting field packs and rifles and wearing ponchos. I said the hell with it and just zipped my field jacket up tight at the throat. Still, wet flakes drifted in at the back of my neck whenever I bent, and water ran off my helmet. Marines slipped and fell heavily under their packs, jamming rifle muzzles into the mud and the snow, and cursed that two weeks of dry weather would turn into this the very day we were moving out. The trucks were late, slowed on the mountain roads by snow, and Colonel Gregory, his bright eyes happily darting as if all this was integral to his plans, called the officers together and told us to stand easy. Someone else said the move was off, that the tents would go back up, that we wouldn't move until the snow melted and the trucks could cut the passes. I sat on my rucksack rolling cigarettes and listening to Scott lecture the section on the aesthetics of rolling a proper field pack. It was amazing what that boy had learned at Yale. Around me platoon leaders drove their men, lined them up, moved them somewhere else, and shouted until their voices grew hoarse and cracked. It was nice not having a platoon at times like these, having only a dozen scouts and interpreters and not forty men, and then I saw Charley Logan splashing through the mud and snow with his new exec, the regular, both of them with soggy sheets of paper, rosters and lists of one sort and another, trying to make them out before the ink ran.

It was even nicer not being an exec.

Then the trucks, which weren't going to come, came, and we climbed aboard and sat there on the long side benches, waiting. The canvas roofs of the trucks were furled, as they always were near the line, so we could see enemy air if it ever came. The snow fell heavy, six or seven inches by now, piling up on our tin hats and shoulders and laps, melting through to the skin, and we sat until one by one the trucks ground up out of the valley in low gear to the road that led south over the pass. We were still in North Korea, had not been out of the enemy's country since Mack and I first arrived at Regiment, and now for the first time we were leaving it, to follow the main line of resistance as it fell away to the southwest and crossed the 38th Parallel and then gently straightened out for its run due west to the Yellow Sea. The trucks climbed steadily to the pass, skidding sideways at the turns, the snow drier and deeper as we climbed, and finally I turned away and leaned back with a carbine between my legs, trying to sleep.

We crossed that pass and then another higher, where there was real snow, winter snow, and the trucks skidded and slipped and their gears screamed, and then we were over it and running downhill and the mountains began to fall behind. Army trucks passed carrying the army troops who were taking over in the mountains from the Division. The marines jeered and there were shouts in return. One of my scouts spat at the trucks as they went by. "They're just shit, that's all, just shit." I started to say something but Scott rapped the man on his helmet. "Watch your damned language," he said. They were the first American soldiers I'd seen over here, and I watched, trying to see their faces, to see if they were different from us, but they were just faces in the snow, faces like ours.

I wondered how they would make out on 749 and the other hills.

The swaying, jouncing motion of the truck, the early wakening, combined in drowsiness, and I half slept, half daydreamt, about the ridges behind us and about being "Shit Trench" and about the big negro who died and about not having said good-bye properly to Chafee and about the cold and Brute Krulak and how Princeton taught me to roll cigarettes and how Hoops called shrapnel "shrapnails" and about the toothpaste foam at the corners of Charley Logan's mouth and how dead men looked hung on the wire.

A mammoth pothole jerked me into wakefulness. The road was just a road now with the snow thinning and the passes no longer passes but undulations through low hills. The pines pinched out, and stunted, wind-teased trees came in, more Asian-looking and exotic, more what I'd expected five months before. The army trucks were still coming counter to us, whipping past in the snow, but they were only trucks and even our scouts stopped taking note of them and just slumped, sleepy and backs bent, trying to absorb the lurch of the road. Then the road became better, and we sped west along what might at one time have been pretty fair highway, stretches of it even paved, but cracked and broken down by tanks and heavy gun trailers and the endless convoys of big trucks. Around noon the snow stopped and there was a halt for five minutes. Men scattered off to relieve themselves against trees or bushes or just into the still air. We climbed aboard again, and men broke into their rations and began to eat, spooning up fruit from the can, drinking the cold, rust-tasting water from canteens.

Early in the afternoon we began to pass the first villages, and we knew we were now far south of the line. The marines whistled and called to women, but these villages had seen too many trucks full of troops pass and there was no novelty to us. Only here and there a child waved or a man straightened from his work to stare. Then I heard a great whooping and shouting from the trucks ahead, and I stood up to see, holding tight with one hand to the overhead frame. There was a kind of ceremonial sign erected over the road, its supports polished wood and the sign itself brightly lettered in reds and yellows, very professionally done. The drivers slowed to let us savor it. "You are traveling this road by courtesy of the U.S. Army. This Division's slogan: 'Sharpen Your Bayonets!'" The Division commander's name was written after it, General "Iron Mike" Something. For the next hour we traveled through the territory of that Army Division. There were lots of soldiers about, eating candy or leaning against buildings, some of them having their boots shined by Korean children. The marines shouted at them a whole hour.

"Hey, doggie, sharpen your goddamn bayonet!"

"Never mind them shoes, kid, sharpen his bayonet!"

"Where's your bayonet, dogface?"

The soldiers didn't holler back, tired out by all the trucks that had passed before us. The marines must all have been shouting the whole time, and by now the soldiers wouldn't even look up. The snow was gone, and except for sore buttocks, we were enjoying the ride. It beat walking, especially when you had the army for comic relief.

Colonel Gregory had briefed his officers the day before. We would not go directly into the line but would set up a blocking position in the low hills just to the rear of the Regiment's other two battalions and overlapping the rear of yet another division. The identity of this other division, the exact site of the blocking position, these things were not divulged. About four in the afternoon the trucks turned off the road and parked under trees, and the Battalion set up on the reverse slopes of three small hills about a thousand yards behind a modest ridgeline I assumed was the MLR. Some men already had tents up and others were going up. There was no snow at all, but the ground was wet as if snow had fallen early in the day and melted, and now again it smelled like real spring and not the false spring of the high mountains. I figured we were seventy-five or a hundred miles west of where we'd started that morning, and thirty or more miles south. There were no bunkers, no trenches, but men had started digging slit trenches next to the tents. A captain from Division came up and saluted Gregory. We could expect some incoming, he said, but until now it had not been heavy. There were 105 guns opposite us, maybe some heavier guns, too. They were all guns the Chinese had taken the first winter or captured from Chiang Kai-shek four years before, all American guns.

So it would be the Chinese now. A new practicality asserted itself, and I called Scott to me.

"Find out if any of the interpreters speak Chinese."

There was nothing in war like being prepared.

The Allied line in this sector was nothing like as imposing or defensible as the high mountain ridges in the east, which was why they worried about the Chinese coming south and why the Marine Division had been moved here to stop them. Here the dominant hills reached only perhaps two hundred meters, and between them ran flat valleys ranging up to a half mile or a mile across—good tank country, good attacking country. So you held the hills as strong points, mined and wired the valleys and registered mortar and artillery concentrations, and established blocking positions just to the rear like this one our Battalion was now setting up. Defense in depth rather than a long thin line. I thought of C. Aubrey Smith in *Four Feathers,* tracing with a finger dipped in claret the "thin red line" at Balaclava. By the time the tents were up and trenches dug and sentries posted and men fed, it was nearly midnight.

Reveille went at five, and by six the rifle companies were

digging into and fortifying the three hills. I left Scott to organize the intelligence section and strolled up to see Charley Logan and Dog Company. McCarty, the new exec, looking very much the professional, was out there chivvying the working parties, slapping a whippy branch against his leg like a swagger stick. The marines had entrenching tools and a few pick mattocks to work with, no real shovels, but the ground was softer here, without frost, and the red earth flew as the shallow trenchlines began to snake their way along the forward slopes of the hills, just below the skyline. As I watched, a chopper came in low and without ever setting down, dropped rolls of barbed wire and steel stakes to the working parties. Logan was up and down the hill a dozen times, looking as tireless as Chafee, and almost fragile without the layers of winter clothing. Watching them sweat, I didn't miss Dog Company at all.

Scott turned up two interpreters who claimed to speak Chinese and a third who knew a few words. I told him to notify Regiment we needed someone to test them, to be sure they weren't just bragging. Then Sasso, the scout from Jersey City, came up at a trot.

"Lieutenant," he said, panting, "there's some son of a bitch out there in the mine fields playing golf."

Sasso wasn't a drinker nor was he shook. I went with him up to the right flank of Dog Company's hill, and there on the low ground between the blocking position and the MLR were two men, one of them clubbing at a golf ball and the other retrieving it. I shouted at them, and the man with the club waved and then bent again over his ball with what seemed extraordinary concentration. He was using a short iron, and he lofted the ball cleanly into the air so that it fell within a few yards of the retriever, who tossed it back with a curious underarm motion. I shouted again, but neither man looked up, so I sat down on the hillside to watch. Sasso stood there, shaking his head.

"The son of a bitch is crazy. Crazy."

Thirty minutes more of this and the golfer shouldered his club and ambled toward us. I got up to receive him.

"Hallo," the golfer shouted, British by the accent. "Decent weather at last. It's been bloody until today."

"Don't you know the maps show mines out there?" I said.

"Mines, mines," the Englishman said impatiently, "people are always going on about mines. Wish I'd never heard of the bloody things. Our people haven't put one up yet. My name's Lonsdale."

"Brady. What outfit are you?"

"Leicestershire Regiment. I'm leftenant. This is my batman, Mooney. Mooney doesn't golf but I say it keeps one in trim. Right-o, Mooney?"

Mooney grunted what I took for affirmation.

"We came out from Hong Kong," Lonsdale said. "Splendid duty, that. Did nothing but play golf, thirty-six holes most days. When they sent the Regiment out here I brought my sticks along. Never know when you'll get in a round. Knew my game would go all seedy if I didn't get in a few swings each day. Right, too."

Sasso just stood there, not saluting or speaking or anything, just leaning forward as if wanting to touch Lonsdale to see if he were for real. The Englishman asked what outfit we were and I told him.

"Oh, I say, splendid. That chap John Wayne, was he really a marine or was that just the cinema?"

I said I didn't know but I thought it was just the cinema.

"I did know a marine once, though. Leftenant. Extraordinary chap. Drunk every morning by ten. Bloody big chap, though, awfully fit even tiddly."

I thought I'd better get it in that we weren't cinema marines or drunks but had been fighting in the eastern mountains.

"Fighting? I'd understood there hadn't been any since last summer. Just demonstrates you can't believe all the gen. We arrived a week ago. Bit of gunnery and a few patrols, that's about the size of it. Damned glad I brought the sticks along."

Before we parted, Lonsdale promised to arrange an evening in their mess. "Like to meet your chaps." I said that would be fine. Sasso said nothing until the two Brits strolled off, and then he shook his head again.

"Golf. What the hell kind of war they think this is, Lieutenant?"

So we had the British on the right flank. I was glad about it, never having met any British and being curious about them, as people and as soldiers. Better than having the army over there, anyway. But golf?

That evening around six the Chinese welcomed us, throwing in about fifty rounds of 105, and Mack Allen and I shared a slit trench. Mack brought along some Asahi beer in his pack from the last reserve, and we drank it lying on our backs waiting for the shelling to end. It tasted good in the spring dusk, and it felt good not to be cold, not to be lying in snow. That night there was a firefight just to our front, the heavy sound of machine guns, the lighter, faster chatter of burp guns, with a few grenades punctuating the argument. I lay there on a real bunk savoring the first firefight I'd heard in weeks. The sound was familiar, even reassuring. Across the tent Allen snored, other men breathed softly in sleep. Outside an easy breeze and not the wind of the great hills pushed gently against the canvas of the tent while the crunch of a sentry's tread approached, pivoted, faded again. The firefight was still going on when I fell asleep.

26

Lieutenant Lonsdale didn't forget his promise. The batman, Mooney, arrived one afternoon with an invitation addressed to me, saluting snappily and handing it over. A half dozen marine officers were asked to visit the British mess the next evening at eight.

"Black tie or white?" Allen asked.

"Golfing clothes more likely. Plus fours." I sent back word we would be delighted.

"You should have written a formal reply," Mack said, "had it engraved maybe."

The marines had also rubbed up against the Brits. They stole their black boots or traded them, they drank with them, they fought them, they told them lies and were told lies in return, they even took them on at soccer and got whipped. Basically, they got along wonderfully. Marines enjoy the exotic, and their relief at not tying in with our own army was so great the British could not miss. It also became quickly apparent that the British Regiment could fight and that Lonsdale's remarks had been charming understatement. There were firefights up and down the line every night. In our blocking position we heard them but weren't involved. The shells shuttled overhead with their freight-train's roar to smash the red dirt hills on both sides of the line. It was not that the Chinese were more aggressive than the North Koreans; it was simply that this was better ground and we were more accessible. Each side sent out patrols nightly and on most nights they drew contact. By day, except for the shells and occasional sniping where the lines closed to a few hundred yards, there was nothing. It was a nighttime war, and both sides observed the ground rules: by day we fenced, by night we fought.

The British officers' mess was a sandbagged bunker, built above ground and nearly ten yards long. At the far end was a bar, with a portrait of the King, nicely framed. Major Nicholson, our new operations officer, went in first. A young British subaltern said good evening.

"Would you mind, sir?" He held out a hand.

Nicholson stared at him and then realized. His side arms. He unhooked the web belt and gave it to the subaltern, who hung it somewhere. We all handed over our gun belts.

"Feels kind of funny without it," Mack said.

"I dunno. More civilized this way."

Lonsdale came up. "Ah, Brady, good man." Then, to Major Nicholson, "Sir, may I present you to the colonel?" He took Nick halfway across the room to where the British Regimental commander met him with a brisk handshake. The colonel had broken veins in his nose and puffs of hair on his cheeks. Introductions were made all around, very chummy, and batmen came up with trays of drinks, platters of hors d'oeuvres. How did they do it, where did this stuff come from? When we all had drinks the colonel raised his glass.

"To our American guests," he said.

"The King," Nicholson said smoothly. He'd been with us only a few weeks but I was proud of him. He'd handled this as Chafee might have done, with a certain style. Mack was talking with an officer named Gwynne.

"Actually," Gwynne was saying, "I'm a Welshman. This Regiment's home is Leicestershire, but you don't have to be from there, actually, though many of the men are. You understand, this is only one battalion of the Regiment. There may be ten or fifteen other battalions scattered about the world, but wherever one Leicestershire battalion is, they *are* the Regiment. You see that, don't you?"

Mack, being a polite Virginian and a student of military history, said yes.

There was a dartboard, and the ritual game began. Our

supply officer was dangerously wild with one shot. "And they took away our guns," Mack Allen whispered. More drinks and more food, followed by more toasts. We toasted the Leicestershire Regiment and the Leicesters toasted the United States Marines. Then someone toasted the Royal Marines. Then a British officer, slightly befuddled, raised a glass.

"To the American Marines and the entire American army."

This aroused little enthusiasm among us. Lonsdale brought a young blond officer over. "I say, Brady, explain just what your marines are anyway, will you, old chap?"

I told him, in some detail. The blond officer looked vague.

"Quite," he said, "a sort of commando. Jolly good."

I started to explain but instead I said, "Is there another Scotch?"

"Oh, I say."

The singing began about ten. By eleven it was totally obscene but notable in that every Brit knew every word of every lyric in the repertory. They never repeated a song, except for one that went, "I just want to hang around / Piccadilly underground / Livin' off the earnings / of an high priced lady . . ." Then I glimpsed someone at the entrance to the bunker. Lonsdale went over and then motioned the colonel aside. There was more chat, and the blond officer, whose name I hadn't gotten, went out, picking up his gun belt and tin hat as he went.

"What's that all about?" Mack wondered.

"I dunno. I'll ask Lonsdale."

"Oh, really nothing, old chap. Some Chinamen mucking about Harlequin Bridge. Peter has the duty tonight, so he's gone down to look about. Be back directly."

Nicholson was not the most experienced of us, but he was the senior American present, so I thought I'd better tell him. Nick nodded and put down his glass.

"We'd better cut these with water from here on out," he said.

Nicholson told the others to cool the drinking, but the party went on. I listened, as well as I could through the singing, and two or three times in the next hour I thought I could hear firing, but each time it died before I could be sure. The marine officers were now singing as loudly as our hosts but not as well. Our supply officer seemed especially fond of a song about "Three old ladies, locked in a lavatory." Just before midnight the young duty officer, Peter, slipped back into the bunker and hung up his belt, making his way to the colonel. En route, I noted with some admiration, he paused to take a smoked oyster from a batman's tray. Then I could see his lips moving. "Nothing," they said, "it was nothing."

I relaxed then. But, Jesus, the way they handled it. A marine going out on patrol to see if "some Chinamen" were out there "mucking about," would have shaken hands, smiled bravely, and handed over a sealed letter to his mother.

Well, the Brits had been at this sort of thing longer than we had.

To the right of the Leicesters was the rest of the British Commonwealth Division: Canadians, New Zealanders, South Africans, Australians. The South Africans had a squadron of fighter planes, old P-51s from World War II, and they used them to strafe; they were too slow to be used for much else. They mounted Klaxon horns on their planes and sounded them as they dove. You had to like the South Africans, half of them square-headed blond Dutchmen with heavy accents and funny first names, the rest proper English types named Nigel or Geoff. Good soldiers. One afternoon I heard there were Australians marching past, and I went out to see, standing on the side of the hill as they passed. The Aussies didn't pay any attention to us, they simply marched by, but they looked good. I hoped they'd sing "Waltzing Matilda," but they didn't. They didn't sing anything, but they looked like soldiers. Marines remembered Australia from the War, and New Zealand, where they had recuperated and rested between the island assaults, and there was no heckling as there had been with American army troops. Firefights broke out every night, along the marine lines and to the east on the British front. A platoon leader I knew came by one afternoon on an errand.

"How are they, Lou, the chinks?"

"Well, Jim, they're pretty good. They know their work. I wouldn't be surprised if they did come south pretty soon. The mud's drying and we're pretty thin and there's a hell of a lot of Chinese."

"And they're good?" I pressed.

"Jim, we killed one guy on patrol the other night. Brought in the body because we wanted proof. You know, they carry this little kind of service book in their pockets. This chink, he enlisted or got drafted or something back in 1936. He fought the Japs for nine years. Then in '47 he fought the Reds for Chiang. Then when Chiang bugged out to Taiwan they just turned him around, put a red star on his cap, and in 1950 he's in Korea fighting us. Now he's dead, sixteen years of professional soldiering and all that combat and the son of a bitch is still a private soldier. I got kids in my platoon got out of high school last June."

"How'd you bag him?"

"He was a one-man listening post right out in front of the MLR. I still can't figure it. We ain't the quietest moving people there ever was or he just wasn't listening."

"Maybe he was tired."

"Jesus," Lou said, "after sixteen years of fighting, I'd be tired, too."

The morning intelligence reports came to me. One wild one said a Chinese body brought in turned out to have been a woman. There were rumors big air raids could be expected, that the Russians had turned over a lot of bombers to the chinks. Some reports said Russians were flying the Migs now, some said it was ex-Luftwaffe pilots. The most bizarre report said one of the enemy voices overheard during a dogfight was that of a turncoat American flying a Mig. We'd never been bombed or strafed, not since early in the war, and I wondered what that would be like. There was talk, too, of tanks, whole divisions of them, but no one ever saw them, and talk of poison gas being used. I hoped that wasn't so, because except for one day's training at Quantico, I'd never worn a gas mask. And in our Battalion, none had been issued.

Pierce Power was being rotated home, one of the last men to have fought on 749 last September. He found out where I was and came by. He looked better now, more the Pierce I knew from college, not as gray and wasted. I introduced him to Mack and the others, and we sat around and had some Asahi beer in the big litre bottles they wrapped first in Japanese newspaper and then sheathed with straw.

Naturally when they learned Pierce had been on 749, people started telling war stories. Pierce listened for a while and then he told one, a good one, and I was proud all over again that we were friends.

"Some Korean Marines were on 749, too," Pierce said. "When we made the top and there were no more gooks to flush out, we dug in, hoping they wouldn't come back. We were thin; we didn't have much left. Across the saddle the Korean Marines were on top, too. The hill was secured, but there was a bunch of KMCs over there shouting and arguing about something. Then they kind of stood back and one of them knelt down, and this guy came up very close behind him and took out a handgun and shot him through the head. One minute he was kneeling there and then he was dead. I was tired as hell, but I stood up and started yelling across the saddle at them. I'm yelling at them to stop and waving my arms, and one of them waves back, being friendly. Later I found out they executed the guy because he was slow getting up the hill. But when I saw him he was on top and none of them had been there very long, so how slow could he have been?

"But they shot him anyway."

It was also Pierce who gave me some detail finally about how Jim Callan was killed.

After he left I remembered how I got Callan into trouble toward the end of Basic School, on a hot afternoon in the Virginia spring, when he was caught reading a book during a tactics lecture. It was a paperback, *Treasure of the Sierra Madre,* that I liked, and I had lent it to Callan. He was summoned up to the stage and the book was torn up in front of us and Jim was given a bad chit. I was sore about the book and Callan promised to replace it, but I said not to worry about it and then he was shipped out in the first draft.

He was a rancher from New Mexico. His mother was dead, and he and his dad ran a two-bit ranch, living with drought and scratching out an existence. Callan was twenty-five, and he told me there had been drought nineteen of those years. But he and his father would get along. They had plans, ideas about how to get water piped in. He only needed the money, and he was saving for it in the Corps. After the war, he'd have enough.

Now he was dead, and I sometimes wondered if it was the bad chit he got for reading *Treasure of the Sierra Madre* that got him shipped out so fast and killed so soon.

We gave a return party for the British. I had the front half of a supply tent cleared out, and we had whisky and the beer. Mack got some saltines somewhere, and I contributed the salami my mother had sent a month before. By trimming away the mold spots it would get by. Lonsdale and Peter and about six others came, and ten or twelve marine officers played host. The party was all right, you understand, but it lacked the smooth of the British party. Still, we were having a good time, the British beginning to loosen up with their choral arrangements, when someone poked me.

"Colonel wants to see you."

I went to the tent flap. Standing there in stocking feet, sleepy looking, was Colonel Gregory.

"Good party, Lieutenant?"

"Yes, sir. Some of the British officers dropped over. Just having a drink or two. Would you like to come in and join us, sir?"

Gregory didn't cackle this time. "Well, some people might think it would have been proper to invite your commanding officer in the first place, some people might."

"Yes, sir, Colonel. That surely would have been right. I'd like to apologize for that, Colonel. That's my fault, plain and simple."

I really meant the apology. The colonel stood there looking frail and old and tired with his stringy neck and his socks. It was damn rude not to have invited him. Would I ever learn?

"Sir, I feel like hell over this. I really do. Would you please do us the honor of stepping inside and joining us? I know the British would very much like to meet you. I'd like to have them meet you, sir."

"Well, now, that's very decent of you, Brady. A little belated, but decent. Yes, I would like that."

We went inside and someone called attention and Colonel Gregory waved a hand and said hello and was handed a glass. The talk resumed and the introductions were made. The colonel seemed to enjoy it, and the British did too, and the colonel never cackled, not once. Even the stocking feet seemed right. The British would probably go back talking about the "extraordinary" CO who took his boots off when he went to receptions. That tickled me, the thought of it, and out of pleasure and annoyance with myself mixed up together, I drank too much and felt myself reeling with my feet planted.

"Brady, I suggest you secure the party now," the colonel said quietly.

"Aye, aye, sir." I sobered. I had fouled things up again, getting drunk as host and while the colonel watched. I announced our regrets that the party must end and apologized, too many times, but it went off all right. The British said thanks, and then everyone drifted out into the midnight chill, and I looked around the empty tent and shook my head hard.

"Brady." It was the colonel, still there in a corner, leaning against some ammunition boxes.

"Yes, sir?"

"I'd get some sleep if I were you, Brady. We may be getting up rather early in the morning." He went out, cackling for the first time that night.

⟙27⟙

Someone was shaking me; a flashlight blazed in my eyes.

"Scott, for Chrissakes?"

"Reveille Lieutenant, early reveille."

I pulled an arm from my sleeping bag. The watch said 2 A.M.

"Scott, it's two o'clock."

"I know, Lieutenant. Something's up. The whole Battalion. Colonel wants to see all officers. Right now, sir."

Scott sensed it was no moment to be amusing.

The colonel sat on a camp stool in front of his tent. His driver held a flashlight on the ground before him where maps were laid out, stones weighting them down. Around Gregory were the other staff officers. The company commanders, someone said, would be along in a few minutes. Gregory sipped at coffee in a canteen cup, and looked around at the ring of dull, sleepy faces.

"My, but we're a bright, shining group this morning, aren't we? Brady here? Ah, yes, Lieutenant, good to see you so alert after having played good mine host."

Charley Logan came up, blinking. "What's up?" he asked someone and got a shrug in reply. The other two company commanders came in.

"All right, gentlemen," the colonel said. "We're all here, I guess. Anyone late can be briefed by the exec. Division is testing the mobility of the line outfits. This Battalion will strike camp immediately, make up full field packs, carry three days' ration, one unit of fire, and be prepared to board helicopters at first light. I make that about 4:45 or a little over two hours from now. We will be flown to Kimpo Peninsula and on arrival will run a field problem, assaulting and taking a hill held by Divisional troops as 'hostiles.' Maps and problem overlays will be passed out to all officers when I secure this meeting. Now, any questions?''

When I got back to my section Scott was waiting.

"They say we're moving out, Lieutenant.''

"They're right. Get them saddled up.'' I felt tired and slightly sick to my stomach and I sat down on the cot. "Get them moving, Scott. There'll be copters here at first light. Two hours.''

Scott knew I wasn't in the best of form. He was very proper.

"Would the lieutenant know our destination?'' he asked.

"The lieutenant would. Kimpo Peninsula, and don't spread that around. Just tell them we're moving out, but not up to the line. It's some damn field exercise.''

"Exercise?'' It was one of the few times I saw Scott shaken. "At two o'clock?''

I waved a hand and he went out of the tent. I lay back for a minute. The tent began to sway. I forced myself up, went over to the helmet turned into a washbowl and poured water into it, splashing it over my face and hair. It felt cold and in the predawn chill I shivered. There was a piece of towel at the foot of the bunk and I rubbed it hard over my face. I wished I could just turn in sick and not go. The idea of getting all this gear stowed, the notion of a copter ride feeling this way, then an exercise at the other end? Those goddamn British. I realized we would not be seeing them again, and I would like to have said good-bye to Lonsdale. Maybe we'd be back this way, maybe not. Maybe this was just smoke screen, this business of a field problem. Maybe this was the start of what Gregory had told me and Mack, maybe we were going to jump off, up the coast somewhere, get in behind the Chinese where we could move and not go up against the damn hills. Maybe that was it. I began to feel better and bent over to drag the rucksack out from under the bunk. Moving that quickly my head spun again, so I rubbed my face hard with both hands and stood there, very straight, until the tent again was still.

Around me were the sounds of camp being broken. The tents were coming down, even the big supply tents; marines were tossing creosote and then shoveling dirt to fill in the heads; wires were coming down or being cut, with only one wire to Regiment and lines to the three rifle companies to remain until the last minute. Scott was shouting at someone. A tinkling Korean voice answered, one of the interpreters. I pulled on clean socks and began to pack, trying to beat the hangover by ignoring it. Sasso stood in the tent flap.

"Here you are, Mr. Brady, three days' rations."

"Thanks, Sasso. Everyone got theirs?"

"Yessir. Where we going, Lieutenant?"

"Field problem, Sasso, that's about all I know."

"Guy handing out rations said Kimpo."

"Sasso, get out of here. I've got packing."

Boy, we really kept secrets, didn't we? The rucksack was nearly filled already and no rations in there yet. I broke open the cardboard cartons. Peaches, pears, coffee, toilet paper, sugar, they went in. The tins of pork and beans, chicken, franks and beans, I looked at them, gagging, then annoyed at myself, I jammed it all into the rucksack, knowing tomorrow I would again be healthy, hungry. I sipped from the canteen, just a little, suspecting what water could do to a stomach like this. The jerrican was cold, and I refilled the canteen with fresh water. It might be hot later on. I lugged the pack over to the tent flap and swung it through. It was still night, a few cigarettes glowing, here and there a flashlight's beam. Men shouted and tents came down heavily, jeeps and maybe a truck or two revved their motors, and you could hear the metallic click of rifles being stacked and unstacked. Overhead were plenty of stars but no moon. The stars were enough to see by, to work by. That was one thing you learned, living out, how much light the stars gave, if you used them, if you stayed away from artificial light and let your eyes adjust. I skirted the tent guy lines and walked over toward the road. There were more lights down there, men loading heavy gear into the trucks: tents and water cans, stoves and cases of ammo, big boxes of rations. That stuff would go by road, meeting us at Kimpo, with the choppers carrying the men and their weapons and packs. I unbuttoned my pants and urinated on the ground. Hell with it, we were leaving and I wasn't going to stumble around looking for a piss tube still operating. Then I thought of the people who would hold this position next, and I kicked a little dirt over the dark stain in the dust. Scott came up to report.

"All squared away, Lieutenant, ready to move out."

It was 3:15. We'd done all this in just over an hour. There was an hour or more to go before light. I was getting sleepy, but the tent was down and furled, and I told Scott to let people crap out for a while but stay together.

"Okay, you people," Scott said, "crap out, *crap!* But stay close."

I wondered what Yale would think these days of Scott. I eased myself down slowly and slumped against the rucksack, my legs out straight in front of me. It was comfortable and I nodded off. Then I woke, chilled in the damp of morning, the sky still dark but the first birds sounding. It was five o'clock and gray daylight when the helicopters came. Runners came around with embarkation orders. The intelligence section would move early, with one rifle platoon going in ahead to set up a perimeter defense. The rest of Fox Company would follow us, then the rest of the staff, the other two companies and the machine guns and mortars and everything else. We were airborne about five thirty. I felt okay now, tired and headachey, but really good compared to earlier. The flight was wonderful. Behind us the eastern sky had exploded into pinks and reds with dark streamers of cloud drifting across the color. We flew low, just skimming hills, over a small river, the Imjin, I figured. We flew over Korean villages, the first farmers up and in the fields, women in their long dresses hurrying out of the houses to see the commotion, a child looking up and waving and then sticking his hand in his mouth, smoke coming from chimneys. Water shone in the puddles, picking up the pinks of dawn. A bony cow with its ribs showing grazed along a paddy's dike. Dirt roads ran like spokes from the villages and then pinched out in the fields. A dog chased the chopper's shadow across the uneven ground. He must have been barking, but above the motor noise you could hear nothing, not even shouted talk. I'd not seen many Korean villages or civilians, and I kept looking down, like a tourist, sitting on the floor near the copter's open door, three other marines in there with me, all of us easy and relaxed and enjoying the ride, trying to see out the door as the slipstream whipped our faces all rubbery and shapeless.

Then we came to a big river, about a mile across, that I figured must be the Han. A steel bridge broken in two slumped into the river mud near the far bank, and a pontoon bridge stretched across, curved nearly double its length by the current. I looked upriver, trying to see Seoul, but it was too far or I had the wrong river. I could only see country and a few villages. We came in over Kimpo Peninsula now, flying low over tilled fields. They must have seed grain in by now, I thought, wishing I knew something about farming. Away off to our left as we banked, you could just catch the sea, the Yellow Sea. That was something to think about, the Yellow Sea with all of China on its far shore. The sun bounced off paddies and huts and the tilled field, and I saw one old gent walking behind an ox, holding the reins. It was wonderful country, really, and it was a shame we had to foul it up. A damned shame.

The helicopter came down in a stubble field near a crossroads. The roads here were dirt too, and now the rotor blades whipped up dust and sent it swirling, and when I jumped out I closed my eyes against it. The copter moved away smartly. It was a half hour's trip, and there were a lot of marines still waiting to be moved. A marine came running over to us.

"Come on, get the lead out. Come on, get off the landing area." Then he saw my bars and snapped a quick salute. "If you could move your people, Lieutenant, that would be a help."

I told him what section we were.

"Yes, sir. Just over there. If you'll set up over there on this slope of that knoll. That's Battalion CP."

"What about my scouts and the interpreters? Orders say I'm to attach them to the rifle companies."

"Don't know anything about it, Lieutenant. Use your judgment, I guess." Some more marines were on the landing area watching their copter climb and bend away to the east again. "Come on, let's move out. Off the strip," the marine shouted.

I waved the men over and they trotted across the field. Sasso and Scotty were there. Now from the other end of the field came two of the interpreters and another scout.

"All right," I said. "We're in operation. That knoll's the CP. Scott, set us up there. Sasso?"

"Yes, sir."

"Those men up the road toward those hills, that must be the perimeter setup. Get on up there and find out. If it is, report to the platoon leader and stay with him. When their company commander comes in, report yourself to him. Stay with them until the problem secures. Then get back to me or Scott. Take an interpreter."

Sasso shouted at one of the Koreans, and the two moved off fast, their packs bouncing as they jogged across the road and into the other field. This was nice flat, dry ground here, like Kansas fields. Scott was staking out a bit of ground for the section. I dropped the pack and wiped my face, dusty over a film of sweat. That was good, the booze was coming out. Better to have it come out that way than, you know, the other way. I took a drink from the canteen. It tasted good this time. Two more copters were coming in now. Scott sat down on his pack and took out a cigarette. I started to sit down and decided against it, feeling embarrassed about feeling sick earlier and wanting to show I was okay now, that I didn't have to sit. Really, I did feel remarkably well. Maybe helicopter rides were good for hangovers, maybe you could patent the idea.

"Brady, I want you."

"Yes, sir." It was the colonel. He looked older and mangy, but he bounced along on those spindly legs and didn't look tired. He had his driver and the executive officer, Keeler. Keeler was out of Birmingham and had a soft drawl. He had his map case open and was laying out the maps, the driver holding them so they wouldn't blow.

"Brady, where's the enemy?"

I showed him on the map and then on the ground where the enemy was supposed to be.

"What do you make it, Keeler, two miles?"

"Two, two and a half, Colonel."

"Brady, I want you to move up there and tell the platoon leader to push on toward the hills. Move fast and spread out. You go with him. Leave one of your people here to simulate an intelligence section while you're gone. Course, we're always simulating intelligence, aren't we?" He was still cackling as I tossed off the order to Scott. The old man was really making me work for having forgotten to ask him to the party. It would be a while before I gave a party again, I guessed, and a good thing.

I slung my pack and began to move up the road at a dogtrot with the scouts and two interpreters. Then I remembered something the colonel had forgotten, that scouts and interpreters were to be attached to the other rifle companies not yet ashore. I sent back two scouts with the message for Scott. God, these field problems were worse news than the damn war.

Through the pleasant morning and the hot afternoon we maneuvered and fought a simulated battle through low hills. At five we secured the problem and marched back down to the valley, where the colonel and his staff critiqued the day's work. I sat on the ground, back curved with fatigue, sweat and dust dried on my face, and thought back. The day Simonis went into the valley and we went down to bring them out was worse than this. But then there had been danger to drive us, the spur of fear and then of hope. Today was nothing but drudgery and heat and choking dust and two hours' sleep and the whisky inside me. For a moment I wished we were back on the line. But it was stupid to feel that way. I ought to know better.

We slept out that night. A good night. In the morning we marched five or six miles north and set up camp in defilade behind a line of hundred-meter hills, just mounds, really. North of the hills was the Han River, where it bent left and flowed to the sea, more than a mile wide here, and with a terrible tide, I'd read somewhere, that rose and fell twenty or thirty feet. On the opposite shore were the houses of a sizable fishing village. The Chinese Eighth and Fourteenth Armies were there, in that village and in the country beyond. I knew that from the maps and the intelligence reports, not from what I saw. Because you couldn't see a thing move.

South Korean artillery just north of us shelled the Chinese every day, and the Chinese returned fire. Now it was full spring, April, with May coming, and except for the artillery it was very pleasant on the Kimpo Peninsula, especially since everyone believed we were here for a reason, that we would soon be going north again, across the Han or outflanking them along the coast. So we enjoyed Kimpo while we waited to go north, and took consolation in the belief that when we moved, it would be by sea, the way marines were meant to move, and not up the forward slopes of the hills, damn them.

28

Throughout April we ran problems, some of them landings on the Han beaches from landing craft, on our side of the river. We left the distant shore to the chinks.

And we tried not to think of what it might be like if it worked out the other way round and it was the Chinese who came south.

If they came and if they would take the losses, they would go through us. Not even a marine division could stop them. We were realists. Twenty thousand good men do not stop two hundred thousand, and that was what the Chinese had in the Eighth and Fourteenth Armies, and behind them were eight hundred thousand more Chinese. The marines knew this and, knowing it, tried to ignore it. We were south of the Chinese Army on the route they would have to take if they came south again, and we would stay there until we were ordered out or the Chinese came over us. It was best not to think too much about this.

So we thought about other matters.

The Bible adjures men to spend their talents wisely, never wasting them, but using them fully and for good. Ramon Gibson, the new air officer with the Battalion, put this biblical advice to better use than any man I'd yet known. His father had been an American diplomat and his mother was Latin American, and Gibson had grown up at various embassies throughout South America and spoke Spanish and Portuguese as well as he spoke English. He was educated as an aeronautical engineer and had flown fighter planes in the War and again in Korea. Between wars was when Gibson had followed biblical strictures so admirably. He got a job with an airplane manufacturer, was given South America as his territory, and for five years he flew around the continent, selling planes, discussing them technically, and convincing prospective customers in their own language he was more than just another *Yanqui* hustler. In those years Ramon Gibson married, had children, and made a good deal of money. Now he was in Korea.

Each marine rifle battalion has one or two aviators who are active flyers but who for brief periods of time are grounded and attached to the battalions to call in and coordinate air strikes or to direct reconnaissance flights over enemy lines. Gibson was put into my tent when we settled in at Kimpo, and we became friends. He was handsome, urbane, older, and the sort of marine flyer you expected to see on recruiting posters. Ramon had been shot down the month before. His plane had gone in over friendly ground, but he had been concussed, so now he was with the Battalion and, at least for the moment, once again a foot soldier. Of course, in a sense, all marine flyers are still infantrymen. This is what the book says, and the Corps tries to make it so, with every flyer reverting for two weeks a year to commanding troops or running problems as an infantry officer. All of them were trained that way in the beginning, at Quantico, but marine flyers, or naval aviators as they are called, sometimes are softened by the good life as pilots. Still, in a pinch, most of them can do a competent job on the ground. Gibson could. Rob Jardine was our other aviator, a loud, gross man, quite funny but undisciplined, totally unlike Gibson. Like most infantrymen who publicly were contemptuous of flyers, calling them "airedales" and "flyboys," I really held them in some awe since they could do something I couldn't do: fly an airplane. I never admitted this, naturally.

Jardine and Gibson and most marine aviators flew Corsairs. "Great plane," Gibson said, "a real workhorse. The bombload they can carry for a fighter, the structural damage they can sustain and still get you home, the way you can't stall them, even at very low speed, their maneuverability."

The problem was, they were World War II propeller planes in a jet age, just too slow. But the Marine Corps had ordered and paid for thousands of Corsairs and wanted to get its money's worth, hating to waste a dollar, and so the Corsairs were still flying.

"The one great worry," said Gibson, "is that one day by sheer accident a Corsair flown by someone crazy like Jardine is going to shoot down a Mig. It'll be pure accident, of course, but in a war anything can happen. And if it does they're going to order 10,000 more Corsairs and we'll be flying them against rocketships in the Second Interplanetary War."

What Corsair pilots had decided, Ray told us, was that if one of them happened to shoot down a Mig, the others would shoot down the Corsair before it could get home and report. I had the sense that if it were Jardine who got the Mig, there would be no shortage of takers.

Gibson and Jardine and the rest of them assigned to ground troops had to fly two hours a month to qualify for flight pay. One morning Ramon told me he was going to check out an O.Y., an observation plane, and fly down to Kimpo Airfield to get some ice from the Air Force. They had ice down there they just put out in the sun to melt, they had so much of it. We hadn't seen ice since we left the mountains, and the Battalion exec told Gibson to go ahead, okaying it that I could go along. Gibson got a jeep and we drove to Division. The plane had tandem seats. Gibson opened the windows to the hot spring weather, and we flew to Kimpo and got a couple blocks of ice. Then Gibson asked if I wanted to fly over the lines.

"Sure," I said, "I'm supposed to be the intelligence officer."

We flew north over the Double Bend of the Imjin River, where a year before the Chinese had chopped the British Gloucestershire Regiment, over the marine lines, just faint scratchings on the low ridges, and out over no man's land. As we flew north Gibson half turned and grinned at me. "Look at that," he shouted. I couldn't see anything.

"What?"

"Flak," Gibson yelled. He looked very happy, a man in his element. I felt less enthusiastic. Now I could see flashes from the ground like sunlight glinting on mirrors.

"Can they reach us?"

"Doubt it," Gibson shouted. "We're at 6,000 feet. They can't get this high with what they're using. They won't use big stuff. They figure an O.Y. like this is up here just to spot their guns, and they don't want to give it away. Anyway, I don't think so. It wouldn't be smart."

For the rest of the flight I hoped the Chinese were being terribly smart. From up here the war looked different, not real. The flak gave it reality, but since it didn't hit us, it had limited value. We flew south again.

"Want to fly her?"

"I don't know how."

"Simple, push the stick forward to go down, pull back to go up. Gently in both directions. You bank just as you'd drive a car. Take it."

I flew the plane for a few minutes. A magnificent feeling. I lost it a few times, and Gibson brought it back level, and then I began to get the feel and it was even better. I'd never felt anything like this.

Gibson swung the plane south, and we came in over the ridges to Division, where there was a short landing strip that could take a plane like this one. He banked and went in low and then, only a hundred feet above the ground, pulled up sharp, and we roared fast over the end of the runway and then skimmed the hill beyond. Ray turned back to me.

"Never be embarrassed to take a wave-off," he said.

The plane banked once more and came all the way around, and we came in again, this time lower, and Gibson brought it down smoothly on the dirt field. I never did figure out what was wrong with the first approach. As we got the ice out and loaded in the jeep I guessed that was one of many reasons Ray Gibson was a pilot and I was a foot soldier.

We sat out the war in Kimpo for most of April. The weather turned really hot and I wondered what it would be in July and August. There was no rain, and sleeping out or under canvas was fine. We ran problems day and night, but these hills were nothing, not after the mountains, and the men were so toughened by winter that, as Hoops might have said, "they cut the hills like there was none." The chinks and our gooks shelled each other back and forth across the Han. I went up a couple of times to the Korean observation posts on the south bank of the river and lay there in a trench watching through glasses the Chinese on the far shore. I was intrigued by the Chinese, the notion that up there were a million of them, digging in, eating their rice, patching their sneakers, and maybe planning to come south tomorrow or the day after. Through the glasses I could just see them sometimes, working parties or people just strolling about. At that distance they didn't look that different from us. But I knew they were.

One day the entire Battalion boarded trucks and drove down to the riverbank out of range of the guns and boarded and went out on a big LST. For an hour or so we steamed up and down the river, like on the Hudson River Day Liners, and then the landing craft came alongside, and we went down the cargo nets into them and turned and swept ashore in simulated beach assaults, splashing through the shallows yelling and screaming, the way marines should. It cheered us to know we were not forgotten, not lost in this great allied army, that we were not just another infantry division of dogfaces, but that we were, and always would be, amphibious assault troops, that we were marines. I know that sounds corny, but it is how marines think. Meanwhile, the rumors percolated. The Chinese would come south, the marines would swing past them on the flank and go north. But neither army moved. We stood where we were and shelled each other and ran field problems. And waited.

Ten miles south of the Battalion was Kimpo Airfield, where Gibson and I had gone for ice. The Air Force kept its jets at Kimpo, gleaming silver Sabre Jets and some newer ones, with swept wings. Whenever the weather was clear they climbed off each morning to fly north, up the west coast of the country to what they called Mig Alley, that corner of North Korea nearest China, where the Migs stayed and fought. Everywhere else the Migs ran and did not fight, but in Mig Alley, close to their bases, they fought. Each day the jets flew north to Mig Alley, 200 miles away, killed and were killed. An hour later they came back, flying over the sea to avoid the flak, and as they neared Kimpo they began to roll, signaling their kills with a long, lazy silvered roll through the blue sky, white vapor trails stretching out through the blue miles behind. Like most marines I felt the airedales were really not fighting much of a war, but despite myself, I was moved and excited to see them come in rolling like this, knowing the distance they had gone into bandit country, what they had done there, what they had left behind them, all within the hour or the ninety minutes. It was a new kind of war, not our kind, but I loved to watch them come rolling in.

29

Toward the last week of April dispatches came in from Division. Mack Allen and I were eligible for promotion to first lieutenant. We were to report at the earliest possible date to a hospital ship riding off Inchon for physical examinations. Colonel Gregory called us in.

"You better go now. You never know when this Battalion will be moving out. We've had it too quiet to last. Too long in reserve. This Battalion's got to go in soon. Get down there and get promoted so we can get on with the war. You'll all be generals at this rate. Go on, get a jeep." He wheezed into a cackle, and as we went he shouted after us, "I want that jeep back. No sidetrips for tourism."

We left next morning, four of us in two jeeps. A lieutenant from Fox I didn't know and Charley Logan, who was a reserve going regular. He was very solemn about the physical. It meant a lot to him. The rest of us were just glad to be on an outing, jouncing along the Kimpo roads choking on Kimpo dust. About ten miles south of the camp, near the big airfield, a bullet slammed into the fender of our jeep. Mack was driving, and he kicked the jeep ahead and didn't stop until we had some trees and a hillock screening us and the road.

"Who the hell did that?" I asked. There was a gouge in the metal of the fender. There was no doubt it was a bullet. A rock tossed up by the tires couldn't have done that. Logan pulled up next to us and got out, looking mournful.

"I'll never go regular. Some damnfool will shoot me on the way."

Mack wanted to spread out and go back up the road to flush out the sniper, if that's what it was. We were only carrying side arms, and I didn't think that was a very good idea. "Besides," I said, "we're near the airfield. Probably some flyboy put a round through his tent and we just happened to be passing."

"No, dammit, it came from above. Look at the angle. It was a sniper."

"Go on, there hasn't been a guerrilla around here in a year."

Mack stalked up and down. He was a bulldog. He didn't like people shooting at him and he was ready to start hunting this guy down.

Logan and I got him back in the jeep. "Some dogface hunting rabbits," Charley said. Finally we drove off, Mack at the wheel, going slow as if to draw another shot and get its direction. After a half mile or so he straightened in his seat and pushed the jeep hard toward Inchon. We never did find out who it was that shot at us or why they fired.

The hospital ship lay a mile out from shore, a big, beautiful white ocean liner with a huge red cross on its hull. There were no big docks at Inchon, only some piers for landing barges and lighters. The tides were too high, the water close in too shallow. Along the waterfront were cranes and trucks and bulldozers, moving goods and arms up from the water to the road, to big tin warehouses or to the narrow-gauge railroad. Here and there spotted along the shore were rusted tanks and a few shot-up barges, jetsam from the Inchon landings of September 1950. I looked up and down the shore and wondered how the marines had come in on those tides and gotten over the seawall under fire. A lighter came in, and a navy coxswain took us out through swells to the hospital ship, sitting there like a hotel, swinging in neatly under a freight hatch with a fixed ladder. The cox shouted to a sailor in whites who looked at us curiously and waved a hand.

"Okay, you guys, make it snappy."

One by one we timed the swells and leaped for the ladder. There was a kind of vestibule inside the ship. The sailor stared at us. I guess he wasn't accustomed to seeing marines unless they were on stretchers.

"What do you guys want?" he said.

"We're marine officers, sailor," Charley Logan said. "Don't they salute in the navy anymore?"

"Sure, sometimes. Whaddya want?"

Mack started to say something fierce, but I stopped him. In a bureaucracy like the navy some little shit like this could make things difficult for you. "We've got orders for promotion physicals. Where's the sick bay? Where do we report?"

"Why din't ya say so?" the sailor said. "Wait here, I'll tell somebody."

We waited in the little steel vestibule for a few minutes, Harvey, the other lieutenant, muttering and Mack, calm now, watching the waves. Logan sat down with his back against the bulkhead. I had to urinate, and I tried opening a door leading farther into the ship, but it was locked. I looked out at the ocean and there was no one there, so I opened my fly and began to piss into the sea. As I did, the door opened and a young doctor in white surgical dress looked out at us.

"What are you people doing here? What do you want?" He seemed frightened to see we were wearing side arms and helmets and canvas leggings, and then he saw what I was doing. "And what do you think this is?" he said, his voice cracking.

Captain Logan shoved the papers at him. The doctor backed away, trying to read what it said on the orders but not really wanting to touch them. I buttoned my fly and looked down at myself. We didn't look all that bad. Our clothes were secondhand but they were reasonably clean, and only one of us had a mustache. I sniffed to see if I smelled bad, but I couldn't pick it up. Maybe we'd smelled this way for so long we didn't notice anymore. The doctor kept backing away.

"All right," he said, "but leave those guns with someone. You can't bring weapons aboard a hospital ship. It's against the Geneva Convention. And you'll have to take showers. No one's going to examine you like this." He turned and went inside, very quickly, slamming the door behind him.

"That's hard," Harvey said, "having to take a shower. I bet they make them do it every week or ten days out here. Probably they get paid extra for it."

Another swabbie came and we handed over our side arms, and he led us inside and down a succession of white corridors, everything neat and clean and shipshape. The showers were wonderful, plenty of hot water and new bars of soap and thick, white towels. We started then to dress, but the sailor told us no, that we would go straight to the examination now, that we should wear our towels. I didn't mind. When after showering I picked up my clothes I got a definite aroma from them, probably from my green shorts, a little yellowed by now. To an unaccustomed nose they might possibly offend. The physical was the usual, and then we sat around waiting on surgical tables and gurneys, naked except for the damp towels. The young doctor who'd done the exam came out with our papers.

"Allen, you check out. You other three fail. High blood pressure."

He ducked back out of the room. Charley Logan was indignant.

"I knew I'd flunk. It was that damned sniper and then that sailor not saluting. Those are the things that get you, that's where your high blood pressure comes from."

He was intent on going regular, making the Corps a career, and he was really upset.

Mack started to laugh.

"Well, what are they going to do with us? If you're not fit to serve as a first lieutenant then how can you serve as a second lieutenant? If you guys flunked then they ought to send you home, stateside. Right now."

"You passed," Logan said resentfully.

"Oh, hell, I'll have him try me again."

Logan was too sore to talk. I went to the door and knocked and the doctor stuck his head in. What was it now? I told him.

"So maybe you should declare us unfit for duty and send us home to recuperate, doc. I mean, high blood pressure's serious, isn't it? Strokes and all?"

"And can you test me again, doc?" Mack said.

The doctor gave us one of those Leon Errol looks that had everything but steam coming from his ears.

"Goddamned marines. Give me the papers. You pass, you all pass! Now get the hell out of here and off this ship. No wonder we have wars with people like you. Go on, shove the hell off."

When we were dressed we found our way back to the landing stage. The sailor who had first met us kept an eye on us. "The ship's store is closed," he said with a snarl. "They wouldn't sell you nothing anyway. It's for ship's crew." We hadn't even asked about the ship's store, but he kept watching us, making sure we didn't steal anything or sneak off, characters not to be trusted. It was rougher now, a real sea kicking up, with spray making the steel plates of the stage slick. We could see the lighter out there through the spray. Someone had sent a signal, and now it closed to about ten yards and then veered away. The coxswain shouted at us.

"I'll come in close as I can and you guys jump."

Logan was unhappy again. Now that he'd passed the physical and was going to become a regular he would drown or be crushed between the lighter and the ship's hull. The lighter came in, rising and falling five or six feet at a crack. Mack was going first. He stood there with his wrestler's legs bent and tensed, ready to jump. But just as he coiled, the lighter fell away, too far.

"Can't do it," the cox yelled. "I'll bang the son of a bitch and catch hell. I'll be back for you in the morning."

He didn't wait for an answer but just turned over his tiller and made for the shore, quickly hidden in spray and a heavy rain slanting down. And so we stayed aboard that night, with Logan talking the officer of the deck into sending a signal to Battalion. "Just in case the shit hits tonight. Wouldn't want old Gregory to run us up on desertion."

They assigned us cabins, with real bunks and sheets and pillowcases and little stainless steel sinks with mirrors and actual wardrobes with hangers. At six we went into the officers' mess for dinner, the food served on plates by Filipino messboys. We were given a separate table, no one came by to talk to us. There were doctors and line officers and even some nurses. I remembered navy nurses from *Mister Roberts* and *South Pacific*, pretty, friendly girls who talked to everyone. No one came near us. The nurses and the doctors and the ship's officers talked and laughed among themselves, shutting us out as if this were some snooty fraternity house dining room and we were some strangers who didn't know the secret Deke handshake. Logan, who had just signed himself up for life in the Marine Corps, the Corps he loved, cursed steadily but low about it. "We're shit," he kept saying, "just shit."

Mack didn't say anything but I knew he felt that way too. Harvey kept watching the nurses. I thought it was rotten, knew it was rotten. The only time we had ever seen the navy they damned near killed us with those eight-inch shells from the cruiser and now the navy was snubbing us. Of course we smelled bad. We weren't stupid, we knew that. Of course we had high blood pressure, how could it be otherwise, living as we did, running up and down hills, eating rations, fighting the chinks, fighting a war. It was so damned mean that not one officer or nurse came over to ask how we were and what it was like or just to say hello and offer a cigarette. Yet that night, when we secured, I lay for the first time in six months in a real bed, with sheets and a pillow, white sheets that were crisply pressed, and I knew we were lucky. The men on this ship would never know what it was really like, what war was, what a simple pillow in a starched pillow slip could mean. They would go home as we would, if we were lucky, with the same medals and with their war stories, but it wouldn't be the same and never could be. We had something they would never have.

And there was something else that cheered me up, and in a way even made me feel tolerant of these navy people. I knew we would not be forgotten on this ship, even when we disappeared in the morning into the great maw of the war, back to anonymity and the hills. It was something Harvey did, after dinner, when the coffee was served, something Harvey said that would be remembered. He had been very quiet, unnaturally so for he was a loud, voluble man, staring at the nurses who sat easily chatting with these crisp, starched young officers. There was one girl who seemed especially to have tugged at his imagination, with a ripe body and a quite lovely face. As she sat there talking, she moved occasionally in her chair, displaying long legs and considerable body action. I thought perhaps she reminded Harvey of a lover, or a wife, and I was touched that this large, gross man should be so moved by a fancied resemblance that he was for once struck dumb. Then, as a sort of calm fell in the mess, a lull in the talk and the clinking of cups, Harvey said, almost thoughtfully, but quite loudly:

"If she only knew it, but that girl's sitting on a gold mine."

In the morning the lighter took us off and we returned to the Battalion, Mack and I first lieutenants.

To a civilian it must sound superficial, shallow, but being promoted in combat meant something, and Mack and I couldn't wait to pin on silver bars. Only problem, they didn't have any, and in the end someone suggested a bit of adhesive tape stuck on the gold bars would look dull silver, so we did that.

I never did get a set of real silver bars.

30

It was about noon, a free morning with some of the platoons being paraded for one reason or another but for most of us little but the endless repetition of garrison chores, cleaning rifles, polishing mess gear, washing clothes, writing letters, sharpening knives. It was hot for this early in the season. Mack and I and the flyer Gibson, sharing a tent, lay on our cots, the skirts of the tent neatly rolled so we got what breeze there was. You could hear shouts from a volleyball game somewhere up the company street, the words unclear. Then there were other shouts, also unclear, but you knew they were different from the volleyball shouting. Scott came into the tent, without even the courtesy knock, which was unlike Scott, a stickler with officers.

"Mr. Brady, there are some gooks out here. They say some marines shot up their village, attacked some women."

I spun my legs off the cot. Mack was up with me. I knew Scott was excited or he wouldn't have said "gooks." He liked to be proper about such things. We went outside, where six or seven Korean men stood, talking to anyone who would listen. One of my interpreters was with them. There were also two women, one of whom looked middle-aged to me, the other very old.

"Ask them what happened."

The interpreter talked some more. One of the men answered and the rest fell quiet, but the younger of the two women whimpered and tugged nervously at her long white

206

dress. The Korean who was talking, apparently the head man of the village, talked for quite a while, and when he paused the interpreter asked another question, and this answer was as long, with gestures.

"All right," I said, "let's not have the story of his life. What happened?"

"He says two marines came to their village this morning. They shouted for women. The people closed themselves in their houses and a few ran into the fields. The marines tried to force some doors but couldn't get in. Then they went to the house of these two women, who are a mother and her daughter. When the women would not open the door the marines fired their guns in the sky. The women were afraid, so they opened. The marines went inside and closed the door. When they came out they went through the village shooting at the houses and telling the people not to tell anyone they had been there or they would kill them. This man knows some English words. He understood what they said. Then the marines left and the people came out. It was agreed they should come to tell what happened and to ask for justice. That is what he says."

"They'll get justice," Mack said, sounding tough.

"What did the marines look like?" I asked.

The interpreter and the head man talked some more. "They were young, in uniforms like yours. One had blond hair. They had carbines, not rifles."

"Is he sure about that?"

There was more Korean dialogue. "Yes, Lieutenant. He knows the difference. He is sure."

"Well," said Mack, "that's something." He stopped and then looked brighter. "Hey, maybe they weren't marines at all, maybe they were soldiers."

There was more talk. "No, he says they had yellow legs." The interpreter looked down at the canvas leggings we all wore.

"Damn," Mack said. So it was marines.

I told Scott not to let anyone leave. Mack and I went over to the executive officer's tent and told him what had happened. He sent a runner to tell the company commanders to muster their men.

"If two men are missing, then we'll know who it is. You believe the gooks, do you?"

"Yes, sir," I said. "I saw their faces."

"Well, don't believe everything a gook tells you."

"No, sir."

"Sir," Mack put in, "they'll be back here by this. Those gooks took an hour to come up to the camp, least as I figure. They were shy about coming up. Couple of marines could have made it from that village in ten minutes."

"Probably right. Still, we'll have the muster."

"Sir," I said, "they had carbines. That makes it like they're headquarters company or machine gunners, or else mortars. Not like they're rifle platoon."

"All right. Colonel Gregory's at Regiment. I'll assign you two investigating officers. Report to me when you have something." He turned to go back inside the tent. "One thing. I don't mind marines being a little wild. And I don't much like gooks. But we're not going to have rape. This Battalion is going to have discipline. They're marines. We won't have rape." He went inside.

"Well, we've got it, whether he likes it or not."

"Yeah," Mack said. "First time we've been billeted near civilians and this happens."

"Come on, let's find out who did it."

We had them by two o'clock. All companies mustered out. But the heavy machine-gun platoon had had gun drill that morning, dry firing without ammo. Two men had been excused. They had been on the loose for at least three hours. We questioned men in their section. The men were reluctant to say anything about their mates. Finally it came out that they had come back in around noon, sweating and one of them looking very nervous. Mack and I marched the two gunners up to our tent.

"Why did you do it?" I asked. I didn't like to look at them but forced myself to watch their eyes.

"Do what, Lieutenant? We didn't do nothing."

"Mack, ask the doctor to come up here. I'm going to have him take a urinalysis."

"Jesus, Lieutenant. We didn't do nothing. We been in camp all morning."

"None of your section saw you from before nine until

208

around noon. That's three hours, plenty of time to get down to that village and raise hell.''

''Jesus, Lieutenant.'' This gunner was doing the talking. The other was quiet, rubbing his hands together. Under his fatigue cap his hair was like straw. The Koreans had said one was a blond.

''What weapons do you carry?''

''Carbines, Lieutenant, you know that. Carbines.'' He remembered me from when I had the machine-gun platoon.

''Sasso, get their weapons and let me know if they've been fired. If they have, don't fool with them. Lock them away somewhere.''

''Jesus, Mr. Brady, I didn't do nothing. I swear it.'' Now it was ''I'' and not ''we.'' I didn't say anything and the blond marine just stood there.

Allen came in with the Battalion surgeon, a plump young man just out of med school. He looked embarrassed but he had two sample bottles.

''Doc, can you get a urine sample from them?''

''Sure, Jim, sure. But you know . . .''

''Well, then, let's do it. Right here. They can do it right here.''

Scott took the bottles from the doctor and handed them to the marines. He jerked his head at them. ''Go ahead, fill them.''

The two men opened their pants and urinated into the bottles. I took them. The bottles were hot, nearly full.

''Scott, watch them. We'll be outside.'' Mack, the doctor and I went out. Gibson followed, not saying anything, just looking stricken and unhappy. He was probably thinking things like this didn't happen in the air wing.

''What do you say, doc?''

''What do you want me to say? You can't tell anything from a test like this, nothing you could use in court. Nothing.''

''Doc, just tell me if there's sperm in those samples. That's all I need. Sperm. Just tell me that.''

''Oh, shit,'' the doctor said. He held the two bottles up to the sunlight. Mack looked over his shoulder, trying to see something himself. I watched the doctor's face.

''Well?''

"Okay, so there's sperm. More in one sample than the other, but there's sperm in both."

I nodded. I'd been so damned sure, it wasn't even a surprise. Mack grabbed my arm.

"Jim, we've got them. That was smart, Jim."

"Not so smart," the doctor said. "They could have had an ejaculation of any sort, could have masturbated. Sperm will show up in the urine for hours afterward."

"Reveille went at six. That's more than eight hours. Could it be there eight hours?"

"There may be specialists in this shit but I'm not one of them!" the doctor said, angry.

"Could it be there?" I shouted.

"No, possible but not likely." He hated this.

"Well, then?" I said. There's a policeman in all of us.

"Look, they could have masturbated since."

"Pretty difficult to find that kind of privacy around here. And I never heard of two marines going off into the hills to jerk off. One maybe, but not two."

"They could be homos. Dammit, Brady, I'm not saying they did, just that they could have."

"Could have, but didn't. Here's Sasso. What about the carbines?"

"Fired, Lieutenant, both of them. You can smell it."

"Okay," I said, very sure of myself.

I started back into the tent. "Bring the gooks in here, the women and the head man."

"Wait a minute, Jim," Mack said, "if you're going to run an identification parade, we'd better rustle up some more marines, make it a regular lineup."

"Boy, you're right. I'm starting to forget things. Sasso, get six marines up here, dressed, with leggings."

Sasso went off. In the tent the two machine gunners were standing close together but not talking. Gibson looked at the ground. Scott was looking at the marines, not understanding, or maybe understanding and not wanting to. I asked them a few more times why they had done it, and the talky one kept saying they hadn't done anything, that he hadn't done anything. The blond one still didn't say anything. Then Sasso was back with the marines.

"Ask them which were the ones who did it. Are they here?"

The interpreter put the question. The older woman looked blank. The head man began to jabber and point. The younger woman looked at them all and put her head down.

"Are they here?"

"She says yes."

"Which?"

The woman looked up and pointed. Then she pointed again. It was the two machine gunners.

"You sure, lady?"

The interpreter put the question. The woman pointed again and then looked down.

"Scott, dismiss the rest of them." I turned to the machine gunners. "You men are under arrest. Jardine, Sasso, take them down to the exec. If he tells you to, take them to Division to the brig. Mr. Allen and I will write a report."

Ramon Gibson seemed confused by the whole business. "What will happen to them?"

"Hell," Allen said, "you're the captain. Haven't you ever gotten mixed up in something like this before?"

"Sure, court-martials. One thing and another. Never a rape case."

"Well, we don't have one every day, you know." Mack was protective of the Battalion.

I didn't say anything. It was still daylight but I was very tired, sitting on the bunk listening to Mack and Ray. Gibson was less shocked now, permitting himself to be amused by it. "Brutal and licentious soldiery," he muttered. Well, it was fine to be amused about it now, but it disgusted me. Marines shooting up a village, terrorizing people, raping those two old women with their faces like baked potatoes. How could they do it, how did they think they could get away with it? This way we were as bad as the Nazis and the Japs, attacking civilians, attacking women. It undid everything we were trying to do, saving their country for these people, giving it back to them. In that village they wouldn't remember that Americans died for their two-bit village. They would only remember their day of horror when two Americans, two marines, for God's sake, raped their women at gunpoint.

211

The blond marine was the son of a minister. The other was up for promotion to corporal. Their records had been excellent and now they faced a general court. This damn reserve, this being around civilians, it was no good. We'd been too long away from the war, losing what we had on the line, the pride, the discipline, the professionalism. Not wanting to say anything to Gibson, who wouldn't understand, or even to Mack, who would, I longed for the clean, hard purity of the line. Dedication and celibacy, harsh and cleansing, puritanic, that was the line, that's where we belonged.

Weeks later we were told the two marines had gotten off. The case had been badly made, in part by Mack and me, and a good lawyer got them off. They were transferred, of course, and we never saw them again.

31

It was evening, and Mack Allen and the two pilots Gibson and Jardine and a few others were there, talking and smoking in a big new tent we had with sandbagged walls four feet high on all sides. The Battalion had come up on the line again on May Day, when the Chinese had fired off all their guns just as we'd done at Christmas. Now it was the second or third day on the line, with the rifle companies holding a hill called 212. The British Commonwealth Division was again on our right, but a different regiment, Canadian this time. On the left we had a battalion of marines. We got the May Day shelling and then some small-arms fire, but otherwise it was pretty quiet considering the low ground. Both flanks of 212 fell away until it was just valley with nothing barring the way south except mines and wire and the men. You ran out of good terrain in these little valleys and you filled in with guns. Bob Simonis was leaving the Battalion, being sent back to some pogue job in the rear. He'd been there when Mack and I arrived and had stayed with Dog Company and his rifle platoon the whole time. We sat around with Bob, talking about it, how green we'd been, how John Chafee must have shuddered when he saw us but never let on, about all Chafee had taught us, how wonderful he'd been commanding green officers.

"No, you weren't that green," Simonis said. "You were good men, both of you, and Chafee knew it, right from the start. Not green at all. You did a job for Dog, we all did."

213

That pleased me, and I think even Mack was pleased. It wouldn't be the same without Simonis, as it hadn't been the same without Chafee.

"Sure it will," Simonis said. "This is a good battalion. The rifle companies are good. So is the staff. And the colonel. You'll do all right. Take care of yourselves. Maybe we'll meet again."

He reached out to touch both of us on the arm. Touching like that meant something to you and the smile that went with it. I can't explain it, but we had been through something together and you touched to remember it. Maybe Simonis was remembering how I went down into the valley that morning to help get him out. Then he was gone, smiling back at us from the truck, not waving but looking back until they rounded a bend in the road and were lost in the dust. Only Mack and I were left now from the old Dog Company. Red Philips was out on that island and Chafee was gone and Ed Flynn and Tex Lissman, stripped bare that night the patrol was called off at the last minute. And Lissman had been a good man. Even good men could take only so much. Now the good men were gone, though, to be fair, most of the new men were pretty good, too. I thought about that as we sat around in the tent smoking cigarettes and talking, and mostly listening to Jardine, the flyer. He was probably a good man too, in the air, but on the ground he was just loud and a bastard.

The next day, or maybe it was two days later, anyway it was the fourth, we had our morning staff meeting on a beaten piece of ground in front of Colonel Gregory's tent. We sat in a circle, smoking and chatting. Somewhere a volleyball thumped and you could hear marines shouting. It sounded nice, hearing a ballgame and sitting in the sun, warm but not yet hot. Mack had his hat off, trying to get the sun on his face. I was rolling a cigarette, the way Princeton taught me, and then the exec came out followed by the colonel, cackling at something the exec had said, but when Gregory came into the circle the cackling faded and the talk died and we were all business. The way it went, this morning and every morning, was that each staff officer would stand up and speak his little piece: Mack would give the personnel situation; I would issue the password for that night and any pertinent intelligence information; Major Nicholson, the S-3, would talk about patrols and other operations; the chaplain would say when services were; the supply officer would give the rations and ammo report; and so on. On this day it all went routinely, as it usually did, and then Jardine stood to give the air report, looking around the circle of officers, and began to recite, in a singsong way: "Hooray, hooray / The Fourth of May / Outdoor fucking / Starts today."

Jardine was transferred back to the Air Wing shortly after that, and he celebrated the event by buzzing the camp low in his Corsair, so low three tents were blown down, and scaring all of us, sending me, and I was not alone, diving into a muddy trench. None of us had ever been strafed that I knew of, but if this was what strafing was like, I wanted no part of it. Later in the spring we heard from someone who knew him that Jardine had come in low like that again, on his way home from a mission, and had clipped one of the last power cables left hanging. He landed safely, but some of his Corsair was left behind. I didn't like Jardine or miss him, almost no one did, and gradually his name faded in the mess, though his Fourth of May poem lived on in the Battalion. That was how it was, a man was part of your life, you liked him or you didn't, but he was there and had meaning. Then he was gone, and after a few weeks his name wouldn't come up. That was how it was getting with Chafee even, although not for Mack and me. Charley Logan had Dog Company, and we sometimes went up to visit with him, but there was no talk with him of Chafee, whom he was self-conscious about having replaced. The platoon leaders had barely known Chafee or didn't know him at all. To them, he was simply a bit of Company history.

The piece of line the Battalion now held was in all respects but one a perfectly normal MLR. The one exception was extraordinary. The truce talks were going on, had been going on intermittently since our replacement draft arrived late the year before. They had become a fact of life and would, probably, go on forever, and they did little to alter the face of war. Except in this sector, where the Battalion stood, and where the truce talks became a tactical consideration.

Sticking out from each MLR, ours and the Chinese, were narrow dirt roads leading to Panmunjom and the straggle of tents and huts where the negotiators met. These two roads, and a small circle around the truce site itself, were considered neutral ground, and it was forbidden to fire weapons in the area. At night a single searchlight blazed vertically into the blackness, warning off planes, and identifying the neutral zone to all of us who could see it. This light became a factor when you went out in front of the lines at night, avoiding being silhouetted against it, using it to guide you. And the roads leading to Panmunjom became a favorite route for patrols entering no man's land from either side. You could use the road so long as you moved away to either side before you shot anybody. An unreal and stupid rule, but both sides took advantage of it. I walked out one day along the road, it having become the thing to do, and I wanted to see the ground close. Weird, being out there by daylight, reasonably sure no one was going to take a shot. I was startled by a fox that burst from some brush and ran across my path. Later, I saw pheasant, and someone else said he had seen deer, all along the ribbon of road leading to Panmunjom. Somehow the wildlife learned that along this little corridor, they were safe. Anywhere else they, like the men, were fair game.

But if the truce corridor was quiet, the rest of the line was not. Maki, who had my old platoon, took a daylight patrol out, using peculiarities of the ground to remain masked from the Chinese lines. But they ran into firing, small arms and mortars, and five men were hit. I had a scout out with the patrol, Sasso, and when they came in I was there to ask him what happened.

"Lieutenant, we got lost."

"What do you mean, lost? Broad daylight. And you weren't five hundred yards out."

"I know, Lieutenant. We had these checkpoints, see. All we had to do was hit the checkpoints and we'd be in defilade, covered all the way. It should've been a stroll on the beach. We kept picking up signs all the way of chinks, how they come up to our line at night, the trails they use. We even found a burp gun out there, and a couple of stiffs. Some other stuff, too. Well, we missed the damn checkpoints."

"How the hell could you miss a checkpoint? Who was reading the map, you?"

"No sir," Sasso said, "that's the point. The lieutenant, Mr. Maki, he was reading the map. He got us lost."

I stopped myself at that, wanting the story but not wanting to be in the situation of listening to an enlisted man criticizing another officer on a serious matter. Then I thought about five men hurt from my old platoon. Sasso was a good man, the best scout I had, and I said the hell with it.

"So he got you lost. Did you tell him?"

"Lieutenant, I told the man three times he was on a wrong leg, and finally he told me to shut up and I did. It was right after that we came under Chinese eyes and we got incoming mortar and some small arms. We missed the checkpoint and were on a wrong leg, sitting out there like ducks on the pond. He marched us into the open and we caught it." Sasso shook his head thoughtfully, as if he still couldn't believe Maki's incompetence.

"Okay, Sasso. Don't go telling that story around. I want to look into it."

"Lieutenant, I don't tell stories around. Not when people get hit. I don't want no arguing with officers. But I don't want to go out with that man again."

"Okay, Sasso, that's enough. Go get yourself some chow."

Dils was one of the wounded, still one of the third platoon's squad leaders. He'd been hit in the groin by shrapnel, and the helicopter had already taken him out. One of his squad, Greaves, had also been hit, but not badly. I went to see Greaves, to ask how it was, and about Dils.

"Son of a bitch, Mr. Brady, it was worth getting hit just to see old Dilly's face when he got it in the balls. You know how quiet he always is, and I thought I was going to die right out there from laughing. I mean, I laughed first because it was funny, someone getting hit that way, and then I see Dils hopping around on one foot pulling down his pants to see how bad it was, and wiping away the blood with his hand to see that it wasn't so bad, that he was still a man. I couldn't stop laughing. That Dils, though, he'll have my ass when he gets back, for laughing when he didn't know if he had a pecker anymore."

I left Greaves and went back to the CP, wondering what

to do about it. I was as full of hate for Maki as I'd ever been for the damned gooks. I thought maybe I should call him out, fight him, and even if Maki beat me, which considering how big he was was likely, I would have had the satisfaction of letting him see my anger and contempt. Then I thought I should just tell the exec or the colonel and leave Maki to official punishment. In the end, I did nothing. Surely even a man as dumb as Maki would be affected by what happened and would use his head next time and not get anyone killed. We all did stupid things; we all made mistakes. It was ironic, Dils being one of the men hit, when a mistake of mine had nearly gotten him killed. I knew only that I didn't want to see Maki again, that I would not be able to talk to him. Maybe Maki would have the sense to ask for a transfer, to get away from these men who knew how he'd fouled up. It didn't work that way. Nothing was ever that neat. Maki came down to the CP a week later and, as he passed, waved to me casually and said "howdy," just as if nothing had happened. Instinctively, I'd raised a hand in greeting and mouthed "hello," and then he'd passed and I knew this was the way it had to be. You could not carry hate too long without it eating into you. No one had named me judge over Maki or anyone else, and whenever there were this many men thrown together there would always be the weak and the stupid and the careless. And we would fight the damned war despite them. I told Mack about it and he said I was right, but it convinced him the colonel was right to keep us around, in case the Division went north, or the chinks came down, because people like this Maki were sure to be killed off early in the first quarter.

"Guys like that never die, Mack. They don't have the imagination."

"Well, Jim, Maki ought to be glad Chafee isn't still here. He would have had him up on charges."

"Maybe that's what we should have done," I said darkly, and when Mack saw my face he didn't like what he saw there. He stopped talking about it and neither of us mentioned it again.

I went out myself on the next patrol, a night stroll out the corridor and a short march into the valley between the lines. There was no firing, no foul-up, the searchlight gave us good bearings, and we came back into the line about two with nothing but some exercise. I thought of those patrols in January and February, shivering, and with the men coughing. Two nights later Cather, one of the new Dog Company platoon leaders, took a combat patrol out the route we'd scouted, crept up quietly on an unimportant bump in the ground called Hill 69 and caught some chinks asleep. Cather and his men dropped grenades into the bunkers and shot them down as they came scrambling out. They killed thirteen chinks and came back without a casualty unless you count a marine who tore his knee on the wire. I went over it with Cather in the morning, the maps and papers and other stuff he'd brought back. Cather was very relaxed and calm about it all, so much so that when we broke, I very nearly snapped off a salute. The man was so young, so new, yet so competent and unexcited about what he'd done. In seven months I hadn't seen an action as good as this one, a perfect exercise, and Cather just seemed slightly bored. Even the colonel had Cather in to shake his hand and tell him what a fine example he'd set for the rest of us.

The same week another replacement officer came down with a bad case of nerves and announced he didn't want to take out any patrols. If a transfer could be arranged he would welcome it. You couldn't have an officer who was shook leading a rifle platoon, and the transfer came through to motor transport.

It was like that. Maki fouled up and got people shot and he stayed on. Cather, even more green, ran a perfect stunt and killed a lot of chinks. A third lieutenant quit. I thought about it for a while, and realized I hadn't been such a bad platoon leader after all, not that much of a sprinter, having stayed the course.

32

There were villages in this sector, real villages, and not the burned out, empty, desolate villages of the eastern mountains, where no one lived, from where populations had been banished. This was farming country, and here in the low hills just north of the Imjin River, people hung on in the villages and farmers worked the fields and a few paddies, in and around and in front of and behind the lines. This was the first real experience the marines had had with civilians. The rapes on Kimpo were an aberration. On Kimpo a mile-wide river, the Han, flowed between the lines, effectively screening us off from civilians in the villages on the other side. Here, around Panmunjom, there were villages all over the combat zone.

From the first day reports began to come in to intelligence of infiltrators, civilians moving back and forth between the lines, of enemy soldiers dressed as civilians, even as women in those long, flowing Korean dresses and aprons. One village at the Battalion's left flank, where the chinks and the marines faced each other a mile apart, quickly became an irritant. It had no name, did not appear on maps. It was too small. But the company holding that sector, Easy Company, kept turning in complaints to Battalion, warning that people were moving through their sector by day and night, compromising security. At the end of the first week Colonel Gregory brought the problem up at the staff meeting.

"Lieutenant Brady, as our fine intelligence officer, I think

220

it would be helpful if you went to look over this village and provide us your best judgment.''

Gregory was a needler and enjoyed addressing me with mock ceremony. I said aye, aye, sir, that sounded like a fine idea.

''You just go in there and have a little heart-to-heart with the head man. And tell him if we catch any Chinese using that village, we'll burn them out. Tell him that, and make it plain.''

I took six scouts and a couple of interpreters, and we stopped at Easy Company to talk with the company commander.

''I smell chinks over there,'' he told me. ''I can't prove it, but there must be. If I were Chinese and held that stretch of line I'd sure as hell use that village moving my people in and out, and the Chinese are smart as me. Maybe even smarter.''

I agreed with him. After a while you developed instincts about these things. Easy sent a squad along to help me find my way. The village was the usual huts scattered around a clearing, smoke hanging low in the heat, a few men working the near-in fields. Farther out were mines, or they thought there were mines, and that kept the farmers close to home. I halted the patrol on a little rise of ground, just above the village, and sent Scott and the scouts out on one flank to cut off the village from the chink lines. I didn't expect any Chinese to be there in daylight, but there was no sense taking chances. I trusted Scott and my scouts because I knew them. The Easy Company squad I did not know and I kept them with me. When Scott was in position I walked over the crest of the rise and went down quickly into the village with the squad spread out behind me. I was carrying a Thompson submachine gun, borrowed from the armorer. It was the first time I'd carried one, and it was heavy with two extra pans, but it seemed a good thing to have if there was any shooting in the restricted confines of a village. When the Koreans saw us coming, there were a few jabbered shouts, and the men working the fields dropped their tools and came running toward the huts. I waved the squad forward at a trot, and we went right through the village to the other side, where Scott waited, the scouts out in a skirmish line. There was no shooting, there was nothing, only the marines jogging through the huts, weapons hanging loose and ready, the Koreans scurrying this way and that, not knowing why we were there and worried, until we prodded them like cattle into the small, central clearing. They stood there, craning a bit to see what we were up to, a few of the women talking nervously, the men moody and silent. Scott came up.

"Nothing, Lieutenant. We've poked into every hut. Unless they're under the floor somewhere, no Chinese here. You see anything?"

"No," I told him. "Get the interpreter up here. Give me Kim." Most of the interpreters were named Kim; most Koreans seemed to be. But this Kim was the best English speaker. He was also tall, and I wanted a tall man.

"Tell them we are marines. Tell them we came here because we were told there are Chinese who come to this village at night. Tell them the Chinese are bad, that they want to take their country. Tell them that we fight the Chinese for them. Make it strong, but what I said."

Kim translated. It took longer in Korean, or maybe he added something of his own. When he finished I spoke again, standing on a smooth boulder off to one side of the clearing, a rock too big for farmers to move. I wanted to get as high as I could, talking down to them and trying to look as old and dangerous as a twenty-three-year-old without a beard could look.

"Listen to me," I said, "there are no Chinese here today. That is good. We are happy our Korean brothers have no truck with the Chinese. But I tell you this, we will come back again, these marines and more, and if there are Chinese here, we will kill the Chinese and we will burn this village and turn you into the fields. Tell them that."

Kim had to ask what "truck" meant, and I was annoyed. It broke the mood. Then Kim spoke again and every face was turned toward him, even the marines, who did not understand his words but knew what I'd said, what Kim was repeating.

"Tell them one more thing. Tell them the marines are the greatest soldiers in the world, that we wear these yellow leggings and are not like other soldiers. Tell them we kill faster and shoot farther and have greater guns than other soldiers. We will come back here and if they are our friends, we will come in peace. If they betray us, the marines will come like the locust, and this village will be stripped bare and burned black. Tell them that, and then we get out of here." I was being melodramatic and heavy-handed but I knew that. It was the tone I wanted.

When Kim finished, Scott fell in the troops, the men moving smartly, as if on the parade ground, knowing the Koreans were watching. We suspected they had often seen Chinese soldiers, and each marine stood very straight, wanting to be remembered as bigger and more fierce than the Chinese. We *wanted* to look dangerous, a matter of pride.

The head man of the village made a little speech when I had the men fallen in. He said it was well known that in this village they were all friends of the yellow legs, that no Chinese would dare come here, that this village wished only to live in peace and cultivate its fields. I nodded, saying "good" in English, and shook hands with the head man. Then we marched out through the village, and I could feel their eyes on my back.

I wondered how soon it would be that the Chinese would know every word spoken that morning in this village.

There was another village, this one closer to the Chinese lines, so close the marines could not get to it without fighting their way in. The Battalion's observation posts had this village under surveillance during daylight, and here there were no doubts about the chinks. They were there, one or two at a time, in uniform. Our people could see them through glasses. Colonel Gregory decided against shelling the village. There were women and children there.

I brought him the observation reports. "So what if there are a couple of Chinese there," he said. "It's practically in their lines. There are plenty of Chinese everywhere, Lieutenant. We don't have to shell that village just to scare a few Chinese. There's no shortage."

"Yes, sir," I said. You don't argue with old colonels.

Then one night the chinks came up and ambushed a Fox Company patrol and killed two marines. The ambush happened near the village. It was pretty clear the chinks had come through there if they hadn't been there hiding in the huts all the while. Colonel Gregory changed his mind.

"I want that village cleaned out," he told the staff meeting the next morning. "What's the best way? I don't want to hit civilians if I can help it."

There was a lot of talk. Some officers didn't seem to care if we killed civilians or not. Others were more cautious. Gregory cut in on them, curt in a way alien to our experience of him.

"One way or another I want that village cleaned out. If there are no suggestions that make sense I'll ask the S-3 to draw up an operation and we'll carry it out."

The meeting broke up. A small village had just had its death sentence pronounced, and no one there knew it. A jeep came by, the two marine bodies lashed aboard. A couple of us snapped off salutes, the jeep blowing up dust on its way through the camp, dust that already shrouded the rolled ponchos in which the dead were wrapped. The dust stung your eyes, and people said the dust was full of parasites that caused infections and gave you worms, so it was hard to keep watching the jeep as it made its way slowly toward the road and the river. I turned away. Mack Allen was standing there.

"Mack, this is some war."

"Yeah," he said, not knowing what I meant, just agreeing.

"We never fight a real battle, we don't win or lose, yet guys get killed, we wrap them up and send them south somewhere. We eat some more, we sleep some more, more of us get killed or lose a leg or go blind, and there's never a real battle and still the war goes on. Wouldn't you think one of us, them or us, would get tired of it and just pack up and go home?"

"You tired of it?"

"Awful tired, sometimes. Then I think about jumping off against them and really moving, chasing them north, breaking through the way we've been taught, the way the Division did last September and the September before that."

Mack rubbed his eyes, reddened and wet, with a dirty handkerchief.

"It'd be sweet," he said.

Before Major Nicholson could get his operation down on

paper, how he was going to clean out that village, someone else's plans took precedence.

A half mile in front of the MLR, just opposite the draw, a tongue of high ground snaked out from the chink lines, licking at the marines. The Chinese were on that tongue, dug in and invisible by day, but they had some heavy mortars, maybe four-deuces, and they shelled us hour after hour, causing casualties, cutting wire, caving in bunkers. The marines shelled back, but it had gone on now for a long time and the chinks no longer seemed to mind. They simply stayed in their holes and called in more mortar and sometimes their big guns, and the tongue of ground had become a thing the Battalion choked on, as if, in some spastic fit, it had slipped back into our throats. The tongue was 104 meters above sea level at its height. There was a village halfway up its forward slope, but dead and empty. We called the tongue 104 and the village was named Tu-mari. Fox Company was given the job of taking it and the tongue.

If the marines could take it and hold it, instead of the tongue sticking out at us, we could turn it against the Chinese MLR. Regiment and Division approved the plan to take 104 and Tu-mari, and now Fox would have to do the job. It was the biggest thing since I'd gotten to Korea, the biggest thing since last September and Hill 749. It was modestly promoted, termed simply a company raid, but if Fox carried it off, it might signal other limited offensives against the Chinese and then perhaps, if we were lucky, a real offensive by the whole Division. The ground was dry, the Division was nearly at full strength, we were ready. Hill 104 and Tu-mari waited.

When Colonel Gregory outlined the operation he suggested creating a diversion at the far end of the Battalion front, to confuse the Chinese, maybe to fool them into thinking the 104 attack was only part of a much larger action. Then they might not concentrate all their artillery on Fox. The S-3 said an attack on the Chinese-occupied village that was bothering us, coordinated with Fox's assault on the tongue, would be constructive. Gregory liked that, even cackled briefly. They sounded not like men deciding life and death but like politicians calculating the vote in an Irish ward.

Easy Company would send a reinforced platoon out into the truce corridor at midnight and take positions on Hill 69, where Cather had pulled off the good raid, and where the chinks came at night and left before dawn. They were to reach 69 about five in the morning, dig in, and direct 4.2 mortar fire on the targeted village, firing ranging shells as a warning and then, when the village was abandoned, burning it out with white phosphorus shells. A whole rifle platoon would go along just in case, this once, the Chinese stayed on 69 beyond the dawn. I decided to go, too.

Before five we knew the Fox Company raid was in trouble. The front was quiet, with only some heavy stuff way off east punctuating the silence of first light. If Fox were on schedule, we'd have heard them already, fighting their way up 104 through Tu-mari, fighting house to house. But there was no firing yet, and I knew they were late and would be making their attack in full daylight. We used to fear night and the darkness; now dawn was the enemy. No one since 749 last September had attacked successfully by day, and on 749 the Battalion lost a quarter of its strength. My Easy Company patrol moved toward Hill 69, no sounds but the rustle of dry brush against our legs, the occasional slap of a rifle stock against web gear, the easy whisper of canteens in canvas against the hip. We were at the foot of 69 when the firing finally began, off to the east of us but not far, mortars and machine guns and the heavy sound of individual rifles, then the *rrrippp* of the burp guns. Fox Company was there and they were too late. It was full light and I think we all knew. Near me a man muttered, "They're fucked. They're really fucked." With silence no longer essential, our patrol leader, a lieutenant named Settle, double-timed his men to the top of 69. There was no one there; the chinks had gone home. I trailed along, trying to read in the sounds how it was going at Tu-mari. Easy platoon worked over 69 briskly, looking for booby traps, poking into the empty bunkers, dank and stinking of rice and sweat and old sneakers. Nobody there, nothing. East of us the firefight raged. We could see smoke now, black and floating upwards in the morning air, but we weren't high enough to see the fighting. Settle got his men into the trenches and took out the radio to establish contact with our four-deuces.

I lay back in the bottom of a trench, looking at the cloudless sky and waiting for something to happen, one ear cocked to Tu-mari, the other listening to Settle. I took a good long drink from the canteen; it was going to be hot. We were wearing these brand new armored vests. They would not stop a bullet but were supposed to be very effective against shrapnails, and the one sure thing, they were heavy and hot. Sweat ran down my back between my shoulder blades and I wasn't even moving. I was skinny and didn't know where all the sweat came from; must be beer, not that I got that much of it. Then there came a single shot, close to us this one, and there was a little cry and some commotion, and I got to my feet, careful to remain crouched, protected by the trench.

"Mr. Settle's hit," someone said. I ran along the trench, bent double, until I got to where they'd laid Settle out in the trench.

"Sniper," a sergeant told me. I didn't know his name or recognize his face. Must be a new man, but he was a cool one. I would try to keep that in mind.

"Where is he? Anyone see a muzzle flash?"

That's what counts first in a firefight, not the casualties but where the fire is coming from.

"Don't know, Lieutenant. Didn't see a thing. Mr. Settle was standing up there talking and then he was falling and the sound came after."

People were working over Settle now, one of them a corpsman with his canvas bag of tricks opened.

"All right," I said, "let's everyone stay in the goddamned trench. What are the orders? What are we supposed to do next?"

"Warn the village. The four-deuces throw in a couple close. Give them five minutes. Then call in the Willie Peter." "Willie Peter" was white phosphorus. It could burn a man's flesh right off his bones, just strip him to char.

"Okay, Sergeant. You're the platoon sergeant?"

"Yessir."

"You want to take over? It's your platoon now."

"Yessir. But since you're here, I'd just as soon you do it." He looked at me. "You've been around awhile, I guess."

"Okay, I've got the platoon. Get your squad leaders over here, the forward observer. And tell that corpsman to give me a report on Mr. Settle. We might want a chopper to evacuate him."

"Aye, aye, sir."

They came crawling to me as beyond us, to the east, the firefight stormed on. More firing now, a lot of it. I guessed both MLRs had taken it up, supporting their people. The smoke was heavier now and drifting up this way on an easy breeze. Four or five marines crouched around me, very alert and paying attention. I looked at them, still listening to the fighting. Here it was quiet, nothing since the sniper got Settle.

"Look," I said, "this is just a diversion. We're to hit that village with four-deuces, that's all. But this sniper, didn't anyone see him, even get a sniff?"

No one had.

"Look, this is stupid. One lousy sniper isn't going to foul up this operation. It's five after six now. We're late. We've got to hit them soon and take their minds off Fox Company out there. Get your riflemen, your BARs up. Sweep this valley. Fire at anything you see moving. There's no high ground within sniper range, so he's got to be down there in the brush and the tall grass. You, observer, tell them they can start with their ranging shots, H.E., around the village. Then we'll give them a couple minutes and fire for effect with W.P. Got it?"

Everyone said yes, sir.

They scuttled away, this way and that along the main trench and into the shallow ditches that served as tributary trenches. The corpsman was still working on Settle, but another marine came up. "Corpsman says he's okay. Got knocked out is all." I said "Good," or something like that. The firing out east kept up, and now the first planes were coming over, dipping into the valley to drop their loads and climbing out very steeply to elude the flak ripping up from the chink lines. They were dropping napalm from the smoke of it, the smell of it, and five-hundred-pound bombs from the sound. The heavy chatter of machine guns and aerial cannon from the Corsairs echoed through the valley. It must have been something and I'd never seen a fight this big. I wished I could see it, but I did not wish I was there.

Another rifle shot crashed very close, another single shot. It must be the same sniper. He had balls to be this close in and taking on a platoon. I knelt there in the trench and yelled.

"Anyone hit? Anyone see him?"

The "no"s came back at me. This was ridiculous. One lousy sniper pinning down a platoon. You'd think we were army troops. I waved the nearest two marines to me.

"Look, get the word along the trench. I'm going to stand up and wave my arms. Tell everyone to watch the brush and try to see him. If he gets a shot off, someone's got to see him."

"Okay, Lieutenant." One of them looked at me as if I were crazy.

I let a minute pass. Now the first couple of 4.2 rounds were bursting around the village, and I peeked over the trench lip. They were good shots, near the village but not hitting it, and people in white clothes began to come out of the huts and run around, not running anywhere in particular, just running. That was how you felt during shelling.

Now I stood up, feeling naked. It was stupid giving him a target, but I couldn't think of a better way. If I really wanted to do the job I ought to climb all the way up on top of a bunker. I started to but my knee buckled. I couldn't do it, I couldn't just stand on that damned bunker. No one expected it of me and I was too scared. I raised one hand and waved, not at anyone, just a silly little wave. I should have waved both arms, standing on a bunker, really given him a chance to get off a shot. But, shit, I just couldn't. I walked a few feet along the top of the trench, exposed. Jesus, how long had I been standing up? Still no shot. The bastard must have known what I was doing and been too cagey to play. Then, after what seemed an hour and was less than a minute, I sank slowly back into a crouch and dropped into the trench. Blood money, you couldn't pay me enough to do that again. I didn't care how long I'd been standing, it was too long. I was really sweating now, not from the armored jacket, from the fear. I wiped a hand across my face and closed my eyes. Then I called out, my voice shaky, or maybe that was just imagination.

"Anyone see anything?"

Again, only "no"s.

The observer crawled back to me. "We've got a good fix on the village. You want to hit her now with the phosphorus?"

"The people out of there?"

"Can't tell. Lot of people shagged ass, but you can't tell if there's anyone left indoors. Can't say. Shall we fire for effect?"

I didn't answer. I moved toward the bunker with the observer following. There was an observation slot, and we went inside and knelt by it.

"Okay," I said, "let's hit it."

The order went out over the radio. Thirty seconds later the first rounds were in the air. When I heard them coming I stuck my head out and shouted at the platoon sergeant.

"Have your BARs zero in on the village. Anyone comes out looks like a chink, hit him."

"Aye, aye, sir."

Now the first rounds slammed in. Beautiful to watch, the red burst and then the firework streamers of burning phosphorus splashing out from the burst. You knew it must be different at the other end, a preview of hell. One hut was hit directly. It was on fire. Another hut started to burn. Phosphorus had splashed it and now someone came out running. I thought it looked like a man, but at this distance, you couldn't tell. He was in a long, white garment. The platoon sergeant shouted in my ear.

"Do we fire?"

"No, hold it. Hold your fire."

"Them chinks, sometimes they dress up like that, maybe. White stuff over their uniforms."

"I know. Just hold it."

More huts were burning, and another figure in white sprinted out and fell. Then the robe began to burn. From another hut came two more figures in white and not the khaki of Chinese uniforms. They ran, fast and bent low, zigzagging across the central clearing of the village.

"Them's chinks, Lieutenant. Women don't run like that."

"Yeah," I said.

There were a half dozen people running now through the village, all in white, one of them on fire, all sprinting away from us, toward the Chinese lines. One was carrying something. It could be a rifle. It could be a furled umbrella. It could be anything.

"Lieutenant, Jesus, let us fire. That's a weapon."

"Okay, Sergeant," I said, "fire at will."

The BARs ripped off automatic fire, heavy and fast. Two of the villagers fell right away, one trying to get up and then falling again. You could see the BAR fire kicking up dust around him. Then a W.P. shell burst just in front of him, and we couldn't see him anymore through the fire and the smoke. The whole village, every hut, was aflame now, and the BARs fired, and another white-clad figure fell. I could still see three or four of them running away, and one of them was on fire. Behind me, in the trench, someone yelled, "Christ, we're killing women!"

I whipped around.

"Who said they're women? How do you know?"

A marine stared at me. His face was twisted and I didn't know him.

"Them's women. You can see the dresses. You can't shoot women."

"They're men," I shouted. "At this distance you can't tell me they're women, not the way they run."

The BARs kept firing, nearly shutting out the firefight up at Tu-mari.

"No, and you can't tell me they're men," the marine said, not shouting now, but still staring. He looked as if he were going to jump me. I looked at him, trying to look absolutely confident, then I turned back to the platoon sergeant.

"Keep firing. They're soldiers, Chinese soldiers."

I was not sure of this, not sure of anything, but I knew the probabilities, and I also knew I was still scared from playing target. I'd made the decision to fire, and I couldn't back off now because a marine, just as scared as I was, was yelling at me. He was guessing, that's all. I continued to kneel there, not really seeing anything anymore, not really focusing. They ran like men, dammit. Women didn't run like that. Behind me the marine was still there. I could

sense him. Without turning, I said: "Go back to your post.
If you're all that worried, don't fire. You don't have to
fire."

There was a sort of sob behind me and a scurrying
movement. I felt funny kneeling there with my back to him.
The marine was shook. Armed. He could shoot me right
here. I forced myself to stay where I was. Then there was
another sound as the marine crawled away.

"Killer," he whispered hoarsely, as if through tears.
Then he was gone.

The 4.2 mortars fired for another minute or two, and then
there was nothing more to fire at, and the observer called
them to secure. There was no village anymore, just a blackened place, smoking and charred. No more people could be
seen anywhere. The BARs shut down and the platoon sergeant crawled up to me.

"I want to thank the lieutenant for taking over."

" 'S'okay. How's Mr. Settle?"

"He's awake. Bad headache. He took a dive into the
trench and got knocked out when he fell."

"Good."

"And begging the lieutenant's pardon, but the lieutenant
did a fine job. There ain't nothing left out there."

"No, nothing," I said. The word didn't mean the same
thing to me that it did to him. He couldn't have heard the
marine who shouted at me about the "women." If he had,
the sergeant would have said something.

You could still hear the firefight on Tu-mari, but it was
fading now. There was nothing more to do here. "Okay,
Sergeant, let's get them up and out. We're done."

I looked at my watch. Not even eight o'clock yet. Back
home people would be eating breakfast, strolling to the
subway, buying the morning paper. We moved out of the
trench on the side away from the chinks. That sniper was
probably still hanging around. Lieutenant Settle was conscious now but woozy. I talked to him for a minute, but he
wasn't really getting it, and two marines came along to walk
with him, each holding an arm. As we went down the hill,
the firing was dying off at Tu-mari and 104. Only a shot or
two and what sounded like a mortar, a little one, a .60. I
watched the Easy platoon work its way downhill, Settle

walking with them, unsteady, like a man who'd taken a few drinks. It was funny that the chinks occupied this hill every night and the marines could come up here by day. A few hours ago, 69 had been Chinese. In a few hours, it would be Chinese again. I rubbed my eyes. I hadn't been thinking very smart. We should have rigged some booby traps, easy to do with grenades and com wire, just a couple of them in the bunkers, stretched across the trench.

I stopped to look around a last time, to be sure we'd left nothing and nobody behind. The last fire team came back down toward me, sweeping the area for the sniper, weapons waist-height and ready, but there was nothing. I let them pass, and then I stepped to the side of the path and unbuttoned my fly and urinated on the dry, reddish clay of the hill. It wasn't much but I did it. We should have rigged a few booby traps, we really should. There was no question about it.

When we got back to Battalion they gave us the score on the Fox Company raid. All four tanks had been knocked out in the first few minutes, one burned out, the other with blown treads from mines. Three of the crews were okay. But forty marines had been hit, and there were eight dead with a couple more doubtful. One of the old gunnies was talking about it.

"Tanks is just shit," he said, "they cain't get out of they own way, they cain't."

That was how old gunnies were. They didn't believe in modern warfare. But after 104 and Tu-mari whenever anyone talked about tanks that was how people in our Battalion reacted. "Tanks is shit, is all. Just shit."

33

I lay in my sleeping bag, unable to sleep. We had the summer-weight bags now, green issue blanketing material sewn up in a sort of coffin shape. Appropriate. It was very hot, the planes of the tent lying sagging and still in the night air. There was no breeze, and the air was heavy with moisture and a rain that might come.

Not being able to sleep, I started to think about women, about having a girl here with me in the bag in the damp heat. That would be okay. I tried not to think too much about women. Sometimes someone got hold of a dirty book and it was shared around, Mickey Spillane and stuff like that, but I usually gave it a pass. Up here where you could get killed was no place to start getting excited. They always said there was saltpeter in the rations, and I was ready to believe it. Months went by when I didn't get aroused. There must be some explanation; it wasn't normal. A healthy twenty-three-year-old and no erections. Boy.

I had a new section chief. Jay Scott had gone home. All the good people were going home. I was going to miss Scott, cool and funny and courteously mocking, one of the few enlisted men I'd really like to see again in civilian life. That was snobbery, I supposed, but there really wasn't a hell of a lot we had in common, most of the enlisted men and me. Princeton, for example, what the hell would I talk with Princeton or Hoops about except the Corps, except the war? Shrapnails and rations, stuff like that. Scott was something else. His replacement, the new section chief, was a regular, a gunnery sergeant with a spiky little waxed mustache and slick hair, like a man in a stag movie. But he was very senior. Scott had been only a corporal when I took over as S-2. To have a gunny as section chief was extraordinary. It just showed how they were pumping people into Korea through the replacement drafts now. The gunny was from another regiment and had come available because the replacement drafts were overstocking with staff NCOs. He was very crisp, very professional, and he told a good yarn.

He told about last fall when we were on the jump and some civilians got caught up in the fighting and came through the lines at night and the gunny's people caught them. They weren't infiltrators, just ordinary, frightened people trying to get out of the way of the war.

"There was this one young gal," the gunny said, "very pretty she was, maybe sixteen, seventeen, you can't tell with gooks except they get old fast. The orders were to send back all civilians under guard, so intelligence could question them, but it was dark by then and I couldn't spare an escort. There was still some fighting going on, and I didn't want my people fooling around in the dark and maybe shooting one another. So I just kept that young lady there and sort of entertained her right there in the foxhole. Entertained her all night. For a fact."

I turned away from his leer. The man was older than I was and a regular, but, Jesus, taking a girl like that, so frightened she'd probably do anything. This was quite a gunny I'd gotten hooked into. I was disgusted when he told the story, but now lying alone in the bag in the hot night, still except for the whir of insects and some low thunder, or maybe it was artillery, I thought about it, about the girl, and it no longer seemed as crude or bad, and I wanted a girl like that with me now. God, it would be nice. Maybe they'd left the saltpeter out of this batch of rations. Maybe it was the heat, that and thinking about the girl the gunny took. I turned on my side to the tent's wall to stare at the dark canvas, but in a few minutes I rolled again to my back. I felt very hot now, the heat of the lowering May night, the heat of a rising sensuality. My mind flashed with erotic imagery, bodies twisting, slick with sweat, colliding one against the other, all sorts of grotesque and impractical positioning. I was a Catholic and now I began to say the old prayers. The words meant nothing, just the rote performance, no thought, just mindless repetition, and still, I felt myself hardening. This was stupid; I could be killed tomorrow and I was caving in to impure desires. Catholics think that way; we really phrase things like that.

In Korea nearly seven months and for the first time I was sexually aroused and close to masturbation. Damn that gunny! Angry with him and angry with myself, I swung my legs off the cot and went to the flap of the tent and looked out. There were no stars and the sky hung low and heavy. A spare helmet sat braced on a kind of tripod just outside the tent. We used it for washing, for shaving, all of us. I took down a water bag from the tent pole, poured the helmet full and scooped water up with my hands to soak down my hair and face. It wasn't a cold shower, but the closest I could get to it, the best I could do. The rolling sound was clearer now, not guns but thunder. Too bad, I thought, we'll have this heat and damp for days. I lay down again, this time on top of the sleeping bag, and finally was asleep.

Now there was real fighting, a lot of it, as if the raid on 104 and Tu-mari had woken the Chinese from a winter's hibernation which had carelessly dozed into spring. Every night now, a couple of hours after sundown, the patrols went out from both sides of the line into no man's land. Sometimes neither side made contact; sometimes they went on until they came up against the mines or the barbed wire of the MLR. Then a tin can would rattle on the wire or a booby trap explode, and the machine guns would start up, reaching out along the outside strands of wire fence, and the mortar shells would drop one after another, bunched together, into the dead spaces where the machine gunners could not reach. A grenade would go off, and another, shouts and curses, broken fire, and the patrol, what was left of it, would gather itself, its goods and its dead, to limp back across the empty places before dawn caught them at its tasks. Sometimes, out there, two patrols would meet, hundreds of yards from their own lines. Then confusion became chaos, and they killed the enemy and they killed each other. Who knew whom you were shooting in the night? The grenade, the knife, the shotgun, even the shovel and the axe were the weapons of the night patrols. It was a throwback, this war. I remembered reading *Journey's End* in college. Sherriff *knew!* Night after night they went out, from both sides, to come back each morning, sometimes with a prisoner, sometimes lugging the wounded, or with their dead. No matter how young, they always looked slack faced and gray and old when they came in in the mornings. I know. When I heard firing in the night, I knew that when they came in, there would be something they could tell me, and I tried to be up before dawn to meet them, to ask questions, to get something useful before it became mixed up in their memories and blurred. I wanted to talk to them before they forgot, not the horror or the fright, but what they'd seen and heard.

Mack Allen, who usually had an idea, came up with one now. He took me aside after the colonel's staff meeting.

"Jim, we're losing too many men on these patrols. I keep the rolls, I keep count. We aren't doing them right. No one understands."

"Yeah?"

"We're sending them out there as if it were a month's campaign. The men carry too much gear, they aren't dressed right, they make too much noise and they can't help that with what they carry and what they wear. They're too easily seen, too easily heard, and they get ambushed. Or our own ambushes are tipped off. What do you think?"

"About what, Mack? Where are you getting?"

"We ought to go out there wearing just skivvy shirts and pants, soft pants like sweat suits, nothing scratchy against the brush, and sneakers, dyed black. No canteen, no web belts, a knife and a couple of grenades, a rifle or a BAR but without the sling, so it doesn't catch, the extra clips in your pocket. Charcoaled up, too. What do you think?"

"Who's going to do all this pooping and snooping? You and me?"

Mack grinned that flat grin of his. "Well, now, I think it might demonstrate the confidence we have in this scheme of ours if you and I volunteered to run it. You know?"

"Hell, Mack, don't foist this one off on me. It's your baby."

He told me I was just pining to get out there on patrol again. I wasn't having any of that. " Come on," I persisted, "seriously, who goes?"

"Well, you and me. Then we ought to work up a special squad, maybe a dozen men, tough babies who've been around. No new replacements and no one who's due for rotation soon. Some boys we both know and we've seen work, people who can move quiet and fast and do the job when they get there."

Colonel Gregory listened to Allen politely. He was not enthusiastic.

"How many people would be on one of these suicide missions?"

"Four, Colonel, maybe six tops," Mack said.

"Who carries in the casualties?"

The Corps brings back its people. That's the tradition.

"Colonel," Mack said, "way I figure it, there shouldn't be any. Just chinks."

The colonel thought awhile, and then the operations officer, Nicholson, thought some more, and finally Mack got the okay to try it and the sneakers and charcoal. The men were easy. There were always a few like Fitzgerald; marines were intrigued by something new, and Mack had the reputation of a good man. He got his dozen without strain. He and I were given four hours a day with them for a week, creeping and crawling in the hills behind the CP, knife fighting and wire cutting, ambush discipline, the lot. Then we took them for a couple of hours each night, compass reading in the dark, maps, jumping each other with a garrote or a knife, stringing booby traps quietly and without light. On May 25 we would have our first run. Then the colonel pounced.

"Allen, your boys can go out tonight. Make it an easy run, close in to the lines, and nothing elaborate this first time."

"Aye, aye, sir," Mack said, rubbing his hands.

"Oh, yes, Allen, and one more thing. Neither you nor Brady goes. I'm not sending officers on six-man patrols. Pick your best sergeant to run them."

Mack argued but it was no good. We did it Gregory's way or not at all. We went up with six men to the MLR in the afternoon and lay at the firing ports of bunkers memorizing the lay of the land and the route they'd take. Mack thought of a dozen things a minute, sheer energy working off the disappointment that he wouldn't be with them. About nine they jumped off. Mack went with them to the wire, squeezing each man's arm silently as he passed through the gate and disappeared down the hill. There was no sound, none at all. It was as if they'd been swallowed by the night in the emptiness out there. I went back into the bunker and sat down to wait, and someone made coffee. Here on the hill there was an evening chill we didn't get below, and the coffee went down fine. I wondered about the patrol, shivering in their T-shirts. It wasn't good on patrol to be cold. You lost concentration, you made noise. I thought of the winter patrols, lying in the snow, the men coughing, and how I shivered, the wind coming across the face of the hill. If there was anything I knew about, it was winter nights on patrol. Mack came inside, really suffering. It was hard on him to work up a crazy scheme like this and then have to send other people to do it.

I didn't say anything. I was relieved when Gregory ruled us out, but I was ashamed to admit it. I didn't have Mack's guts.

Thirty minutes after they went out, no longer, there was an explosion in front of the lines. Mack jumped up, banging his head against the overhead logs.

"Oh, goddammit, a mine, a lousy mine. They hit a mine!"

We knew it was a mine. They weren't out far enough to have hit chinks, not yet. Of all the stinking luck.

It was midnight before we got them all in. Mack and I went out with some riflemen and brought them back. There were three hit. The sergeant lost a leg. Mack walked all the way back with the stretchers, talking to them all the way, trying to comfort them, saying he was sorry it was them and not him. The marines, even the sergeant, doped up and lashed to a stretcher, kept telling Mack it was all right, no one could have helped it, it was just bad luck. The choppers from the aid station were waiting when we came off the hill.

The colonel disbanded Mack's outfit the next day. He

was understanding, saying it wasn't Mack's fault or mine or anyone's, that it might have happened with any patrol he sent out, big or small. It was just rotten luck. No one knew where the damned mines were; no one could help it. That night I bought a half bottle of Old Forrester from the supply officer who kept a small bar locked in his sea chest. Being a supply officer, he charged us list. Mack and I nearly finished the half bottle, though we weren't drinkers.

It was the only thing you could do when you had luck like that.

34

On Sunday at four o'clock precisely, Chinese guns began firing all the length of the marine lines. The targets were behind us, the marine Divisional artillery batteries. The Chinese intelligence was very good, and they hit in or around every battery but two. I was asleep, and Mack was wrestling outside the tent with Buscemi, the football player who was now communications officer. It was just a routine, peaceful Sunday afternoon, and then the shells came over. It only lasted a few minutes, but I was lying facedown in a slit trench, and Mack and Buscemi were tangled up in another trench. No one was hit in the Battalion; they weren't aiming at us. Casualties were light all along, only a couple of artillerymen killed. Still, it was disturbing when things like this happened. You hoped the chinks weren't that good, that coordinated. But they were.

The next morning, at the staff meeting, the colonel talked about the shelling. He said Regiment suggested the Chinese must have pretty good observation posts to be able to pull off a stunt like that. They were probably getting good information from infiltrators and the natives. When I heard that I felt pretty good about having burned out the village.

"Lieutenant Brady, are there Chinese on Yoke?"

Yoke was a modest hill halfway between the lines, directly in front of 212, where Dog Company sat, about a mile out in front of the line. I started to make a little speech about Yoke, not knowing really. This was something I had

241

a tendency to do when I lacked knowledge, make a little speech, but Gregory wasn't having any of it.

"Are there or aren't there?"

I fell back on honesty. "I don't know, Colonel. We haven't seen any, but that doesn't mean to say they aren't there."

"Thank you, Mr. Brady. It's always helpful to have expert opinion." The colonel could be cutting when he chose.

"I suggest, or rather Regiment has suggested to me, that we send a patrol out there to see if there really are any Chinese on Yoke operating an observation post. When Regiment suggests something, I generally go along." He permitted himself a brief cackle.

Nicholson had obviously worked this out. He outlined the battle plan. A full rifle platoon would go out, supported by a section of light machine guns. The guns would set up on the last little hump before Yoke and cover the platoon as it climbed the hill. Simple enough. Afrer that, well, that would depend on whether there were Chinamen there. The patrol was scheduled for that night.

"What do you think, Brady?" the colonel said.

"Sounds fine, Colonel. Fine."

"Now, Brady, since you're the intelligence officer of this Battalion and since you don't know if there are Chinese out there and such information might interest you, don't you think it would be a nice idea if you went along?"

The colonel was a lot of laughs at staff meetings. "Well, yes, sir, I guess it would."

"That's dandy. You might take an interpreter along, just in case those Chinese you don't think are there play us a dirty trick and be there when you arrive."

I was cleaning and oiling my .45 when Mack came in.

"The old man got something against you?"

"Oh, he just likes to needle, and on this one he's right. I don't know what's out there and I guess I should."

We were jumping off at 2 A.M. so we'd be on Yoke before light. I climbed the hill to Dog Company alone, just before dark. Two of my scouts and two interpreters had gone ahead.

It was dark on the hill, with stars. There would be no

moon, which was good. Stars were enough to find your way; a moon showed you up. It was nice being back with the Company. There weren't too many people I knew anymore, but there was the familiar feel of an old neighborhood. McCarty, the exec who succeeded me, was still there and so was Maki, but this wasn't his patrol. I was glad about that. I didn't see him and that, too, made me glad. Charley Logan still had the Company. One night in reserve Logan got drunk and blubbered about how Mack and I and the old-timers were always comparing him to Chafee and how it hurt. He was right. We did. But it was nothing personal. We would have felt that way no matter who replaced John Chafee. It was even good seeing Charley again, especially since he wasn't brushing his teeth.

Logan and McCarty had me to dinner, the usual cans heated over a burner, and coffee. Their bunker had a port, and you could see Yoke out there in front, a black bulk looming, no details. I'd seen it plenty; I was just refreshing myself. There was still a high-tension steel tower on Yoke, a leftover from the Japanese power grid that was all shot to hell now, and that was how you could easily pick out Yoke by day. After dinner we lay around the bunker, a bit crowded, smoking cigarettes and talking. The first sergeant said he was taking his bag down to the supply tent for the night so I could sleep for a couple hours before going out. I thought I wouldn't, that it wasn't worth it, but by nine I was yawning. I lay down on the bare ground, my field jacket buttoned up, my face toward the sandbagged wall and away from the candlelight and the low murmur of Logan and McCarty's talk. McCarty had decided to go along with us. He was being transferred soon, and being a regular he wanted to see as much as he could this last tour on the line. He'd always wanted to make a big patrol and this might be his last chance. He had a new movie camera, a Jap jobbie, and he hoped to get some shots of the chink MLR from the crest of Yoke. I didn't care if I never went on patrol again; McCarty was eager to go.

I didn't fall asleep immediately. I kept yawning but sleep didn't come. That was nerves. You never knew when you went out through the lines, you really never knew, and for the first time, I'd begun thinking about being rotated home.

It was obvious that I was never going to become a rear-echelon pogue, that so long as I was in Korea I would be with a Marine rifle battalion on the line. Now I had nearly seven months in and not many more to go, two months, maybe three or four tops. I could count. Quantico was turning out platoon leaders by the hundreds, and for the first time in two years the Division had enough lieutenants. They were still short of certain NCOs and a few specialists and captains. But they had plenty of lieutenants. It might mean going home this summer. Now I was going on patrol, as I'd done that first tour when I was scared because I didn't know anything. Now I knew a lot. And I was still scared. I turned again on the hard ground of the bunker, and that was the last thing I remembered until Logan was shaking me awake and shoving a can of hot coffee into my hand.

McCarty and I went outside. Logan came after us, clapping us both on the shoulder. I think Charley was glad he wasn't going. Never mind the heat of the day, now it was cold outside. The day's heat had drained off into space, and from a clear, cloudless sky, heavy dew fell on the hill. I shivered, part of that the sudden waking, and I was glad I had worn my field jacket and wasn't going out there in a T-shirt, like Mack's people had. I tightened my gun belt, having lost a few pounds since the weather turned hot. McCarty held out a couple of grenades.

"Want them?"

"Sure." I shoved them into the breast pockets of my shirt. They hung there heavy, like breasts swollen with milk, but cold and dead. Then, on impulse, I stripped off the field jacket and gave it to Logan to keep for me. Even with the night chill, we might be out there all day and it was going to be hot. By morning I'd be sweating and tired in a field jacket; this way I was cold at the start but would warm up. The armored vest was enough to wear, and I let it hang open. I had the .45. They'd taken personal weapons like my .38 Smith & Wesson and locked them up months ago. Too many accidental discharges, too many people shot. The .45 was a joke but you wore it. Close enough, you could knock someone down, maybe even kill him. Fifty yards away, you couldn't hit shit. The carbine wasn't much better and it was silly carrying a rifle. If we got into a firefight, there would be rifles around. Plenty. I'd learned that much.

The platoon was moving through the wire, quiet at the start, placing their feet cautiously, not to slip on the shale of the forward slope. Jack Rowe had the platoon, a replacement from Philadelphia, a slim, nice-looking boy who'd graduated from Villanova. Rowe was only a second lieutenant and green, but on a patrol both McCarty and I, who outranked him, would be under his orders. I fell back with my scouts to the rear of the single line the patrol had assumed. Only the machine gunners were behind us. We moved out briskly, the stars giving plenty of light. Once your eyes adjusted stars were enough. We went down the hill with very little noise, and onto the flat, sixty men and their weapons moving quietly and fast. Yoke loomed black ahead of us.

The line snaked out across the valley and I could see neither head nor tail. But you began to sense the accordion effect as we spread out, the rear end of the file closing suddenly on the people ahead, then the head of the file opening up so that men had to trot to keep up. Anytime this many men moved in file on rough ground you had the same problem. Still, it wasn't so bad, the stars giving light, and no one fell. But we were beginning to make noise. We were no longer moving quietly. I knew we were making a hell of a lot of noise, no talk, nothing really loud, but the sum total of sixty men on the march, carrying machine guns and BARs and wearing web gear, created a steady rasp and rattle that had to carry. I hoped it didn't carry too far. I didn't think there were chinks on Yoke but I wasn't all that sure. Before me the file began to climb the lower slopes of Yoke, the first people on Yoke itself, the point that led every patrol. I was still on the flat but it was only three o'clock, not bad time. We would be at the top before dawn caught us. Now I began to climb, Sasso with me and Wrabel, a scout corporal and a good one, a big, rangy kid. The two of them moved quietly, if no one else did. The machine gunners had dropped back to set up, and I could hear metal on metal as they ran belts through the guns and set up for overhead fire. Somewhere a bird chirped, the first to wake. No distant artillery rumbled, masking sound. All along the line the night gunners had gone to bed and the day gunners had not yet risen. We'd crossed the open flat without difficulty and now were on Yoke, and it looked as if the chinks weren't there, maybe never had been there. For once, we were lucky.

The first explosion was so shocking, I thought we'd set it off ourselves and wondered why we were so stupid and noisy. Then I wondered if it had really happened. One moment the night was black, the next brilliantly lighted, then dark again, the sound fading into echoes. It lighted the hill and then died, just bright enough to blind us for the confused seconds that followed. I knew by now it wasn't imagination. Someone must have hit a mine, some point man got it. Then there came a *rrripp* of burp guns from above, and I realized it wasn't a mine but a grenade; there were chinks up there. There were more crashes, grenades, and shouts in English, and the start of firing back. I'd dropped prone and lay there, head up, trying to see, but not giving a target. Up ahead someone called for the third squad to move up. Behind me and around me men got to their feet and started heavily up the incline. I looked around. Wrabel was nearest me. It was his first firefight.

"Wrabel, okay?"

"Great, Lieutenant. I didn't think we'd be this lucky first time out."

Well, that was a healthy, positive attitude. There was more firing, and when I turned right I could see the sky had cracked and the light was coming, the stars fading and the black turning dull gray. Oh, shit. It was going to be Tu-mari and 104 all over, caught by daylight assaulting a Chinese position. There was plenty of firing, grenades and the burp guns and our stuff, too, plenty active up ahead. I got to my knees.

"Wrabel, Sasso, get the interpreters. Let's go. We'll act as an independent fire team. Watch me."

We got up and began to climb the hill, no one behind us now but the machine gunners a few hundred yards back, out of sight. Up the slope I found McCarty. There were marines lying all over the hill, rifles and BARs pointed uphill. The firing had died down.

"What happened?"

"They got the point man," McCarty said. "Dead. I don't know if it was a grenade or a trap. They're up top, on the crest. You'll be able to see from a little higher up. Rowe has two squads up there trying to take them. We're reserve."

"Did he call in the machine guns?"

"Not yet. Not till Rowe gives it a try or stalls. If he gets stalled I'll call in the machine guns. Can't shoot now, with Rowe trying to crawl up there."

Now the firing erupted again, with grenades going off in strings like firecrackers on the Fourth. It was real dawn now, gray, and the grenades no longer lighted up the place. There were some shouts and then the cry.

"Corpsman, corpsman!"

"Well," McCarty said, "I don't think they made the top."

He got up very slowly, his movie camera looking silly slung around his neck. I didn't think he was going to get much use out of it.

"This fire team come with me," McCarty ordered. Then, to me, "Want to come?"

"Sure." We started up the path again, easy to see now without straining for footholds. There was very little firing. Before we'd gone very far we met marines coming down. The first three were bloody, but you couldn't tell how badly they were hit. None of them were crying or looked to be in shock. They were just bloody and they were walking back, doing all right. I nodded to them as they went past, but they didn't look at me.

"Where's Mr. Rowe?" McCarty asked.

"Up there," one of the wounded said over his shoulder. "He got hit."

McCarty and I went up until we reached a bunch of wounded marines lying on the hillside while off to the right and left of them a skirmish line of marines was lying prone. Every so often someone squeezed off a shot. I don't think they had targets; they were just firing.

"Here's Rowe," McCarty said. He was lying flat. His face was hit and there was something wrong with his hands. A corpsman was kneeling over him doing something. I called Rowe's first name, "Jack?" but he didn't move or answer. I turned to look at McCarty.

"He's bad. You want to take it or shall I?"

"What the hell," McCarty said, "I just came along for the ride, to take pictures. Whatever you want."

"Okay," I said, "you're the exec and you're senior. You take over. Just tell me what you want done."

"Swell," McCarty said. "Sergeant, how many Chinese up there?"

A marine crawled over to us. He was bloody, too, but I couldn't see where he was hit. He talked fast, excited, but he didn't seem badly hurt.

"Could be a platoon, probably less. We got up to the wire and then when we started through they hit us with grenades. They got grenades up the ass. They was throwing them down and we was throwing them back. That's how Mr. Rowe got it. He caught a grenade and it went off. He's shy an eye and it looks like some fingers."

"How many dead have we got?"

"Just the point man so far, unless some of these hit guys croaked. But we got a lot of woundeds. Just about everyone picked up something in the wire."

I looked up and could see the wire, a triple-apron fence. I wondered why we hadn't seen it before, from the OPs, through glasses. It would have told us the chinks were here, maybe. McCarty was taking a head count, and then he sent down for the last squad to come up.

"Give me the radio." He called the machine gunners. "Look, we got chinks on the crest of the hill, the very crest. You think you can hit them and not hit us? We're just below the wire. Can you see the wire now? Got enough light?"

He turned to me. "The machine guns can see us. They say they've got light." He punched the radio button again. "Okay," he said, "hit them."

Both machine guns began to fire, and I crouched lower, head down, neck bowed. It was instinctive. At this range the guns fired with extreme accuracy, and anyway their target was fifty yards or more above where McCarty and I had set up. You could hear the bullets hitting earth, or sandbags or logs or whatever they had up there. Occasionally one hit the steel tower and whined away. Now it was four o'clock and full light, and I wished I could back up and see what the crest of Yoke really looked like. Here we were under it and too close to see. There was no firing from the Chinese. The radio squawked at McCarty and he put it to his ear. "Sure," he was saying, "sure. If they think they can lay it in and not hit us." He put down the handset and looked at me.

"They can give us 105s, too."

"We're pretty close for 105s," I said. Boy, that was an understatement.

"Well, they say they've got a good fix on the crest and they say they can do it. What the hell, they know their stuff. I say let them try."

"Okay," I said, "you've got the wheel."

I didn't like this at all, but McCarty seemed relieved to have a second opinion and that I was going along with him. "Tell them give us one round of 105. We'll adjust."

There was a weird silence, the machine guns stopped, probably changing belts, cooling the barrels so they wouldn't get stoppages. Then the first shots from the 105s came in over our heads, sounding like freight trains, to burst forty, fifty yards up the hill, near the crest.

I'd been looking over my shoulder when it came. "God, I never realized you could see them."

"Well," McCarty said, "I guess you can. That one was perfect. I'm going to tell them fire for effect. Okay?"

I nodded, thinking about the way the shell had looked when it came in above us, black and small and moving very fast, faster than a jet even, and looking very low and close to us and then going out of sight, too fast to see as it passed us, hitting into the hill with the familiar crunch. I'd heard plenty of incoming; this was the first time I'd ever seen the shells. A short round, that was all we needed. Don't give us a short round. McCarty was on the radio now, telling them to fire for effect. He put the radio down and yelled to the marines around us.

"Stay low, the 105s are coming in."

Someone gave a halfhearted cowboy yell, a little cheer, but I lay there on my stomach flat against the upward slope of the hill, my helmet feeling wonderful, thinking how nice it would be if all of me could fit inside it. The first salvo of shells was on the way now, and there was a drawing-up feeling in the small of my back. I watched them over my shoulder, black and fast and low; three of them this time, and I could see all three. They shuttled in, very loud, to smash into the hillside above us. I could feel Yoke jerk under me. I thought maybe I should pray, and I started to, Hail Marys, but I never finished one, short as they were. I would start and then another three shells would come in over me and bang into the hill and shake me like a rat. My body would try to absorb the shock, and I forgot where I was in the prayer and had to start again. I stopped watching the shells come; it was too much watching them and worrying, and I just lay there flat as I could, my face in the dirt, shoulders hunched and my neck screwed down tight between them, trying to squeeze more of me into the helmet.

Shells came in like that for maybe three or four minutes. You couldn't really judge time; it had no meaning in a situation like that. Toward the end there was a short round, only one, and it was really short, falling below us, halfway down the hill. Dirt fell lightly on us, feeling wonderful, being only dirt and pebbles and not hot metal. Then the guns secured. I think that short one shook the gunners up, too, if their forward observers saw it. McCarty was on the radio. "Give us machine guns on the crest again. Now!"

The two guns resumed their chatter, typewriters gone mad, with McCarty shouting. "Keep their heads down, pour it on." He was looking around at the rest of us. Along the skirmish line individual marines were squeezing off single rounds now, the firing ragged compared to the disciplined bursts of the machine guns. McCarty looked around to me.

"I think we ought to go up there. How about it?"

"Hell, yeah, Stew. Let's take them." I was thinking about Jack Rowe's eye and the point man dead and the bloody marines coming down the path. Now that our shelling was over I wasn't even frightened, only sore and wanting very badly to go up and stand on top of this damned hill.

McCarty yelled orders to the marines within hearing. "On three we go," he shouted. "One, two . . ."

We were up and running, all of us, Wrabel next to me, running uphill but not feeling the grade or being winded or leg weary, just sprinting up. There were marines all around me. Some of the wounded must be coming with us, going up a second time. I didn't recognize anyone but Wrabel, but it didn't matter, we were attacking Yoke together, in daylight, assaulting a hill, and we were going to get there. I had the .45 out. It was silly, because you couldn't hit anything and I couldn't see a chink, but I remembered how few men actually fire in combat, how they seize up, and I thought I ought to be shooting the damned thing. Around me other marines were firing, their rifles and BARs at the hip as they ran. They couldn't be hitting anything either, but we'd be keeping their heads down, the chinks. I fired without aiming, just firing vaguely toward the crest of the hill. It felt good to be running and firing. I fired again. Around me there was shouting. I picked up the shout.

"No prisoners!" I yelled. "No prisoners! Kill 'em all!" That's what I was shouting, what others were shouting. Everyone took it up now, everyone near me anyway. It was stupid shouting stuff like that. My job was to get prisoners. Dead chinks didn't help anyone. But it just seemed to be the thing to shout at that moment, and since it felt good I kept shouting it. So did the others.

"No prisoners!"

When we reached the wire, I went right through it. I can't say just how, whether I dove over it, somersaulting, or vaulted it, or just got lucky and ran through a patch the 105s had cut, but I was through, kneeling on the hard scrabbly dirt of the hill looking up. Other marines were through, too. Now there was maybe twenty yards to go for the top. I could see what looked like the top of a bunker with a firing port cut into it dead ahead. I squeezed off one very carefully aimed shot, the first I'd taken slowly, aiming at the firing port. With a .45 even a twenty-yard shot was guesswork, sheer optimism, but dust was whipping up from the crest, all the way along, as if windswept. Everyone must be shooting now. I hoped it wasn't our machine guns, because we were going to be on that crest pretty soon. I was still carrying the two grenades and was momentarily taken with fear a chance shot might hit one of them and explode it against my chest. I pulled one out and then the other, lay one on the ground and pulled the pin and tossed the first. Before it exploded I had the second in the air. I had a good arm and they both made the crest, exploding with a satisfying crack.

I got up from my knees and started again. Twenty yards to go, nothing. The ground was gritty, dry, and it crunched under my boots as I moved. I looked around to see how many were standing, who was going to the top with me. Just a couple. I looked for Wrabel and then a grenade exploded very close. And another. Without willing it, I was lying on the hill now, looking toward the crest, that damned silly automatic in my right hand, and now I could see grenades in the air, as I'd seen the 105s, only these were bigger and slower and coming at me. One grenade seemed to be trailing something, tied up with rags. I couldn't understand that. A grenade went off right in front of me, stinging both hands and my face. Dirt, it was just dirt. Fragments of the grenade would have been hot. I didn't feel anything beyond the stinging, so I couldn't have been hit. I fired again. More grenades were in the air, more going off to both sides and above me. A burp gun ripped off a quick burst. I looked around. Marines sprawled like me on the slope just below the crest. Only Wrabel was standing, wrestling with another marine. He seemed to be taking the man's rifle away from him. I didn't understand that. Now Wrabel was using the rifle to fire uphill, still standing, but in a crouch. I wondered where Stew McCarty was and whether anyone had gotten to the top. Another grenade exploded in front of me, then one behind. I still didn't feel anything.

"Pull back," a voice came up from below. Sounded like McCarty. "Pull back, get out of here."

I stood, still facing the hill, and then turned and sprinted back toward the wire. This time I knew how I got past it, diving through the air to clear the apron and then rolling, tucked, when I landed. I spun back then to face the hill. Other marines were coming through the wire, carrying and helping other people. I fired off the last rounds in the .45, just covering, not hitting anything. Then I rolled to my side to shove in a fresh clip. Next to me a marine was lying prone but not firing. I edged over to him.

"What's the matter, you hit?"

"No, rifle jammed."

"Gimme." I took the M-1. The safety was on. I slipped it off and began to squeeze off single shots at the crest of Yoke. "This rifle's fine," I said, but the marine just lay there, not listening. Wrabel crawled to me.

"You see that guy up there, Mr. Brady? Wasn't shooting or nothing. I took his damn rifle. A corporal and he wasn't shooting." He joined me firing at the crest. Now McCarty crawled up to us.

"Well, the grenades stopped us," he said. "You hit?"

"No. You?"

"Not a bit, but if I land on this camera again I'm going to have broken goddamned ribs." He paused. "Well, where do we go from here?" For the moment, there was no firing.

I put down the rifle and looked at McCarty and then around me. Nearly every marine I could see was bloody, some of them really hurt, others, like me, just scratched up a bit. Some of the wounded were crawling down the hill, dragging themselves along, still with their weapons.

"Well?"

"Look, Stew, whatever you say. We can give her another shot, go up again, maybe try to get a squad around to the right and get in behind them. Only thing is, if we get any more hit, who's going to get these people back home? Some of them are going to have to be carried. If we get more people hurt, won't be anyone to do it. That's what I think."

McCarty looked around, not excited and still looking relatively neat and clean, as regulars should. Then he nodded.

"Okay," McCarty said, "that's good enough for me. This isn't supposed to be a combat patrol anyway. We'll go down. But there's a BAR lying up there and I wanna get that."

"Sure, let's go." I hadn't been afraid since the last 105 shell had come in. It was very strange, being calm and not afraid, not even now. McCarty called for covering fire, and the two of us crawled uphill again. At the wire we stopped. Wrabel and a couple of others were there. McCarty nodded at them and started to wriggle through the wire, under the sagging strands, parting the wire carefully with his hands and moving on his back, squirming along but pretty fast. I squeezed off a round from the M-1, and the others took it up, a ragged tattoo of fire. Up above, a burp gun answered, but not aimed, nowhere near us. The chink was probably sitting on the floor of the bunker, firing blind through the port without ever getting his head up. McCarty was coming back now, with the BAR. He was a cool one. When he came through we all turned and started down the slope, two men at a time covering us, picking up men as we went. Sasso was there, bleeding from the arms and the chest but looking chipper.

"How is it?"

"Great, Mr. Brady, just shrapnails is all. Not bad." We went down to where I'd last seen Jack Rowe. The others who were still there, a corpsman and a couple of marines, they took extra rifles and let the wounded lean on them. I had two rifles now and a bandolier of cartridges I'd taken from somebody, the green cloth soaked with blood drying to a rust color, slung around my neck. There was no more firing. We caught up with Rowe on the floor of the valley, just below where Yoke began. He was lying there on the ground, looking very bad. Some people were coming toward us now from the MLR, stretcher parties. You couldn't land a chopper out here. I looked at my watch. Almost five o'clock. They'd gotten help out here pretty quick. The sun was hanging higher but still oversized, the way it looks in the morning, and it was going to be a fine day. When they got Rowe on a stretcher McCarty said, "Jim, do me a favor. Count heads and see we don't leave anyone out here, dead or alive."

I said sure and took Wrabel, and we counted off people and checked with squad leaders, the ones who were still moving. There were marines scattered all over the lower hillside and the flats at the foot of Yoke. Checking numbers meant getting off the paths and crossing paddies and little fields and cutting this way and that, and it was then I started being afraid again, not of the chinks, but thinking about mines, the way I used to be. It'd be a hell of a thing to do what we'd done this morning and then step on a mine. I took up prayer again and didn't stop until we finished the count. Long lines of men were moving across the flat now, in both directions, empty stretchers coming out, loaded ones going back. Overhead the 105s were flying again, hitting way up on Yoke and well back into the Chinese MLR, discouraging them from shelling us as we came out. I hustled along the line of men to catch up with Rowe's stretcher.

"How is he?"

A corpsman was giving him blood, holding the bottle and walking along beside. Rowe looked dead. They'd cleaned his face a bit, but his right eye looked gone, nothing there but a wound. I didn't look at his hands. No one answered my question, so I answered it myself. "He's okay," I said, "he'll make it. He's a Villanova wildcat, that boy. He'll make it, you'll see."

No one said anything, and I stopped talking, having the feeling I was making an ass of myself. The hell with it. I wasn't talking to them; I was talking in case Rowe could hear me.

I moved along the file of men, and then we stopped at the little knoll where the machine gunners had set up. McCarty was jotting something in a notebook. Later he figured out sixty-four of us had been on the patrol, with forty-eight actually going up Yoke, and thirty-two of us had been hit. I sat down, relishing the break as we picked up the machine gunners while the corpsmen fussed, bandaging wounds. Sasso sat there cross-legged, his shirt off. "I told you, Lieutenant, not bad."

"No stateside for you, Ace," someone said.

"Shit," Sasso said, laughing. Unless you were hit the way Rowe was, you felt pretty good, having gone through all that and being able to make jokes.

We were in through the MLR about eight. I hurried through the Dog Company position and down the other side of 212 to the CP. Colonel Gregory was waiting, and Nicholson, the S-3. They both shook hands with me.

"I'm sorry about that, Brady," the colonel said.

"Well, sir, nothing to worry about." I stopped and thought for an instant. "Anyway, there are chinks on Yoke. We found that out."

"How many do you figure?"

"Could be anything, platoon to a fire team. I'd say a squad. With plenty of grenades."

"Only a squad and they did this?"

"Yessir, they just sat there in the trench and tossed grenades downhill at us. They didn't do anything fancy, just rolled grenades down on us."

"We get any of them?"

"Colonel, I'd be a liar if I said yes. Maybe we hit a couple out of sheer luck, maybe the 105s got some. I'd say we must have gotten a few. But I couldn't swear to it, couldn't give you a count."

He put me on the phone to S-3 at Regiment, and I gave them the same report. The major I talked to sounded incredulous we'd taken all those casualties without giving him a single chink.

I stopped by the aid station, where they picked rock and dirt out of my hands and face and cleaned out some bad wire cuts on my right leg. I didn't even realize I had them. Too excited. When I took off my pants some grenade fragments fell out. Shrapnails. In January the snow had muffled the explosion that blew up Fitzgerald and me. I was starting to think of myself as fortunate. Back at the tent Mack shook my hand but didn't say much. The bloody bandolier was still slung around my neck, and I took it off and dropped it on the dirt floor next to the cot. I thought about trying to sleep for a while, but I was still too excited.

I don't know how anyone who hasn't been shot at up close in a real firefight can possibly understand how good you feel afterward. Men have been killed and hurt, the fight has been won or lost, but there is only the one truly significant fact: that you are still alive, you have not been killed. Later, I was sure, I would mourn the dead and the damaged. But not now. If you were not truly happy at a moment like this when you had just come down off the line walking, perhaps you never would be.

Then Buscemi came by and said they were getting up a volleyball game and asked did I want to play. My right leg stung, but that was mostly iodine, and otherwise I felt fine, so I went out and played a couple of games. Later I went over to talk to people who'd been on the patrol and who were still being treated, who'd been hit but not so bad they had to be evacuated. Mostly, it was grenade fragments, that and bits and pieces of rock from Yoke, gouges from the barbed wire.

By now they seemed to have figured it out about the grenades that came at us looking like they were wrapped in rags. Someone brought in one that didn't explode. It was in an old sock. The chinks tried to increase the explosive effect of the grenades by putting them in old socks full of black powder. I told Mack about it.

"So they even threw their socks at you," he said.

Mack thought that was very good, throwing their socks. Good line. Point was, the chinks outsmarted themselves doing it. The extra charge just blew the grenades to pieces, not into nicely sized fragments that could kill you. That was why so many were hit but not badly, the fragments were too small. Well, you fought and learned.

We heard from Division that Rowe would make it. They put him up for the Navy Cross and he was going home. The other badly hit man didn't die either. Only the point man, the first marine hit, was dead. All that firing, all that fighting, all those people hit, and one marine was dead and I couldn't swear to it there were any chinks dead.

That night the supply officer played his radio in the tent, and the armed forces news said there had been fighting at several points along the front that day but that enemy casualties were much heavier than ours. It was nice to hear. Then after the news the Australian Hit Parade came in and we got some good music. The Australian Hit Parade was always four or five months behind the American, but so what, the songs sounded fine.

=== 35 ===

No one I knew who had been there long enough missed the winter, regretted the cold. But this fighting in the heat possessed its own dimension of horror. You could see the wounds, see what killed people, the explicit manner of death and injury: a leg severed at the knee, a mangled arm, how startlingly white a man's ribs looked sticking out from under a flak jacket, pink at the splintered ends with little bits of meat attached. I could see what my own legs looked like, and the backs of my hands, when I came down from Yoke peppered with rock and grit and shrapnails.

All winter you were so muffled in clothes, layers and layers, swaddled against the cold, that a man could be all shot to pieces, literally sieved, but unless you were a corpsman you didn't have to look at the broken bones and the torn flesh and see blood pulsing from cut arteries and veins. The bodies were just as hurt, just as broken, but it happened under a couple of pairs of pants and an oversized parka. Men died more neatly in winter, modestly covered instead of naked and obscenely ripped apart. Those heavy clothes gave death a certain muffled discretion. A man could die in decency.

I can't explain how even after the bad times like Yoke we would play these endless games of volleyball down at Battalion. There was something manic about it. All you needed was a few yards of flat, beaten ground, a net and a ball. I can't explain either how we had so much energy and had to work it off. Maybe we were trying to distract ourselves with games. Maybe it was that we were living outdoors, or all the protein in the rations, or that we were young and scared and didn't want to think about reality. We played endlessly. Buscemi, who'd been a blocking back for Buddy Young at Illinois and had played football in the Rose Bowl, was the big organizer. I got very good at it. We played what they called "Raiders' Rules," which meant no damned rules at all. You could hit over the net and bang into a guy on the other side and do just about everything but bite and gouge. My right forearm was all scarred from the top of the net. When we broke for a breather Buscemi used to tell what it was like being a Big Ten football player at the Rose Bowl with all those California girls out there wanting to meet them and the newspaper men hanging around to interview Buddy Young. It sounded all right, the Rose Bowl did, and it took our minds off the strongpoints and the night patrols and the Chinese waiting for us, Rose Bowl memories and playing volleyball by "Raiders' Rules."

And it was good to know that some jocks, like Buscemi, were out here with us, and not back at Quantico playing football on the base team. Bradlee, who'd played at Harvard, had been picked to play ball, but he wanted to go to the Division, and some general, who was a famous jock, got sore. Doug was shipped right out and got killed almost right away in last spring's push. We all knew ballplayers who'd stayed behind. And men with political connections. There was one like that, the son of some big noise in Washington, who got off the troop ship in Japan while the rest of the draft went on to Korea.

And there were men like Taffy Sceva, married and with kids, who pulled strings to get himself *into* combat. Taffy was having a fine war and told people he had absolutely no regrets at what he'd done.

And men like Allen Dulles's son, whom I didn't know. He was a Princeton graduate, and his father had run the OSS in Europe during the War, and his uncle was John Foster Dulles, who, they said, if Eisenhower ran and was elected, might be the Secretary of State. So young Dulles had connections, but he didn't use them. He was hit in the head during the fighting in 1951 and invalided home. Men who knew him at Quantico kept in touch with the family, and they said this bright young fellow from Princeton, with all those marvelous Bourbon connections, was in a fine private hospital, where they took very good care of him, supplying him with building blocks and coloring books and simple toys suitable for a child. That was what young Dulles had become, through head injury, a brilliant mind turned childlike, but without a child's capacity for growth.

After Yoke I thought harder and longer about the accident of battle, the heads or tails of combat. This wasn't the ignorant fear of those first weeks of war; I knew too much now to be frightened by everything and too much ever to turn smug. Yet combat was still a great mystery, mingled fear and exultation, a sense of accomplishment offset by neurotic guilt, sheer joy at coming through a firefight, and nauseating terror. Wanting to flee the battle, you were drawn to its furious center. No one who had not fought could possibly imagine the contradictions or the nuances. Some fled battle and others embraced it. That was the enigma.

I was one of those torn in both directions.

By now I could see contour and read country, sensing invisible draws and cover, knowing where to lay a gun or register a mortar concentration, where to string wire and where mines might be laid, where the chinks were and where you could move safely. It was an education, a post-graduate course in survival, in skills I would never use again but skills that were required here. I'd become a professional, and still knew enough to be afraid.

The fighting on 104 and Tu-mari and now Yoke seemed to wake up the entire line, ruffling the calm like a whirlwind across a small pond whipping up eddies. Strategy didn't enter into it; the armies did not move, the maps remained the same, no famous battles were fought or martial reputations made or lost. The truce talks droned on at Panmunjom, not ending the killing but freezing the armies in place, harnessing them to lines established the previous autumn. There was no great interest in the truce talks or much faith, but neither side wanted to break off negotiations by starting a real offensive. This did not mean there was no fighting, just that it was limited to vicious little collisions like those on Yoke and 104, small-unit stuff, companies, platoons, squads, fire teams. It was small and it was bloody.

Each night as May gave way to June, the Chinese came up against the marines, sometimes in delicate little probes, other times smashing against us in waves. They came, died in the wire, ebbed, and came back again the next night. We didn't fight by day. The artillery, on both sides, was too good, too deadly, had been zeroed in for months on every promising dip in the ground. So we fought by night. There were those early in the war who said Americans couldn't fight by night. They were wrong. Marines fought by night and successfully. This did not mean we always won these fights, but it was not the night that beat us; it was the enemy.

Four nights the Chinese came up the hills all the way to the MLR, and two of those nights they got inside the wire and there were short, nasty scraps in the trenches, on top of the bunkers, up and down the ridgeline. We lost men. The MLR was too thin to let this go on, and Division ordered the rifle regiments to push forward of the MLR to establish outposts against which the Chinese probes would spend themselves. Our Battalion put out three strongpoints, on Hill 69, on the machine gunners' knoll in front of Yoke, and on another pimple south of 104 and Tu-mari. A platoon manned each outpost. They went out by night and were supplied by night and every three days they were relieved by night. You couldn't cross these valleys by day; there were doubts you could live in the outposts by night. The platoons holding the strongpoints ringed themselves in with wire, artillery and mortar concentrations were laid all around them, 360 degrees. Mines were sown and booby traps hung and extra machine guns and BARs issued, and crates of grenades went out by gook train in the night. We didn't like running gook trains in front of the lines, but this was special.

The platoons went out on a quiet night to set up the strongpoints, and that was the last quiet night they had. The chinks seemed surprised the first time they came up against the strongpoints. They were en route to the MLR by their usual paths, moving quietly, observing good march discipline, when they were hit by automatic fire from two sides.

261

The Chinese patrols broke and ran, which you didn't see often. The next night they probed, knowing our people were there and trying to figure out precisely where and in what strength, gauging the feel of the outposts, their dimensions. On the third night, they hit. Gregory saw it coming.

Mack and I and the air and naval gunfire officers were in the operations bunker with Nicholson. Gregory wanted everyone there and we would not be anywhere else. You do not put 120 men out in no man's land like this and just go to sleep and not think about it. Around ten the chinks hit the knoll in front of Yoke, the place where we'd rested on our way home, where our machine guns had worked. For two hours the Chinese swarmed around and against the knoll. The firefight was just tremendous. Our one platoon had six machine guns and they were all going. Artillery fire was coming in all around the knoll. The chinks had gotten behind it and were coming in at all angles. They must have thrown in a couple of companies of infantry. The knoll was holding, but they were taking casualties. There hadn't been time in a couple of nights to dig bunkers, and the men were in trenches. The operations officer had an idea; he would try to have some steel plating sent out that the gooks could lay atop the trenches, so the artillery could fire airbursts and sweep the knoll clear of anyone not under steel. Sounded like a great idea except that we didn't have any steel plates and even if we had they weren't out there on the knoll. Toward midnight the Chinese hit the pimple in front of 104. Here the assault was less furious. Hill 69 they left alone. The fight on the knoll lasted until two and then the Chinese pulled back, carrying their dead and wounded. Three marines were dead, six wounded. One man was missing. He had been in one of the forward trenches, and they must have gotten to him, dragged him off. I didn't like thinking about being captured. Being killed was the horror you knew or thought you knew; being taken prisoner was the unknown, and that was always worse.

They hit all three forward positions the next night. Hill 69 was our strongest position, with bunkers the chinks had dug, and on 69 they were quickly thrown back. On the pimple, there was another probe, hardly enough to be called an attack. There was a fresh platoon holding the knoll, the people of the night before having been pulled out to rest. Someone had rigged a sort of loudspeaker in the ops bunker, and you could hear the conversation between the platoon leader out there and Battalion, and the internal communications on the knoll itself, between squad leaders and the platoon commander. It was fascinating to listen to, horrible and scary and entirely gripping, so that if you had tried, you could not have shut your ears to it.

The outposts got through that night and the next, with hard fighting, casualties, but nothing disastrous. Then, with another new platoon in position, the chinks really came against the knoll. They seemed to have worked it out, when we sent out a relief platoon. The replacement had been effected just after dusk, and the old platoon was still on its way back up 212 when we heard the first firing on the knoll. The platoon leader was called Byrne, a new man to the Battalion. Now Byrne was on the radio. We were there in the operations bunker, listening. It was like hearing a very important football game on an old receiver: static, breaks, the roaring in the background; you were terribly excited about the game and couldn't quite figure out which side was ahead. That's how it was with Byrne. You didn't know the score, and this was no game.

"Gib, Gib, where are they?"

"Coming up, about thirty men looks like. We're getting burp. Give us mortars, Lieutenant."

"Mortars. Gibson wants concentration right out front. Give it to him. For effect. Now. Now!"

"Mr. Byrne. Leibling here. They're on this side, too. I'd say a squad. My first fire team is hitting them now. We're getting grenades."

"Okay, okay, lemme know. Hello, mortars, for Chrissakes where are the mortars? That's concentration eleven, repeat eleven."

"Mr. Byrne, I'm getting movement. Can't see anyone yet but they're coming. Right up the ass, right up the rear door. Can I have mortar?"

Byrne's voice came on again and again, answering his three squad leaders, passing on their calls for mortars to company, asking questions, getting broken answers, shouting at the squad leaders. Over his voice came the static and over the static, the firing. Now Gibson, the first squad leader, was on again.

"Byrne, Byrne! They're through the wire. They're in with my first fire team, Jesus, right in the trenches. Oh, God, I'll call back. Can't talk."

"Gib, Gib," Byrne shouted, "stay on the fucking line. Here are the mortars, oh, you babies, right on. I can see gooks now, they're on the hill, up here with us. They broke through Gibson. Hello, Gib, hello, Gib Gib Gib. I can't get him. Bring down the mortars thirty yards. Hit Gibson's position. They're in there with him. Hit Gibson, oh Jesus, hit him!"

The mortars were chunking out every few seconds. Now the artillery officer said something to Gregory and Gregory said, "Hell, yes." They started firing 105 concentrations all around the knoll, air bursts. It was a chance they would hit marines but you had to do it. On the radio one of the squad leaders was calling Byrne. I couldn't tell if it was Leibling or the one whose name I didn't catch.

"Byrne, Mr. Byrne, they're coming through the wire. Do you read me? I got Chinese in the wire. We're hitting them with machine gun. That's it, babee! We're stopping them with the gun. We got 'em, we got the bastards."

Byrne was on the horn again, his words muddy, filtered through the firing. You didn't know if it was the radio or if he was shaken. Maybe it was both. He was talking too much, as you do when you're excited. Or scared.

"Okay, you got Chinese. All right, that's what we're here for, you babies. Hit them, hit them. Use the grenades. Jesus, are those mortars beautiful. Give us another flare if you got 'em, keep the flares coming. We can use them. Gib, Gib, can you hear me, Gib?"

The 105s smashed in now and the voice went completely. I thought I could hear yelling over the radio but I wasn't sure. I hoped they hadn't caught a short round out there. There was more yelling, louder. Maybe it was just one of us in the ops bunker making noise. Maybe I was yelling myself. Then Byrne was back on.

"Good God, they're through. They're in on us. I lost first squad. They're gone, all done. Give me artillery. Give me

105s on the position. Give it to us. We'll take our chances. Give us the son of a bitch. Now, now! Give it to us."

"Byrne, it's Leibling. They're coming in the back door again. I got a jammed gun here. One dead. Byrne, do you read me?"

"We're holding here, Mr. Byrne. Don't let 'em take us from the side." It was the third squad leader, the one whose name I didn't know. He still sounded pretty cool.

Then it was Byrne again, not cool at all. "It's me, Byrne. We're getting 105 now on the hill. Are they short rounds or are they on us? Keep it coming, we want it right on us. Oh, baby, that was close. Give it to us. I got chinks in this trench. We lost one squad. Platoon sergeant's hit. Give us the 105s, that's it, oh, baby, close but oh, baby. Leib, Leib, come in!"

"Aye, aye, sir."

"How is it, Leib?"

"I dunno, Lieutenant." He sounded sleepy, as if a child dozing off.

"What do you mean? Are you hit, Leibling? Are you hit?"

"Hit, Lieutenant. Sorry, no good. Can't see. Chinks. Incoming." The voice faded.

"Leibling, Leib? Someone get Leibling's radio. Is there anyone there? Anyone?"

There was another very loud crash and Byrne stopped talking. Then he came on, sluggish, dulled.

"105 on the trench. Think I'm hit. Here's platoon guide. He's got the wheel." A familiar drawl came on. Hoops. Now I realized this was my old platoon.

"Yes, sir, I'm on here, if I kin get this gadget working."

Major Nicholson cut in to ask Hoops how it was.

"Well, sir, tolerable. Could be better. We're pretty busy. I figure we got about twenty people hit, but the rest, they're keeping up the fire pretty good. I think you could secure them artilleries now. They's jest gonna kill us all."

"Hoops, this is second squad. Leibling's out. We're okay. The 105s caught them in the wire. Ain't much wire left, but the chinks is shagging ass now. Looks pretty good to see."

"This is Hoops. What you got there?"

Another squad checked in. "Got chinks, Hoops, what the hell you think we got?"

"Well, I mean, you gonna pitch 'em out of there or jest what?"

"Hoops, I can't even see the wire for the chinks we got dead around here. We got 'em held, I think. But I don't like to say if they come back."

No one had heard from Gibson. There was some more firing and more radio talk and then toward two o'clock a scare the chinks were coming again, but that's all it was, a scare, and they didn't come. Before dawn they ordered Hoops to bring the platoon back in, starting while it was still dark. They would put a fresh platoon out there at dusk, if Division insisted. It seemed to some of us we couldn't hold strongpoints like these. They weren't strong enough; we didn't have time to dig in properly and build bunkers. Fighting out of trenches with no overhead protection was bad. If we wanted these little pimples and knolls, we ought to push the whole MLR forward and really hold them.

Hoops came in with the platoon, and stretcher bearers met them more than halfway. Lieutenant Byrne was okay, just concussed. Gibson, the squad leader, was dead. Only two men were left of his squad, both wounded. They'd been under the bodies of other marines when the Chinese went through their sector of the trench. Leibling was dead, too. There were fourteen dead in the platoon. I stayed with Hoops, talking to him after he was debriefed. I asked how he felt.

"Just fine, Mr. Brady. They made me guide again, you know, last month. Even Mr. Maki, before he left, he said I was doing good."

"No, Hoops, I meant, how are you after last night?"

"Well, Mr. Brady, I'd be a liar if I said chipper. But it ain't never too bad if you come back. But that was a pretty fair firefight, pretty fair. Old Princeton, he would of loved it."

"Would he, Hoops?"

"Shit, no, Mr. Brady. I didn't even hardly enjoy it myself."

36

On one of the Chinese bodies they found a leaflet urging the capture, alive, of American marines. "Yellow legs" we were called, after our canvas leggings. The fortunate captor was to be given a ten-day furlough and 10,000 sen.

"That's about a buck ninety-eight," Sasso announced.

A public information sergeant came up from Division to ask about the leaflet. He wanted to write a piece about it for *Stars & Stripes* and the hometown papers. The PIO sergeant was foisted on me. "What are marines saying about the offer?" he asked, notebook out. "They say it sounds pretty damned cheap," I said. That was about it. Two weeks later I began getting clippings from people at home, a story in which I was quoted:

" 'Pretty damned cheap for me,' says New York marine."

The next time a PIO guy came up, someone else could talk to him.

Hard fighting continued through June, with Hill 69 and the pimple hanging on, but we abandoned the knoll in front of Yoke; it was just too damned far out and it cost too much. Battalion strained itself to come up with ideas. They issued flamethrowers, which I'd never seen in action before, and extra BARs, so that every other marine out there had one. They actually did get steel plates, rupturing God knows how many gooks carrying them. The ops officer, Major Nicholson, came up with a splendid scheme. They rolled barrels of napalm out and set them in around the strongpoints, hooked to electrical wires, and when the chinks

267

came up they fired off a blazing napalm all over the place. You could smell cooked flesh all the way back to the MLR if the wind was right. So we barbecued some Chinese, but still they came on, and the Battalion continued to lose men, and in the end we abandoned the knoll.

That was the worst fighting the whole time I was there, as primitive as when men stormed castles and scaled crenellated walls and had boiling oil poured down on them from the battlements. And this was 1952, the nuclear age.

The Battalion was pulled off line for five days' rest, and then we took over a position just to the left of 212. It was quieter here because the two MLRs were closer together with very little room for strongpoints to argue over. But every blessing brings its burden. Snipers from both sides were at it constantly, and in the rifle companies you couldn't leave some of the bunkers in daylight without being shot at. Men defecated in cardboard ration boxes and then emptied the stuff at night. It reminded me of Operation Clam Up. We had some infrared sniper scopes sent up so we could shoot chinks in the dark, so presumably it was even more miserable over there than on this side. And there was always a marine with a scheme. Somewhere we'd picked up a fifty-calibre machine gun. They weren't issued and I believe it was stolen from the army. The gunner who had it tended it like a first child, fussing over it and polishing it, but mostly what he did was zero it in on one particular firing port in one particular Chinese bunker about a thousand yards away. He sandbagged the legs of the fifty-calibre so it wouldn't move, and by day he fired off ranging shots, just one every couple of hours, watching through a scope where they hit. Then, when he was sure he had the chink firing port targeted perfectly, he would wake once or twice during the night, using an old Big Ben alarm clock, to fire a single shot blind, through the night, at the chink bunker, hoping someone would be passing by the firing port or had gotten up to take a leak and the single shot would hit him in the head. He lost a lot of sleep trying to kill chinks he never saw, but he was intense about it, and if anyone came near the gun, he growled them off, accusing them of trying to screw up his range and windage calculations.

It was real summer now, very hot and dry, the rains not

due until October, and fat flies buzzed around the outdoor heads and the piss tubes, and you had to cover your mess gear as you ate, waving them away. Once or twice a week a couple of truckloads of marines would go down to the Imjin River, near the Double Bend, where the chinks had slaughtered the "Glorious Gloucesters" the year before, to swim and wash. I went down once and it was very pleasant, swimming and sporting on air mattresses. There were only a few leeches. Other days I practiced my volleyball. There was another divertissement, a rumor the gooks were going to break off the truce talks suddenly one day and kidnap all the allied negotiators. This rumor led to creation of another great plan, one called Operation Snatch.

When the talks were on, the negotiators went out each morning, the brass flying along the truce corridor by chopper to Panmunjom, and the lesser lights and war correspondents going out in jeeps. Marines never really saw a war correspondent on the line, because they got their information from Division or even farther back, but after a while the marines got over being impressed and waved hankies at the press jeeps as they went by. I felt we were being unfair. James Michener, who wrote *Tales of the South Pacific,* had actually spent a week with our Battalion in the mountains last winter. I never saw him, but men swore he was there. Anyway, the gooks were supposed to be plotting to capture or kill Admiral Joy and all our other brass, and even the war correspondents, and that would signal a big Chinese push south on Seoul. To be prepared for that, we had Operation Snatch. I really hoped I'd be around to see it, because it sounded like the damndest thing marines had done since Inchon, and people still spoke of that in hushed tones.

The key to Operation Snatch was a full rifle company of marines set up in defilade just behind the line and adjacent to the Panmunjom road. They had a dozen tanks and about fifteen or so other armored vehicles, and if the word came, the marines were to scramble up on top of the tanks and into the armored vehicles and head north at flank speed. The engines were always kept running while the negotiators were out there, and a rifleman didn't dare take a leak without being threatened with a general court. Half the Division artillery had concentrations preset all around

Panmunjom, and there was always an O.Y. up there buzzing around carrying an artillery observer. Just out of sight four Corsairs were kept in the air during the talks, ready to come in strafing if anything happened. Marines are easily bored, and even with the fighting for strongpoints and the sniping where we were now, people were pretty excited about Operation Snatch and wanted to be around the day when those tanks and armored vehicles went roaring up the Panmunjom road with all guns firing, and the artillery let off with the 155 guns even, and the Corsairs came in low, strafing and shelling, and everyone along the line started firing. And in the truce village itself admirals, generals, colonels, war correspondents, flunkies and jeep drivers would all be overturning tables inside the tents and jumping through windows and punching guys and running toward the tanks and trying to scramble onboard, and the chinks and the gooks would be shooting and getting shot. All hell would be breaking loose, and along the MLR marines would be laughing and applauding the way kids did at Saturday matinees.

It would be something to see, all right, but it never happened, and that was, most people agreed, a damned shame.

I was no longer the Battalion 2. A senior first lieutenant, a regular actually trained in intelligence work, came in on the last replacement draft, and Gregory gave him the job. The new man was tall and trim and very handsome with a pencil mustache. I even rather liked him, though I didn't like losing the job and my scouts. There were rumors I wasn't going to be there much longer, that if there were a big summer offensive as Colonel Gregory kept hinting, I wasn't going to be in it. I had mixed feelings about that. Most marines did, I guess. You didn't want to be a rear-echelon pogue, you wanted to be with a line outfit, but once you'd seen combat and lost people and had the usual close calls, for most of us, that was sufficient. Princeton, for example, my old platoon sergeant, never made any secret of wanting to get a transfer out of Dog Company and back to Division, and he'd done just that. He'd done his share of fighting, had done it well, and he wasn't going to push his luck. I guess that was pretty much how I felt.

Mack Allen heard the rumors, too.

"They say you can extend if you want, put in for another

three months. I'd do it today if they'd give me a rifle company."

"Why, Mack, just why?" This was just dumb and being stubborn, and I was angry with Mack for saying it.

Mack screwed up his face as he did when he was thinking hard and being serious about something.

"Jim, having a company, a good company like Dog was when Chafee had it, that's the culmination of everything we've done out here. Being a platoon leader is wonderful, but I've done that. Being exec or on the staff this way is nothing. I've wanted a company since I was a scared replacement PFC on Okinawa, and all the time at VMI I kept thinking about it. Sure, I'll extend if I can get a company. I'd never forgive myself if I let it slip. What's three months? Nothing. Not when you put it up against commanding a company of the best soldiers in the world."

The words may have been corny but not the way Mack said them.

A few days later I got my orders. I was to join a rotation draft on July 4. That was funny. I'd spent Memorial Day on Yoke, damned near getting killed, and now they were sending me home on the Fourth of July. Mack put in for the extension, the colonel telling him he couldn't promise a company right away but that he'd get the next rifle company that opened up. I tried to argue Mack out of it. It was too vague; who could say what the hell would happen in this rotten strongpoint fighting? Mack shook his head and said he was going to take it, and he did.

One last funny thing happened. Colonel Gregory and Major Nicholson took the Regimental commander up to the OP on 212 to look over the lines one morning, and a chink shell, just lobbed up for nuisance value, exploded right in front of the bunker while they were inside looking out the observation port. All three officers were hit with shrapnel but only scratched, most amazing thing. Their helmets and the bunker saved them, and they came down off the hill dabbing at their cut faces with handkerchiefs and being very jolly about the whole thing. They were all regulars, and it was considered very good for your record and your career to have the Purple Heart. I overheard one enlisted man talking about it.

"They was all happy as pigs in shit," he said, laughing.

I was to leave the following day, and I went around shaking hands and saying good-bye to people and asking if they wanted anyone phoned in the States and taking names and numbers. Mack Allen was already back up on line with Dog Company, and I saved him for last. I climbed the hill to where it fell away into a saddle and there for about fifty or seventy-five feet you were in the open. I started down the saddle, and a shot whipped into the dirt fairly close, and I put my head down and ran like hell. There was another shot, but I didn't see where it hit. Mack was in a bunker, and I had to crawl along a trench to get to him. There were snipers along here.

"Mack, you ever going to dig some decent trenches around here?"

"Jim, you don't begin to appreciate the things I've got to do to make this place livable. You'd think doggies held this hill before. It's enough to make you ashamed."

Mack was very happy being back with the Company. We sat on the floor of the bunker with the sun coming in through a firing port. It was cool and shady inside, a small bunker but trim and quite nice. Mack made coffee and I smoked a cigarette, and took the phone number of his father in Lynchburg, Virginia.

"Be sure you tell him you're calling for me," he said, "so that Yankee voice won't confuse him."

"Mack," I said, "you remember that day we wrestled in the snow, rolling down the hill, and you washed my face?"

"Surely do."

"We sure were green," I said.

"No, Jim, we were just happy."

We shook hands. I wanted to do more, maybe to hug him, but between men you shake hands and what else is there? I backed out of the bunker on my hands and knees and he followed.

"You take care, Mack, you take care."

Mack just nodded and waved a hand at me, not saying anything. He knew what I was really saying was, "Don't get killed, Mack."

I crawled along the trench to where it bent and looked back. Mack was sitting there in the sun in the doorway of the bunker, a rifle across his lap, smiling at me with that broad, flat, close-lipped smile of his. I turned the bend then and went quickly across the open section of the saddle, and this time no one shot at me, and I walked home.

Home? That's what Battalion was and had been for a long time. Hard to realize "home" would soon have another meaning.

Princeton came up from motor transport to see me.

"Heard you was leaving, Mr. Brady."

"When are you going, Prince?"

"August, maybe September. Still short of staff NCOs."

"You were a good platoon sergeant, Prince. I want to thank you. You were a big help."

"Hell, you was okay, Mr. Brady. Okay."

We were never really friends and we weren't now. But I said, "Prince, can I call your wife or something?"

He didn't say anything for a moment and then he shook his head.

"No, sir, I don't think I should give you my wife's phone number. Thanks, anyway."

When he'd left I thought about it, remembering the erotic photos Princeton's wife sent. He didn't trust me. Not even after all this time on the line and sleeping in the same bunker. I was annoyed at Prince, and then I started feeling sorry for him and angry with a woman I'd never seen and would never meet.

I said good-bye to the rest of them, to the colonel, who cackled and showed me his shrapnel wound. He had been in Korea before I got there and would be there after I left, and I knew he was a good and a plain man who tried to do the job right and had not been afraid or a phony. Youngdahl had been flashy and false; Gregory, never. I laughed at him sometimes, but I had an idea that years from now, when I thought of him, it would be with gratitude, maybe even a sneaking admiration. The scouts were polite about my leaving, trying to express regret, but the new S-2 had them working hard on map and compass problems, the sort of thing I tended to slough off, and they didn't have much time for me. I probably should have worked them harder, but I had the rifleman's bias against the staff, that it was a joke job, and you could work on your volleyball or your letter writing. But the scouts had done a job for me when it counted, and I would never forget Sasso, covered with blood, and Wrabel, wrestling with the marine for his rifle, that morning on Yoke. The gunny said good-bye, a bit flowery about it. He knew I didn't like him. Out of politeness I asked when he thought he'd be rotated home.

"Well, sir, I thought I'd put in for duty on Formosa, training chink marines. I don't have much waiting for me stateside, and if Chiang ever goes back to the Mainland it would be a chance to kill some gooks." He paused. "They say those chink girls are something, the young ones."

At dawn on the Fourth of July we boarded trucks at Battalion and drove off down the road. Behind us as we went there was a little firing, not very serious, just a few shells being thrown up across the line. Reveille for the chinks, perhaps, or a farewell to the rotation draft. Probably it wasn't either, but it was nice to know it was a sound I might never again hear for the rest of my life. South of Division they loaded us onto a narrow-gauge railroad train, in boxcars that still smelled sweetly of manure and hay. It was a hot day, and we traveled with the boxcar doors slid open, marines sitting in the doorways with their legs dangling, like kids on an outing. The train moved slowly through the green countryside, past villages and farmers working fields, past oxen pulling plows and children waving from the hillsides. I breathed deeply, trying to retain the small details of this last day. There was the smell of mown grass, of manure, of leather and gun oil and trains and wildflowers and men, all of it very different, all of it smelling so good.

The embarkation point was called Ascom City, which stood for something but I never figured quite what. Five minutes after we got there, marines were calling it Ashcan City. There were Quonset huts and company streets and men scrubbing garbage cans and mess halls with lines of men outside them, just like any garrison in the States. A nervous major with a twitch was the draft commander, and when he called an officers' meeting, I got a company, 400 men. It was called Charley Company, and it was only a rotation draft outfit, but it was funny to think I'd gotten a company before Mack Allen did. The major was neurotic. I wondered if he'd been in the bad fighting but I learned later he had been in charge of a supply depot the whole time. I had four master sergeants in my company, all regulars, and ten officers. I told them what had to be done and got out of the way and they did it. It was sweet being a company commander, at least in a rotation draft. It was also interesting how simple things could be when no one was shooting at you. That night the major said there was no discipline in the camp, that the men looked like vagrants, that some of them had gone over the wire looking for women and drink. He would not tolerate it, he said. Charley Company was assigned mess duty until we sailed. A man from Charley was already on report for spitting in front of the major. The man had a Navy Cross but he was still on report, Navy Cross or no. The major would not stand for impudence. Things were not as simple in Ascom City as they first seemed.

At dawn on the sixth we fell out in formation in the company street. I had a few things to say, and so I climbed up on the roof of a truck. I told them they'd fought as marines and would go home as marines. I wanted no shit. That's all I had to say, and I got back down off the truck, hoarse from shouting. One of the master sergeants came up to me.

"Was the lieutenant in a line outfit by any chance?"

I said the lieutenant had been in a rifle battalion the whole time.

The master sergeant smiled. "Well, sir, I'll put that word out quietly among the men, with the lieutenant's permission, and we won't have no trouble. Some of the wild ones don't take too kindly to rear-echelon pogues, you know. Sir," he added.

Trucks carried us down to Inchon. On the way we passed other trucks going in the opposite direction, carrying the replacement draft. Their uniforms looked very nice, neat and clean. The men going down shouted.

"You'll be sorreee!"

It was what other men had shouted at us a year ago. It was fine being on the giving end this time. Inchon looked the same, the hospital ship still riding at anchor way out, or maybe it was another hospital ship that just looked the same. We marched out, two thousand men, onto a very long dock, carrying full field packs, heavy with goods. We stood there for a while without orders. There were no boats to be seen, and then I said, what the hell, and gave the order to drop packs and sit down. The major came along after a while, and he chewed me out for doing this without permission, but then he went away again without having told me to get the men back on their feet, so it was all right. Around noon we were still sitting there, a few men dozing, when some army troops marched onto the dock, maybe a thousand of them bound for Japan. That woke the marines up, and there was some chatter and shouting, and that drew the major again, and he went up and down the dock, very angry, and really twitching now. I looked out at the sea and avoided his eye.

An LST came in and nosed up to the dock. It had a Jap crew, and they started right in unloading the ship, ammunition and other things. The marines sat there watching, enjoying seeing other people work, and then there was some shouting on board the LST, and men stood to see what was happening, to pinpoint the shouting.

"Fire," someone shouted, "the goddamn LST's on fire."

I couldn't see anything and then I could, smoke rising and men running. Some of the Japanese began to jump overboard into the harbor. Bullets were exploding on the forward deck, and then a rocket went off and sailed over the dock trailing white smoke. It was pretty, but it was dangerous, and there were more explosions now, none of them big, but a lot of them. Some of the Japs hadn't jumped. They were still onboard and fighting the fire, throwing water on it and wrestling a hose and moving crates and barrels out of the way. I stood up. There was no way you were going to get three thousand men off the dock fast without a stampede. I told the first sergeant to get our men to put their helmets on. That was the one thing we could do with all this shit flying around. Then I sat down again, wishing we were off this damned dock. None of the marines moved; they just sat there on their packs with their shoulders hunched under their helmets while the ship burned and the rockets and bullets went off. Some of the army troops at the end of the dock nearest shore began to edge away from the LST, moving toward land and off the dock. Still none of the marines moved. I know it was dumb, but I felt very proud of them, and I kept thinking what a thing it would be to die on this dock just before going home, and concentrated on staying cool, the way Chafee would have. Everyone who was close to the LST was scared, and it would have been stupid not to be with shells exploding and rockets arcing overhead. "John wouldn't panic," I told myself, quickly changing it to "Chafee." Even now, no first names. I'd learned that from him, and, thinking of Chafee, I was cool now. Finally, out of the whole damned war I'd retained something. I may even have grinned, thinking of Mack and Logan and the rest of them up on the line if I died here, and how, when they heard about it, they would surely have found humor in the irony.

Finally the Japs got the fire out. They were good men to have stayed aboard like that when the others jumped. I wondered if I would have jumped.

Around five in the afternoon we were still sitting on the dock, waiting, and it began to rain. Some men put their ponchos on. Some broke open their rations and were sitting there eating them in the rain, the water dripping off helmets into the cans of food the way it always did. I didn't bother with my poncho. I'd never been great at making up a neat pack, and I thought if I started to pull things out, I'd never get the damned thing taut again. At nine o'clock lighters arrived at the dock and the marines started to load. At 11:30 exactly I stepped onto the ship's ladder and climbed aboard, checking my watch, wanting to know the precise time. It was one of the old President Liners, but now it was called the *General Meigs*. We were assigned staterooms, twelve officers to a stateroom, the bunks stacked three high. I took an upper and hoped the ship wouldn't roll too badly. One of the officers in this stateroom had a full case of liquor, a real pogue, fat and sleek, and I could not figure how he carried the booze on board. He must have bribed people to help him. I began to think how we could get some of those bottles away from him. It would be a long voyage home, and it wasn't right that a rear-echelon pogue had all that liquor to himself.

37

I lay in the berth, enjoying the novelty of electric light and the sheets and the pillow and the shiny white paint of the ceiling just a few feet above me. Even the rows of rivets were strange and quite wonderful, simple joys. The stateroom was nearly still now, one man still stowing his gear. I was very tired, and now I could sleep with no one waking me to go outside and be shot at. I guess most people were anxious to get home, but I hoped for a long crossing, a leisured transition from one life to another. It was pleasant thinking about getting home, but I could not focus on it, not yet. I was still thinking about the war and the people in it. Princeton and Hoops and the colonel and Mack Allen, most of all of Mack, still there, still fighting, still and always the good ol' boy from VMI and Harvard. Remembering was one way of keeping people alive, and the least I could do. I wondered what it was like tonight on the outposts, whether Mack would be out, if the chinks would be coming across the valley and climbing the slope, their sound covered by the rain. Rain always made night defense bad. It was weird now not hearing the guns. There must be guns but I couldn't hear them.

It wasn't my war anymore; it belonged to other men. I hadn't done badly. I'd been frightened, I'd made mistakes. But I'd done things that had merit, had gone into the valley after Simonis and had gone up Yoke and was ready to go up again. Had I been right on Hill 69, about the chinks dressed as women? I still thought I was. But how could you be sure? I hadn't lost any men through stupidity or from fear. If you summed it up, that was the real achievement, what you had to keep with you. I was going home whole, that was something pretty important, too. My name would never be recalled as one of those who changed the direction of the war. But no one could take away memory. I lay near sleep thinking about the war and how I would not have missed it, not for anything. War gave you a new perspective about things, even painted ceilings and orderly rows of little bolts.

Now the lights went out. Around me and under me, the simple, comfortable sounds of sleep, the smell of men, the sound of snoring and a fart, the easy movement of the still-tethered ship. I thought of that pogue with his case of booze, the fat boy who had the whisky and didn't deserve it. I was contemptuous of pogues and felt superior, very tough and competent and not all that civilized, ready to do whatever I had to do to get that whisky, or any other damned thing, if I decided I really wanted it.

No, that was bullshit. I was still myself and when I got home would fall back into patterns of behavior, maybe even be civilized again. War changed you but you remained the same person. Did that make sense?

I thought about what little fighting I'd actually done: tracking that wounded gook through his blood in the snow; going into the valley for Simonis; standing up to let myself get shot at on Hill 69; this last time on Yoke when I got through the barbed wire somehow and saw the grenades flying at me and watched the 105s coming in over my shoulder. Things like that had to change you, didn't they?

Yoke. The biggest fight I was ever in, and there'd been, what, maybe a squad of chinks? Some battle. Some war. Small and mean and cold and all the war I ever wanted. As Sergeant Wooten said, it wasn't much, but it was the only war we had.

The *General Meigs* swung gently at anchor on the beginning of a flooding tide as rain fell over the Yellow Sea and across the peninsula we'd left behind. On the line they would be standing a 50 percent watch while in the rice paddies and the valleys the Chinese moved squelching through mud toward the low hills.

I used to read how old soldiers sometimes went back, to walk over the ground. They even had organized tours, men from World War I going back to Flanders to trace where the trenches had been, where they had crouched and fired, where friends had died, tours for men from the Second War revisiting Normandy and walking the beaches, seeing again Monte Cassino and places in the Pacific. When they flew Mack and me out from California last November we'd stopped at some of the islands, Kwajalen and Guam and for refueling at Iwo Jima. Kwaj was just an atoll and a lagoon with rusted tanks and smashed landing craft, Guam a big, tropical place with palm trees and an officers' club, and Iwo black ash and a small hill hardly worth noticing, which was Mount Suribachi, and nothing else, only the wind blowing over the ash, moaning.

I knew I would never go back to Korea, never sign up for an old soldiers' tour. I didn't want to see the hills again or feel the cold or hear the wind out of Siberia, moaning. I didn't want to disturb the dead.

For all the firefights, for the little swagger I now permitted myself, I knew how raw I still was, as a soldier, as a man. I wondered whether anyone ever became really good at war. An unnatural act, killing, and trying to kill. Yet that was what I'd been doing since last November, when on the very first day there, in the first hour, I made my peace with God.

Now I had a lifetime to ponder the mystery of who lived and who died, but even as I lay near sleep in that crisp, clean bunk I knew it wasn't ability or courage that had gotten me through as much as extraordinary good fortune. I was warm and safe. And alive! And I had been neither incompetent nor a coward.

To be twenty-three years old and alive seemed a miracle such as I would never know again, no matter how long I lived.

Then I was asleep, to dream of ordinary things without significance, lulled by the vibration and the easy motion of the sea, and did not realize the ship was moving, with the war drifting slowly astern.

Epilogue

The war ended a year later, in the summer of 1953, pretty much along the same line we were fighting on when I got there and when I left, and the same line they fought over for another year. All that fighting, all the dead, and the damned line never moved. And finally they made a truce.

Two more things happened in 1952, after I got home.

In the fall a letter arrived from Lynchburg, Virginia. I was afraid to open it and then I did and it was okay. Mack Allen was back, and he was taking a job as town engineer of a place in Alabama. But he was going to try to get to New York first, on a visit, to see me.

Then, while it was still summer, the Marine Corps notified me my footlocker had been shipped and I could pick it up at Grand Central Station. My brother, who was eighteen and on his way to the seminary, drove over to help me with it. It was stored in the depot's cellar, down there where they held freight and kept lost luggage and such. I handed a paper to an employee of the railroad, and he led us deeper into the cellar. There, along with lost baggage and my footlocker, were the coffins from Korea, stacked and tidy, each with its American flag neatly lashed on.

Like Mack and Simonis and Captain Chafee and me, they too were home.

Index